KU-201-099

French Popular Culture
An introduction

Edited by
Hugh Dauncey
University of Newcastle upon Tyne, UK

U.W.E.L.
LEARNING RESOURCES
ACC. No. 2318060   CLASS 121
CONTROL 0340808 306
DATE 8 MAR 2004
WITHDRAWN

A member of the Hodder Headline Group
LONDON
Distributed in the United States of America by
Oxford University Press Inc., New York

First published in Great Britain in 2003 by
Arnold, a member of the Hodder Headline Group,
338 Euston Road, London NW1 3BH

http://www.arnoldpublishers.com

Distributed in the United States of America by
Oxford University Press Inc.,
198 Madison Avenue, New York, NY10016

© 2003 Arnold

All rights reserved. No part of this publication may be reproduced or
transmitted in any form or by any means, electronically or mechanically,
including photocopying, recording or any information storage or retrieval
system, without either prior permission in writing from the publisher or a
licence permitting restricted copying. In the United Kingdom such licences
are issued by the Copyright Licensing Agency: 90 Tottenham Court Road,
London W1T 4LP.

The advice and information in this book are believed to be true and accurate
at the date of going to press, but neither the authors nor the publisher can
accept any legal responsibility or liability for any errors or omissions.

British Library Cataloguing in Publication Data
A catalogue record for this book is available from the British Library

Library of Congress Cataloging-in-Publication Data
A catalog record for this book is available from the Library of Congress

ISBN 0 340 80881 0 (hb)
ISBN 0 340 80882 9 (pb)

1 2 3 4 5 6 7 8 9 10

Typeset in 9.25/14pt News Gothic by Dorchester Typesetting Group, Dorset
Printed and bound in Malta

What do you think about this book? Or any other Arnold title?
Please send your comments to feedback.arnold@hodder.co.uk

Contents

Contributors   vi

Acknowledgements   ix

1 Introducing French Popular Culture   **Hugh Dauncey**   1

2 Language   **Nigel Armstrong**   17

3 Press   **Denis Provencher**   34

4 Radio   **Geoff Hare**   48

5 Television   **Hugh Dauncey**   62

6 Cyberculture   **Gabriel Jacobs**   77

7 Music   **Chris Tinker**   90

8 Fiction   **Martine Guyot-Bender**   104

9 Cinema   **Phil Powrie**   119

10 *Bande dessinée*   **Ann Miller**   135

11 Leisure   **Bert Gordon**   150

12 Sport   **Phil Dine**   165

13 Food   **John Marks**   178

14 Fashion   **Caroline Weber**   193

15 Advertising   **Sophie Bélot**   206

Index   221

Contributors

Nigel Armstrong researches French and sociolinguistics in the University of Leeds, UK. Current projects focus on variation and change in the spoken French of the Hexagon. Recent publications include: *Social and Stylistic Variation in Spoken French: A Comparative Approach* (Amsterdam and Philadelphia: John Benjamins, 2001); and (editor, with Kate Beeching and Cecile Bauvois) *La Langue française au feminin. Le sexe et le genre affectent-ils la variation linguistique?* (Paris: L'Harmattan, 2001).

Sophie Bélot teaches French and French civilization at the University of Sheffield, UK. She recently completed a PhD on gender representation in French advertising.

Hugh Dauncey is Senior Lecturer in French Studies, University of Newcastle upon Tyne, UK. He is the co-editor (with G. Hare) of *France and the 1998 World Cup: The National Impact of a World Sporting Event* (Ilford, Essex: Frank Cass, 1999); *The Tour de France, 1903–2003: A Century of Sporting Structures, Meanings and Values* (Ilford, Essex: Frank Cass, 2003); and (with S. Cannon) *Popular Music in France from Chanson to Techno: Culture, Identity and Society* (Aldershot: Ashgate, 2003). He has published a variety of articles on French popular culture, especially television, radio, the new media and sport, and, with G. Hare, is editor of the *Web Journal of French Media Studies*.

Phil Dine is College Lecturer in French, National University of Ireland, Galway. He is the author of *French Rugby Football: A Cultural History* (Oxford: Berg, 2001) and *Images of the Algerian War: French Fiction and Film, 1954–1992* (Oxford: Oxford University Press, 1994). He is currently working on a history of French colonial sport.

Bert Gordon is Professor of European History at Mills College, Oakland, California, USA. His books include *Collaborationism in France during the Second World War* (Ithaca, NY: Cornell University Press, 1980) and (ed.) *The Historical Dictionary of World War II France: The Occupation, Vichy and the Resistance, 1938–1946* (Westport, CT: Greenwood Press, 1998). He helped create the internet discussion list H-Travel in 2003, is currently its co-editor, and serves on the Bureau of the International Commission for the History of Travel and Tourism. He has written on war-related tourism in France and on the emergence of 'mass tourism' and Mediterranean tourism. Current research focuses on gender and its depiction in cinema imagery in relation to tourism; and tourism in relation to the May–June 1986 Paris student revolt.

Martine Guyot-Bender has taught post-war French literatures and cultures at Hamilton College, Clinton, New York, USA, since 1991. She has published two volumes on Patrick Modiano: *Poétique et politique de l'ambiguité* (Paris: Archives des

Lettres Modernes, 1999) and (co-edited) *Paradigms of Memory* (New York: Peter Lang, 1998). She is the author of articles on popular culture: 'Fiction at Twenty Thousand Leagues Above the Sea: *Hemispheres*' Fantasies of France', *Sites/Sites* (summer 2001) and 'Seducing Corinne: The Official Popular Press during the Occupation', in J. Goslan and M. Hawthorne (eds), *Gender, Fascism and Popular Culture in France* (University Press of Lebanon, New Hampshire, New England, 1996).

Geoff Hare recently retired from his post of Senior Lecturer in French Studies at the University of Newcastle, UK. He has also worked at university level in Paris, Bradford, Leeds and Aberdeen. His main research interests remain in the study of sport and broadcasting – especially radio – in France. He has published widely on French radio and television and sport, notably *Football in France* (Oxford, Berg, 2003) and (co-edited with H. Dauncey) *France and the 1998 World Cup: The National Impact of a World Sporting Event* (Ilford, Essex: Frank Cass, 1999) and *The Tour de France, 1903–2003: A Century of Sporting Structures, Meanings and Values* (Ilford, Essex: Frank Cass, 2003). With H. Dauncey, he is editor of the *Web Journal of French Media Studies*.

Gabriel Jacobs currently holds the Chair of Business Management in the European Business Management School, University of Wales Swansea, specializing in information and communications technologies. He was previously Senior Lecturer in the French Department at Swansea. He has researched and published extensively in French culture, business information technology and digital music.

John Marks is Reader in French Studies at Nottingham Trent University, UK. He is the author of *Gilles Deleuze: Vitalism and Multiplicity* (London: Pluto Press, 1998) and is co-editor of *French Cultural Debates* (Newark: University in association with University of Delaware Press, Monash, 2001).

Ann Miller is Lecturer in French at the University of Leicester, UK, where she specializes in language teaching, *bande dessinée* and cinema. She has published a number of articles on *bande dessinée* and is currently completing a PhD on the subject.

Phil Powrie is Professor of French Cultural Studies and Director of the Centre for Research into Film and Media (CRIFAM) at the University of Newcastle upon Tyne, UK. He is a general editor of the journal *Studies in French Cinema* and has published extensively on French literature and cinema, including: *French Cinema in the 1980s: Nostalgia and the Crisis of Masculinity* (Oxford: Clarendon Press, 1997); *French Cinema in the 1990s: Continuity and Difference* (Oxford: Oxford University Press, 1999); *Jean-Jacques Beineix* (Manchester: Manchester University Press, 2001); and – co-authored with Keith Reader – *French Cinema: A Student's Guide* (London: Arnold, 2002). Two co-edited books are currently in preparation: *The Trouble with Men: Masculinities in European and Hollywood Cinema* (with A. Davies and B. Babington) and *The Films of Luc Besson* (with S. Hayward).

Denis Provencher is Assistant Professor in the Department of Modern Languages at the University of Wisconsin at La Crosse, USA, and recently completed a Postdoctoral Research Fellowship at the Center for 21st Century Studies at UW-Milwaukee. His published work focuses on the intersection of language, gender and sexual identities in contemporary literature and popular culture genres in both France and the United States. Current research explores the coming-out experience of French gay men.

Chris Tinker is Lecturer in French at Heriot-Watt University, Edinburgh, UK. He has teaching and research interests in modern and contemporary French Studies, popular music, film and media. He has published articles on the singer-songwriters Georges Brassens, Jacques Brel, Léo Ferré and Serge Gainsbourg, and is author of *Post-war French Song: Personal and Social Narratives* (Liverpool: Liverpool University Press, forthcoming).

Caroline Weber is Assistant Professor of Romance Languages at the University of Pennsylvania, USA. Her speciality is eighteenth-century French literature and culture, and she has recently published *Terror and its Discontents: Suspect Words and the French Revolution* (Minneapolis: University of Minnesota Press, 2003). Her next book project is a study of Marie Antoinette's clothing.

Acknowledgements

Thanks to:

Elena Seymenliyska and Eva Martinez at Arnold for believing in the project and for their patient support and Geoff Hare for his friendship and encouragement.

Every effort has been made to trace all copyright holders of material. Any rights not acknowledged here will be acknowledged in subsequent printings if sufficient notice is given to the publisher.

CHAPTER 1

Introducing French Popular Culture

Hugh Dauncey

This volume is an *introduction* to an aspect of the contemporary reality of France – 'popular culture' – which, for various reasons, has often been relatively inaccessible to those interested in French society and French culture. Until quite recently, French 'popular culture' has suffered from a kind of invisibility in academic circles, both in France itself and in Britain and the United States, and, even now, the majority of research and teaching on French society and culture in universities focuses not on anything which could really be classified as 'popular', despite moves away from traditional interests in *canonical* literature, art, music and more latterly cinema.

The diffidence displayed by researchers and teachers towards the cultural forms and activities which contribute to making up the 'other' France of 'culture' understood in a wider sense is all the more surprising – although it can be explained – given that the image of France and of French culture in the world is now, and arguably always has been, communicated by cultural symbols which are not high-literary, high-artistic, high-musical nor high-cinematic. In other words – and keeping simply to the nineteenth and twentieth centuries – for every Sartre there is a San Antonio, for every Colette a Coluche, for every Gautier a Gaultier and for every Barrault a Renaud (the examples are debatable, but that is just an illustration of the permeability of categories and definitions in this area). To change the examples for comparison, perceptions of France and French culture outside France have always been as much – if not more – about can-can and music hall as opera, as much about sailing and rugby as classical dance, as much about *boules* as Boulez, as much about Barthez as Barthes. So what people outside (and inside) France think of as defining (in whatever sense) French cultural identity has often been ignored in discussions of French culture.

What people in Britain and the USA know about French culture is, of course, necessarily incomplete and partial, given the barriers to cultural exchange posed by language and other factors. French popular music has had to overcome the hurdle of translation to succeed in the USA, for example, and relatively few French singer-songwriters – Aznavour, Chevalier, Trenet and Piaf, for example – have succeeded in introducing their work in non-Francophone contexts. French television shows have had even less success in imposing themselves outside France. So what is understood by 'French culture' is nowhere near the whole picture: the traditional bias towards *la grande culture* or 'high' culture (despite the celebrity of much 'low' French culture internationally) compounded by linguistic and cultural obstacles to the diffusion of French 'popular culture' abroad has produced a distorted image of the cultural realities of contemporary France.

But developments in popular artistic forms, commerce and technology are also contributing to making French non-elite culture better known. Popular music in the form of 'French touch' techno music typified by Daft Punk and Air has relatively recently brought French music to a wider audience, either by being essentially word-less or by mixing tracks from English-speaking artists (such as Barry Manilow). Commercials from French advertising agencies now appear (to mixed reactions) on British television. British television has suffered the assault of Antoine de Caunes's and Jean-Paul Gaultier's *Eurotrash* programme (Channel 4) in a complicated and satirically self-aware intertextual play on national self-perceptions. Satellite and digital television and radio are increasingly making French (and other Francophone) TV and radio pro-grammes accessible to new French- and non-French-speaking audiences worldwide.

It will not have escaped notice that the terms 'culture' and 'popular' have thus far occurred surrounded by protective inverted commas. This is simply because the pre-cise nature of 'popular culture' is something which properly escapes the brief of this book itself. There is a very extensive literature discussing culture and definitions of elite culture, mass culture, folk culture and popular culture, to which readers may address themselves, and there is not enough room in a book like this to rehearse the histories of the concept of 'culture', although those coming to the study of the forms of 'popular culture' presented here should have at least a nodding acquaintance with the issues. Some excellent introductory discussions of 'popular culture' and how to study it are suggested as 'further reading' at the end of this chapter, so here we will simply graze the surface of the debates.

The term culture was often used historically to describe phenomena which belonged to a social elite, phenomena produced for and consumed by the dominant social classes, and which were often used to distinguish that (cultivated) social elite from the vulgar (*vulgus* in Latin meaning the common people, *le peuple* in French), those who did not have the 'culture' (or education) to appreciate or understand what cultured people did. Up to the mid-1970s, say (although it is difficult to put a date on the process of cultural change that was kick-started by the events of May 1968), *la culture cultivée* in France included classical music and 'literature' (the literary canon), but not *yéyé* pop or rock music (see Chapter 7), 'industrial literature' such as roman-tic novels or *roman noir* (see Chapter 8), radio and television (see Chapters 4 and 5) and so on and so on. These latter cultural phenomena would be consigned to the category of *culture populaire* or *culture de masse* as an inferior product, of value neither as an activity or 'cultural' product nor as an object of academic study.

It is worth at this point trying to distinguish between the terms 'mass culture' and 'popular culture'. Mass culture is a term that was coined at the time of the rise of 'mass society', that is western societies that were being moulded and manipulated, or so it was feared, by the new mass media, the mass-circulation press, radio and later television. The term was often used within the context of a critique of modern society and has therefore taken on pejorative connotations – evoking uniformity, standardization and impoverishment of cultural experience. Like 'mass culture', the term 'popular culture' is also defined against 'high culture' (*la culture cultivée*) but is often (though not always) less judgemental. It has come to mean the culture of the non-elite majority, of 'ordinary people', the culture of the people. Like 'mass culture', popular culture has sometimes been looked down on as banal or unchallenging, per-haps even harmful or subversive (see the various moral panics about rap music or youth radio phone-ins).

The notion of standards, as sometimes used by critics of aspects of popular cul-ture, raises the issue of how we measure achievement in popular culture, how we judge its artistic quality. Of course, this in itself limits the definition of culture to a product (whether artefact or performance) that is to be consumed by a (passive) audience, therefore part of 'consumer culture', whereas there are other aspects of culture that may be defined as a process, the process of creativity, and which are more interactive – such as community arts (called in France *animation socio-culturelle*). There are those who argue indeed that popular culture is essentially inter-active, which would explain both the working-class rejection of the democratization of high culture via the *maisons de la culture* (Gaullist attempts to spread the prod-ucts of high culture to the populace) and the recent growing popularity on radio and television of audience-participation programmes, so-called reality TV.

Some critics argue that high culture is essentially about difference, what Bourdieu called *la distinction*. The tools to appreciate 'legitimate culture' are summed up by the term 'cultural capital', Bourdieu's term for the knowledge, tastes, values and indeed language that are just as important as economic capital in maintaining social hierarchies, at least in so far as cultural capital also signifies membership of a par-ticular social group. In terms of culture as belonging, each cultural grouping (or sub-culture) will have its own cultural capital, which in the case of 'youth culture' might be termed, in English, 'street cred'. (Suggestions for the French equivalent of this on a postcard – postcards being another form of popular culture.)

So does radio – for example – belong to 'high culture', 'popular culture' or 'mass culture'? In a sense it belongs to all, since it has become less and less monolithic as a medium, although nowadays, of course, such elitist distinctions are no longer so automatically a part of the dominant ideology; indeed they might easily be labelled politically incorrect. Cultural activities or cultural productions associated with a given social class or community are viewed from the 'cultural studies' perspective as being equally valid expressions of that class or community. French culture ministers, for example, now quite happily promote French hip-hop and rap in the name of 'cultural democracy', where in the 1960s Malraux's *maisons de la culture* were an attempt to democratize culture with a capital 'C'. A related transformation in thinking is that, nowadays, postmodernists see high and low culture as inhabiting the same space and being appreciated by the same individuals. Indeed, evidence for this might be seen in the transformation of *Le Monde*, the paper of the French elites (see Chapter 3), which, since 1998 (when France hosted and won the soccer World Cup), has a significant sports section as well as its long-standing 'culture' columns containing reports on 'high cultural' spectacles such as opera, art exhibitions and modern dance. In the 1950s and 1960s, media studies in British and American universities, as the forerunner of cultural studies, began the legitimation of popular and mass culture as worthwhile objects of serious study, and this democratization also has its intellectual champions in France (Baudrillard, Bourdieu and others).

The forms of popular culture studied in this book are complex hybrids of practice, which share an importance in the everyday life of ordinary French people. The concepts of the 'everyday' and the 'ordinary' are themselves of course problematic – whose ordinary everyday are we talking about? – but their common-sense meanings take us far enough into the world of French 'popular culture' to learn more about some of the practical and sociocultural realities of the lives that most of our French counterparts actually lead. Introducing his book *Everyday Life and Cultural Theory* Ben Highmore discusses Sherlock Holmes. As those who know their late nineteenth- and early twentieth-century British popular literature are aware, Conan Doyle's brilliant but troubled detective was a cocaine addict, and Highmore describes the way in which Holmes escapes his depressive boredom by uncovering the bizarre and extraordinary features behind the humdrum details of the crimes he investigates: 'To the mystery of the everyday, Holmes brings the disenchantment of rationalism' (Highmore, 2002a: 4). Highmore's discussion of Holmes posits 'boredom', 'mystery' and rationalism as forces which combine to figure the everyday as simultaneously known and unknown, comfortable and uncomfortable. Contemporary everyday life – for Highmore – is *boring* in the institutionalization of time, learning and work and bureaucratic rationality, and it is *strange* in the way that the richness of interpretations (*à la* Holmes and *à la* Freud, for example) produces 'mystery' through explaining the banal, and in the way anyone's everyday is bizarre and exotic to anyone else's. These are thought-provoking perspectives, and Highmore develops discussions of important theorists of 'the everyday', such as Simmel, Benjamin, Lefebvre and de Certeau.

However, this volume of introductory analyses of aspects of French popular culture has no ambition to contribute to the *theorizing* of 'the everyday'. In a way, though, it is Holmes's famous remark that what is significant is the fact that 'the guard dog did not bark' – and therefore that the intruder was known to it – which can introduce a volume of studies like this. Making a similar point to Michel de Certeau's assertion that the everyday exists 'between the lines' of what is written and archived about society and culture (Certeau, 1988), the aspects of 'popular culture' in France that are described here have suffered a neglect both from French specialists on French culture and English-speaking specialists on the particular domains we cover. However much the phenomena and practices described here make up the everyday experience of life in France – listening to the radio and watching TV while getting up, choosing what clothes to wear, buying a daily newspaper and a weekly magazine, deciding what to eat at lunchtime, booking a holiday using the Minitel or internet, and so on – they have often been largely ignored. As John Lennon once said, 'Reality is for those who can't cope with drugs', so like Sherlock Holmes, but without the cocaine, we should indulge in a little study of some features of 'real' life in France.

FRANCE 1945–2000: A SOCIOCULTURAL BACKGROUND

One of the recurring questions from contributors as they wrote their chapters was 'Will people reading the book know about May '68?' The answer was, of course, 'Maybe. We'd better cover that in the Introduction'. As well as the 'events' of May–June 1968 when student and worker protests against the Gaullist regime para-lysed central Paris and threw the government into turmoil, there are a number of factual and conceptual 'building blocks' which may help readers better understand the treatments given in individual chapters.

How far back should we go? Both for the sake of providing a manageable treat-ment of the topic and for conceptual and theoretical reasons, our coverage is restricted to the period since the Second World War, and, while this period is in many ways accepted in historical periodization, there are, obviously, themes, issues and events from French politics, culture and society in the nineteenth and early twentieth centuries which inform the artefacts and practices of French popular culture after 1945. As well as May '68, for example, France's experience of the Popular Front gov-ernment in 1936–8 reverberates down the following decades of popular culture in ways which are picked up by several of the chapters in this book. So, as well as try-ing to provide a convenient summary of the sociocultural backdrop – from 1945 to the present day – of French popular culture, this Introduction also has to suggest the longer-term factors which contributed to structuring society and culture in twentieth-century France.

Michael Kelly has suggested that in France there are 'three dominant zones of social identity around which cultural exploration has turned, summarized in the Republic's motto, "Liberté, Egalité, Fraternité" but also in the Vichy alternative to it "Travail, Famille, Patrie"' which criss-cross French politics and culture (Forbes and Kelly, 1995: 1). These are national identity, class identity and gender identity. Certainly, the questions of popular culture can partly be answered in these terms –

for example, French (popular) culture is threatened by the cultural hegemony of the USA; popular culture is denigrated as the culture of the masses; popular culture can be gender-differentiated – but there also other explanatory concepts and processes, such as socioeconomic modernization, which underlie, transect and overlap these 'zones'. We try to bring out some of these in what follows, as we present some of the major themes that have informed the development of popular culture since the Second World War.

LES ANNÉES FOLLES AND THE POPULAR FRONT: COMING TO TERMS WITH LOSS

France during the 1920s and the 1930s had to find her feet. France's experience of the Great War (the term *la grande guerre* seems more appropriate than the simple ordinality of 'First' and 'Second') and of the 'twenty-year armistice' (Marshal Foch's judgement on the Versailles Peace Treaty) of the inter-war period informed developments in popular culture in various ways. The trauma of citizens and society brought by the horrors of modern warfare pushed a nation where men were missing, mutilated or altered by their experiences of trenches and death towards new thinking on life, nation and society, culture and class.

Novels such as Henri Barbusse's *Le Feu* (Under Fire, 1916) and Raymond Radiguet's *Le Diable au corps* (The Devil in the Flesh, 1923) translated some of the social and emotional upheavals of the conflict into popular literature, and cinema addressed new questionings of old values of nationalism, patriotism and class in films such as Jean Renoir's *La Grande Illusion* (The Grand Illusion, 1937) and *La Règle du jeu* (The Rules of the Game, 1939). Developing industrialization – accelerated by the war effort – and growing urbanization, combined with the rise of communism and socialism, provided fertile subjects for literature, cinema and music, particularly in the social-realist and poetic-realist films of the 1930s of Jean Renoir, René Clair and Marcel Carné. Stimulated by political tensions between left and right during the 1920s and 1930s and by the growing class rivalries spawned by industrialization – which eventually culminated in the Popular Front – films such as Renoir's *Le Crime de Monsieur Lange* (The Crime of M. Lange, 1936) and *La Vie est à nous* (Life is Ours, 1936) presented working-class protagonists struggling against bosses and exploitation.

The admirable summary of the culture and society of the 1920s and 1930s given in *French Cultural Studies: An Introduction* (Forbes and Kelly, 1995) stresses how popular culture during this period experienced innovative organization and expansion of popular culture, which was frequently the result of new technologies. Music, cinema and sport in particular were transformed. Music and cinema advanced through new recording techniques allowing talkies and musicals, and street singing, sheet music and the café concert were challenged by the music hall and new (increasingly mediatized) star performers such as Mistinguett and Maurice Chevalier. Popular music was encouraged by radio, which grew during the 1920s, moving from news and sports broadcasts towards concerts and popular music in general. In a country demographically and physically shattered, searching for new distractions, sport assumed a new importance beyond its usefulness – as *la gymnastique* – in keeping the nation's citizen-soldiers fit to defend the Republic: sports federations (rugby, soccer) were founded; the Olympics came to Paris (1924); France won the Davis Cup tennis competition (1926); and French cyclists dominated the Tour in the 1930s. Sport became more popular, more mediatized, and linked to national prestige, as the 1936 Munich Olympics in Nazi Germany were to underline. The Popular Front was instrumental in fostering the development of leisure (by legislating paid annual holidays) and encouraging sport (by creating a ministry and sporting infrastructures nationwide). Perhaps less concretely, as a 'popular' government (it was a fragile coalition of left-wing parties engendered by the perceived menace of the militant right) whose election was marked by wild celebrations and whose policies were awaited with hopeful anticipation by the working classes, it created an image of *fête* and of the possibilities of popular action which have inspired portrayals of it and popular culture in general ever since (see Weber, 1995).

WAR, DEFEAT, THE 1940S AND 1950S: COMING TO TERMS WITH RESPONSIBILITY

As well as his 'La Chanson du maçon' ('The Mason's Song', 1941), which contributed to his reputation as a collaborationist, one of France's most famous popular songs is Maurice Chevalier's 'Ça fait d'excellents Français' ('What Excellent Frenchmen they Make', 1939), which explains how soldiers of all ranks and political persuasions go to war to defend France. While the message of the song is socially and politically consensual, the list of officers and other ranks and varying political attachments (or lack of them) which forms the lyrics well describes the divisions and contradictions of France in the inter-war period. As Lloyd has explained, Chevalier himself experienced the years of defeat and collaboration in France between 1940 and 1944 in similar confusion (Lloyd, 2003) and, escaping execution during the Liberation, symbolized the difficult political responsibilities of popular artists.

Defeat in 1940 – though swift – was traumatic, and the collaborationist Vichy regime of Marshal Pétain attempted to provide stability and certainty for French people through the authoritarian, anti-semitic, anti-communist Etat Français (replacing the Republic) and its alluringly simple motto of *Travail, Famille, Patrie*. The authoritarian nature of the Vichy regime – and its state-led programme of *Révolution*

nationale – arguably stifled the development of popular culture, although both collaboration and resistance gave rise to pamphleteering and popular literature – such
as Vercors' *Le Silence de la mer* (The Silence of the Sea, 1942) – and cinema produced a number of classics. Perhaps the major effect of Vichy was to concentrate
the minds of France's intellectuals on their political and artistic responsibilities –
Sartre's *Qu'est-ce que la litterature?* (What is Literature?, 1948) was a prime example, which became the recurrent theme of political engagement during the 1950s
and 1960s, but another legacy was France's memory of Vichy itself.

As Rousso has demonstrated in *The Vichy Syndrome* (1991) the memory of Vichy
has figured and informed politics, society and cultural production through the follow-
ing decades. In popular song, Chevalier's ambiguous behaviour during the
Occupation was typical of the problems of dealing with this compromised past, but
other singer-songwriters such as Brassens also dealt with issues arising from Vichy.
In cinema, the archetypal example of the problems of remembrance was Marcel
Ophuls' documentary drama of life in Clermont-Ferrand during the Occupation, *Le
Chagrin et la pitié* (The Sorrow and the Pity, 1971); this film was only allowed on
French TV under the socialists in 1981, such was the rawness of its treatment of a
sensitive past. Other directors have naturally chosen to exploit this rich seam of troubled national identity and melodramatic morality: Louis Malle's *Lacombe Lucien*
(1974) and *Au revoir les enfants* (Goodbye Children, 1987), François Truffaut's *Le
Dernier Métro* (The Last Metro, 1980) and Audiard's *Un héros très discret* (A Perfect
Hero, 1996) and many others. More latterly, television has joined the Vichy memory
industry, with documentaries and other programmes which renegotiate remembering
and commemoration. This trend towards the televisual discussion of contemporary
history is marked and problematic, and has included what is arguably the single other
major event (apart from May '68) which has informed and influenced cultural production during the post-war decades: the Algerian War.

Before we discuss decolonization and the national trauma of the Algerian War, we
must however consider the socioeconomic background to the cultural and sociopolitical tensions surrounding both the remembering of Vichy and the inventing of
decolonization. The Fourth Republic (1946–58) in particular – born from post-
Liberation recreation of politics and provisional governments led by de Gaulle, and
thus replacing both the Third Republic (1870–1940) and the Etat Français (1940–4)
– was a period of frenetic economic reconstruction and modernization. The success
of growth and modernization was such that the sociologist and economist Jean
Fourastié coined the term *les trente glorieuses* to describe the period from 1945
until the oil crisis of the mid-1970s, suggesting that these 30 glorious years of
growth separated two entirely different Frances (Fourastié, 1979). Modernization
came through accelerated industrialization and changes to agriculture (mechanization, land reform) which were not without social costs. Inhabitual (for a France accustomed to a stable population) demographic expansion accompanied economic

growth, and shifts in population from rural to urban areas and of wealth between classes created social tensions. An example of the problems of reconstruction and growth was France's housing crisis of the post-war period: the plight of the homeless led to the famous Emmaüs movement of the Abbé Pierre, dramatized in the film *Hiver '54* (The Winter of '54, 1989). After the return of normalized patterns of politics (left–right animosity) in the early 1950s, *la guerre franco-française* again became a permanent feature of French politics, society and culture.

THE ALGERIAN WAR AND THE 1960S: RESPONSIBILITY, GAULLISM, FRANCE IN THE WORLD

The Fifth Republic replaced the Fourth Republic in conditions largely created by France's difficulties in deciding what to do with Algeria, the most populous, richest, closest and most important of her colonies, which achieved independence in 1962. France's – eventually unsuccessful – attempts to hang on to Algeria through military 'pacification' of the Algerian nationalists' armed insurrection were costly in economic and human terms, and politically and morally. Just as the experience of war and collaboration in the 1940s had informed intellectual and popular-cultural life through new questionings and concerns, the questionable ethics of France's treatment of Algeria – particularly the army's use of torture – and the way the Algerian issue revealed continuing doubts over the loyalty of some in the army to republican ideals, created an Algerian 'syndrome' which eventually led to novels, films and songs reviewing France's past in what was once vividly described as a 'savage war of peace' (Horne, 1985), but which for a long time the French government insisted was simply 'peacekeeping'.

From 1958 until 1969, when de Gaulle resigned from the presidency a year after the events of May '68, France was governed by Gaullism: the new Constitution of the Fifth Republic was designed by Gaullists, and a Gaullist-dominated parliament, Gaullist government and Gaullist president often led to feelings that France was somehow stifling under the Gaullist project of modernization and the search to rebuild France's reputation after the Fourth Republic's perceived weaknesses in government and society. Modernization of society and the economy became even more an ardent objective of national planning and government policy, and the suffering caused by the changes it wrought were increasingly reflected in popular culture, rural depopulation and the loss of rural life's traditions being lamented, for example, in Jean Ferrat's song 'La Montagne' ('The Mountain', 1967).

Such social tensions, and feelings of suffocation and 'boredom' – the term was coined in a famous headline in the *Le Monde* newspaper, describing France's mood just before May '68 – coincided with a period when the demographic boom of the years after 1945 produced young adults (in work or education) whose ambitions and interests often conflicted – radically in such decades of change – with the values of older generations. Such a cultural 'generation gap' was seen in popular music (new singers, new songs, new musics), in sexual behaviour, in leisure and holidays, and in literature and film (where new, young writers and directors appeared with other questions and themes). An extreme example of these trends is perhaps the song 'Annie aime les sucettes' ('Annie loves Lollipops') written by Serge Gainsbourg for France Gall in 1968; accounts differ whether the young and innocent-looking France Gall knew if she was singing about sucking lollipops or something else, but the younger half of those watching must have wondered whether the rest of France was getting the joke. This demographic encouragement of new forms and new energies in popular culture also took place against a background of technological developments which fostered new creativities and freedoms. The role of the portable transistor radio in allowing troops in Algeria to add their own information to what they were told by officers is often cited, and radio and television were significant players in the events of May '68 itself. In almost all fields of popular culture during the late 1950s and 1960s, France's more youthful population, growing prosperity, social and economic modernization and technological development combined to encourage expressions of popular culture. But it was arguably only post-May '68 and post-de Gaulle that popular culture really began to flourish, initially under the more 'liberal' presidency of Valéry Giscard d'Estaing in the 1970s and then, increasingly, during the 1980s.

De Gaulle's preoccupations with France's rightful place in world affairs (her *Grandeur*) focused attention more closely and consistently than in previous decades on the military, political and *sociocultural* relationship between France and the USA. Ross has brilliantly unpacked some of the influences of the USA and of modernization during the 1950s in particular (Ross, 1995) and this 'special' relationship has always troubled France. Ever since the Great War and the presence of a million US soldiers on French soil, the impact of jazz music, Josephine Baker and *la revue nègre* in the 1920s, and the redefinition of the international system brought by US leadership of Allied victory in 1945, France had been increasingly aware of American power and culture. The late 1940s had seen Franco-American cultural relations partially and controversially recast by influxes of US films (codified by the Blum-Byrnes Agreement, 1946) and the conditionally offered economic assistance of US Marshall Aid (1948–51). The strength of communist support in France during the post-war period led, naturally, within the context of the Cold War, to increased sensitivity to real or imagined American 'imperialism' of military (NATO), economic (the dollar), linguistic (diplomacy, films, music), technological (computing) or more broadly cultural (books, music, food, ideas) forms. Gaullism and communism shared a concern with the perceived dangers and drawbacks of 'coca-colonization'.

MAY '68 AND THE 1970S:
PREFIGURATIONS OF A NEW FRANCE

May '68 was many things, but it started as student protests against higher education, taken up and amplified by militant groups, which then struck a chord with workers in industries and trades unions, dissatisfied with conditions of employment, the
attitudes of Gaullist governments and the distribution of the fruits of France's industrial growth. At their height, the events of May and June paralysed central Paris,
touched hundreds of provincial cities and towns and sparked a general strike of 10
million workers. The unhappiness of students and workers was channelled to a certain extent by trades unions keen to use the events against de Gaulle and prime minister Georges Pompidou, but at a basic level the protests and outpourings of support
for new ways of organizing society, social and interpersonal relations and politics
reflected younger people's alienation from the society in which they were becoming
adults. Much of the social and cultural commentary which arose during May '68
focused on consumer society – criticized for its reductive constraints on life – and the
perceived political and social authoritarianism of the heavy-handed Gaullist state.

Various accessible treatments of May '68 deal with its events, significance and
interpretations (Hoffmann, 1974; Caute, 1988; Reader with Wadia, 1993). These
studies may sometimes differ in their assessments, but everyone agrees that May
'68 is only beaten by 1945 as a reference point of the post-war period for French
people. 'Failed revolution' or not, the concerns about personal freedoms, civil rights,
sexuality, culture, government, information, work, leisure and consumerism
expressed during this period did much to set patterns of developments in the 1970s
and 1980s. Particularly in the field of popular and youth culture, May '68 remains a
touchstone for artists, authors, musicians and the general public.

After the brief presidency of Georges Pompidou (1969–74), France's coming to
terms with politics and society post-de Gaulle and the contemporary world was accelerated by the seven years in office of the independent republican Giscard d'Estaing
(1974–81). As France's most youthful twentieth-century president (48 when elected,
whereas de Gaulle was nearly 80 when he departed in 1969), Giscard recognized
the need for sensible changes to the style of government and the functioning of society – his election slogan was 'change without risk' – and was inhabited by a reform-
ing zeal to bring legislation and practices into step with the new social and cultural
realities of modern France. Although the death penalty remained (until the socialists
arrived in power in 1981), Giscard legalized abortion, brought greater recognition to
the rights of women, gays and lesbians, initiated moves towards greater plurality of
information by breaking up the state radio and television organization, created a
measure of comprehensive secondary schooling, overturned the ban on Paris elect-
ing its own mayor and generally – through his writings and policies – attempted to
address dissatisfactions voiced in May '68.

Doubly constrained by the world economic crisis of the mid-1970s and by problems with the majority Gaullist element of his parliamentary support, Giscard achieved less than he hoped. His presidency coincided with the painful end of *les trente glorieuses*, the challenge of demographic and ethnic changes in the French population (produced by the post-war baby boom and by the growing presence of second-generation immigrants) and the growth of new social and political trends such as regionalism and environmentalism. Popular culture both reflected and portrayed the maelstrom of sociocultural developments in the 1970s: the films of the period were either American imports or French analyses of the new complexities of – say – relations between men and women, or the difficulties of life in a increasingly post-industrial society. Newspapers such as *Libération* were created and flourished in the new more 'liberal' atmosphere; information on television was liberalized – slightly – by the separation of the news services of the main two state channels. The long-established satirical weekly *Le Canard enchâiné* used its freedom to criticize government as never before, seriously damaging Giscard's image. The electorate's disappointment in Giscard – he promised change and struggled to deliver – added to the desire for political 'alternance' between the right (in power since 1958) and the left, captained by the socialist François Mitterrand, led to the latter's victory in the 1981 presidential elections.

SOCIALISM AND LANG IN THE 1980S; THE FREE MARKET CONSENSUS IN THE 1990S

By the early 1980s, some of the aspirations of May '68 and some of the changes to structures that had been made during the early 1970s began to reach maturity, and some actors of May '68 were occupying positions of influence in government and the cultural industries. The socialist governments of the 1980s (and the right-wing government headed by Jacques Chirac 1986–8) presided over developments in the economics and organization of (popular) culture and over far-reaching changes to the ways the state conceived of culture as an object of policy. Two trends in particular may be seen to dominate this period: a new governmental readiness to apply a wider, more inclusive, more democratic and popular definition of 'culture' than hitherto; and the explosion of the audiovisual media as a prime site of debates over popular culture and French cultural identity. Both these trends were to continue into the 1990s and beyond, but it was during the first presidency of François Mitterrand that they arguably first arose as driving forces in popular culture.

The Socialists knew that after the socioeconomic and cultural transformations of the 1960s and 1970s more than Malraux-style *beaux-arts* policies concerning culture were needed. The prime mover in policy that evolved – aiming at stimulating creation (of all kinds), pluralism, decentralization, abolition of divides between 'high' and 'low' culture ('decompartmentalization') – was Culture Minister Jack Lang. Lang is usually associated with the ways in which the state moved towards recognizing 'popular' cultural forms as part of its new mission to support French 'creativity' wherever it was to be found (policies which became known as *le tout culturel*). There were essentially two kinds of 'popular creation' to be found: firstly, minor popular arts such as cooking and circus, which enjoyed the status of 'art' (of a subordinate kind) but which had eluded ministerial definitions of 'culture' and had therefore missed state aid; secondly, the 'popular culture' of the cultural industries (music, television, radio, *bande dessinée* (BD), advertising, fashion and so on) often condemned and patronized as 'mass culture' by previous official interpretations of culture. Cooking, for instance, was ennobled by the invention of the Ecole Nationale Des Arts Culinaires (the National School for Culinary Arts); the image of circus skills was raised by the creation of the Centre National de Formation aux Arts du Cirque (the National Training Centre for Circus Arts). And concerning mass culture, there was a particular focus on youth culture, exemplified by considerable encouragement of pop and rock (and other genres) and interest in BD (rightly or wrongly perceived as a young persons' culture). If 'youth culture' was predominantly 'mass culture', Lang was forced to address the traditionally negative view of mass-cultural, industrially produced forms of culture held by French elites and the state. Accepting the validity of popular music, advertising and fashion as culture and therefore opening the way to state subsidies of these cultural forms in the same way that high culture had traditionally been funded was a necessary corollary of both *le tout culturel* and of concerns to stimulate France's economic competitiveness in an area – culture in general – where she was felt to be strong. It was during the 1980s that changes started to occur in the economic organization of popular cultural production which transformed sectors such as radio, television and music.

The audiovisual media were transformed in France during the 1980s and 1990s by the July 1982 law stating that 'la communication est libre'. In the 1980s in particular under socialist and right-wing governments, the application of this 'freedom' led to the creation of a broadcasting regulator that kept government at arm's length in the management of radio and TV, to the licensing of hundreds of small radio stations (many of which were later bought up in the creation of large national music networks, although many local, regional and community stations survive), and television saw the invention of three new independent commercial channels and the privatization of the top audience channel TF1, which its critics would argue rapidly went downmarket in its 'spectacularization' of programming. The 1990s saw the flowering of over a hundred cable and satellite subscription channels, including thematic channels devoted to pop music, sport, news, horse-race betting, erotica, teleshopping, American shopping and many other specialist interests. Since the 1980s, technology and commerce have been driving forces of popular culture in France to a greater extent – arguably – than ever before.

Conclusion

There are thus a number of recurrent themes in the individual chapters which follow. Sometimes these themes are discussed explicitly and sometimes they provide the background to the discussion. Foremost among these themes are: economic and social modernization during the *trente glorieuses* and beyond; France's obsession with American culture and the beliefs of her elites that French culture needs protection against coca-colonization; the influence of politics – wars, processes, personalities – on culture; the influence of economics and commerce on the organization of the culture industries; the increased standard of living and extra leisure time that the French enjoy. Although the question could form part of the next section, this is an appropriate enough point to ask how ever-closer European integration and the globalization of the culture industries (the recent rapid rise and fall of Vivendi-Universal is a case in point) are likely to affect your favourite kind of popular culture.

SUGGESTIONS FOR FURTHER THINKING AND READING

There are two main strands to the general thinking that students of French popular culture can undertake to supplement the material provided here. Firstly, there are the treatments of popular culture as a concept and as an object of study available in most university libraries; secondly, they can learn more about French society, politics and culture (varyingly defined) by studying a number of recent excellent coverages of cultural developments in France.

Popular culture as a concept and as an object of study is dealt with by numerous works. Here the most we can do is to mention three or four recent approaches which might help inform a complementarily theoretical reading of French popular culture. A good place to start might be *Cultural Theory and Popular Culture: An Introduction* (Storey, 2001), which mixes theoretical exposition and explanation with examples of analysis in an approachable and stimulating way. Likewise, *An Introduction to Theories of Popular Culture* (Strinati, 1995) and *Cultural Populism* (McGuigan, 1992) discuss differing perspectives on popular culture – the Frankfurt school, Marxism, structuralism, feminism, postmodernism – and look at various examples of popular cultural practices. On one aspect of approaches to the 'popular', we have already mentioned *Everyday Life and Cultural Theory* (Highmore, 2002a) and its critical and historical discussion of the concept of the 'everyday', to which can be added *The Everyday Life Reader* (Highmore, 2002b) for its useful compilation of a range of original texts dealing with concepts and debates. Choosing a book on popular cultural theory really depends on how this current volume is to be used, and readers should – with advice, perhaps – find a treatment which suits themselves. Studies of France and of French culture which complement an introduction to French popular culture are easier to recommend.

Culture and popular culture in France are dealt with by a number of studies, but here the choice is more restricted. Two important books which could perhaps form a useful bridge between the more 'theoretical' discussions of 'culture' and its study recommended above are the excellent *Popular Culture in Modern France: A Study of Cultural Discourse* (Rigby, 1991) and the equally good *The Politics of Fun* (Looseley, 1995). Rigby starts from the Popular Front and looks at the ways in which intellectuals and academics in France have conceptualized culture and created discourses – or ways of talking – about cultural issues. In so doing, he blends considerations of cultural value, political ideology and cultural nationalism in an invaluable survey of concepts and themes. Looseley gives a very clear and readable account of changing government perspectives on culture and state cultural policy in France, and in a sense provides a complementary coverage to that of Rigby, by concentrating more extensively on how discourses about culture actually influenced government policies.

Two comprehensive coverages of many of the issues, individuals and policies discussed in this chapter and in those that follow are the invaluable *Encyclopedia of Contemporary French Culture* (Reader and Hughes, 1998) and *French Culture and Society: The Essentials* (Kelly, 2001) which both provide – in encyclopedia and glossary form – overviews of twentieth-century developments in culture (both 'elite' and 'popular'), politics, economy and society. These will provide added information on some of the details alluded to perhaps too fleetingly in the short analyses permitted by this current volume. Interest in French-speaking culture outside France may be satisfied by *Francophone Studies: The Essential Glossary* (Majumdar, 2002). More standardly narrative treatments of the evolution of French culture during the last century are provided by the excellently clear *French Cultural Studies: An Introduction* (Forbes and Kelly, 1995) and *French Culture since 1945* (Cook, 1993). Both of these volumes address more than merely popular or mass culture, placing the issues and phenomena studied here within the wider context of artistic, literary and other more traditionally high-cultural forms and the social, political and economic conditions which have determined their development. The highly recommendable *Contemporary French Cultural Studies* (Kidd and Reynolds, 2000) does much the same, but provides arguably more explicit coverage of aspects of popular culture, such as advertising. *Popular Culture and Mass Communication in Twentieth Century France* (Chapman and Hewitt, 1992) provides 15 analyses of specific topics of which many can be read in conjunction with those provided here (for example on language, radio, advertising, cinema and comic strips).

BIBLIOGRAPHY

Caute, David (1988) *Sixty-Eight: The Year of the Barricades* (London: Hamish Hamilton).

Certeau, Michel de (1988) *The Writing of History* [1975], trans. Tom Conley (New York: Columbia University Press).

Chapman, Rosemary and Nicholas Hewitt (eds) (1992) *Popular Culture and Mass Communication in Twentieth Century France* (Lewiston, NY: Edwin Mellen).

Cook, Malcom (ed.) (1993) *French Culture since 1945* (London: Longman).

Forbes, Jill and Mike Kelly (1995) *French Cultural Studies: An Introduction* (Oxford: Oxford University Press).

Fourastié, Jean (1979) *Les Trente Glorieuses, ou la révolution invisible* (Paris: Seuil).

Highmore, Ben (2002a) *Everyday Life and Cultural Theory* (London: Routledge).

Highmore, Ben (ed.) (2002b) *The Everyday Life Reader* (London: Routledge).

Hoffmann, Stanley (1974) 'May 1968: Drama or Psychodrama?' in *Decline or Renewal? France since the 1930s* (New York: Viking).

Horne, Alistair (1985) *A Savage War of Peace: Algeria 1954–62* (Harmondsworth: Penguin).

Kelly, Michael (2001) *French Culture and Society: The Essentials* (London: Arnold).

Kidd, William and Sian Reynolds (eds) (2000) *Contemporary French Cultural Studies* (London: Arnold).

Lloyd, Christopher (2003) 'Singing in the Occupation', ch. 11 in H. Dauncey and S. Cannon (eds) *French Popular Music since 1945* (Aldershot: Ashgate, 2003).

Looseley, David (1995) *The Politics of Fun: Cultural Policy and Debate in Contemporary France* (Oxford: Berg).

Majumdar, Margaret (2002) *Francophone Studies: The Essential Glossary* (London: Arnold).

McGuigan, Jim (1992) *Cultural Populism* (London: Routledge).

Reader, Keith and Alex Hughes (1998) *Encyclopedia of Contemporary French Culture* (London: Routledge).

Reader, Keith with K. Wadia (1993) *The May 1968 Events in France* (Basingstoke: Macmillan).

Rigby, Brian (1991) *Popular Culture in Modern France: A Study of Cultural Discourse* (London and New York: Routledge).

Ross, Kristin (1995) *Fast Cars, Clean Bodies: Decolonization and the Re-ordering of French Culture* (Cambridge, MA: MIT).

Rousso, Henri (1991) *The Vichy Syndrome: History and Memory in France since 1944* [1987], translation of *Le Syndrome de Vichy* (Cambridge, MA: Harvard University Press).

Storey, John (2001) *Cultural Theory and Popular Culture: An Introduction* (Harlow: Pearson).

Strinati, Dominic (1995) *An Introduction to Theories of Popular Culture* (London: Routledge).

Weber, Eugen (1995) *The Hollow Years: France in the 1930s* (New York: Norton).

CHAPTER 2

Language

Nigel Armstrong

LANGUAGE AS CULTURE

Perhaps the most striking thing that emerges when we think about non-standard French – *français populaire* or *familier* – is that, although language is a phenomenon of a very different order from other expressions of culture, people have similar attitudes towards non-standard French as towards other types of non-standard or popular culture like music, cartoons or football. The obvious difference between language and other popular-cultural manifestations is that we are all practitioners as well as consumers of language.

Here we look at non-standard French mostly on the level of vocabulary, since it is at this level that French is most lively. But we try first to define 'non-standard' French, and explain why language that deviates from the norm is such an issue in France. We then locate popular French within the wider context explored elsewhere in this book – focusing on the tension, especially noticeable in France, between 'everyday' and 'standard' French, and looking at examples of this tension as it appears in some forms of popular culture.

When we 'do' or perform linguistic acts, it is often in a very intuitive way, compared to other types of cultural behaviour. That is, we are usually less conscious of producing language; we monitor ourselves less, although this is less true of vocabulary, as we shall see below. Language is wired in as part of the personal and social identity of all speakers; for example, there is now evidence to show that babies in the womb can recognize what will be their native language. One result is that there is a sharper tendency to say one thing and do another in language. We use language intuitively, but we have attitudes that are more superficial, because they are acquired later on. This dichotomy is perhaps more vividly noticeable in French, as we shall see below. We have moreover to distinguish between the various 'linguistic levels' when making this claim. Linguists commonly study the 'levels of analysis' of vocabulary, grammar and pronunciation. Non-specialists recognize these levels intuitively, and the vocabulary level is usually most obvious. One very neat example concerns a 12-year-old boy talking to school-friends, who used the exclamation *putain!*, equivalent to 'bloody hell!' He then said, as if to himself:

(1) j'ose pas dire le mot parce que c'est en train n'nous enregistrer

  'I can't say the word because it's recording us'

The speaker seems to be using *oser* here to mean *avoir le droit* 'to be allowed to'. What is interesting for our discussion is that the boy is aware of the disapproval that a word like *putain* attracts, while at the same time seeming not to notice other features of non-standard French like the missing *ne* in *j'ose pas* (part of the grammar) or the missing consonant in *en train n'nous* (pronunciation).

FRANÇAIS POPULAIRE, FRANÇAIS STANDARD

The term *français populaire* is unsatisfactory. For the English speaker, there is the risk of being led astray into thinking that *populaire* means 'popular' in the sense of well liked or widespread. The phenomenon is certainly widespread, but, when combined with *français*, *populaire* means 'of the people', as in 'populace', so a literal translation could be 'working-class French'. The label is used by French monolingual dictionaries like the *Petit Robert*, and reflects the *prescriptive* intent of compilers of dictionaries, and beyond that the attitudes of many French people. That is, the aim is to prescribe or lay down the law on language use, especially that of other people. It is perhaps significant that, where the French dictionary provides a label based on supposed social-class origin, bilingual dictionaries like the Collins-Robert or Oxford-Hachette provide a *style* label – *populaire* usually translates as 'casual'. This seems to reflect the more relaxed attitude in the UK to non-standard language, compared to France. The UK approach is quite sensible, as words labelled *populaire* are in fact used by all social classes in France in casual or colloquial speech styles. But, alongside the reality of this behaviour, there are strong views, shared by very many French speakers, about what is and is not 'good French'. An extreme expression of this is a phrase like *c'est pas du français, ça* ('that's not French'), where some speakers actually try to exclude from the language a word or expression they find unacceptable. This reflects what French linguists call *l'imaginaire linguistique*: perceptions about language, as opposed to actual linguistic behaviour. We use the term non-standard French from now on, except where we need to distinguish between *français populaire* and *français familier* (colloquial French).

   The French linguistic situation is one of the more extreme examples of what happens in a society that has a *standardized* language. The process of standardization involves the ongoing attempt to stamp out variation or difference, in language as in any other area of activity. We call it a process because it is never complete: those who disapprove of variation (and change, which results from variation) try to stop it, of course in vain. It is in the nature of a language to vary, since it is used by social groups who can differ from one another very considerably in behaviour and attitudes. From variation stems change; we need only look at earlier states of French and English, as shown in their literature, to see this is so. Standardization has however arrested change in written French more successfully than English: a comparison of Racine and Shakespeare shows this very clearly. French writers seem to take more heed of prescriptivists than their English counterparts.

Standardization is less successful in stopping change in speech, but it does produce a kind of double-think; endless hours in the classroom learning forms of verbs and different types of clauses – French children are still taught grammar in a way that is rare in the UK or USA – seem to have convinced them, in part of their minds at least, that there is a 'correct' French they can never hope to practise properly. The term for this attitude is the 'ideology of the standard', which sees the standard as the only real language and all other varieties as imperfect approximations to it. The odd thing is that the ideology of the standard is taken on board not only by the elite, but also by those who gain no advantage by doing so. The ideology of the standard produces some interesting effects at the official level, and we discuss these below. One part of the problem is that teachers often don't tell their pupils that the French they learn in the classroom is suitable in formal writing but sounds pompous in speech, so that children are left wondering why hardly anyone they know speaks the sort of language they are tortured with in the classroom. The answer that comes back may have to do with inferiority: my family and friends don't speak that sort of French because socially they're at the bottom of the ladder. A more refreshing response, and common among speakers who see they have no chance of getting into the mainstream of French society (assuming they ever wanted to), is outright rejection of standard French, and espousal of the sort of values, and the sort of French, we look at below.

Standardization therefore produces ambiguous attitudes in speakers towards their language. Several studies have shown that many people are ashamed of their way of speaking, and the fact that speakers approximate to a more prestigious language variety in formal situations (job interviews, etc.) shows they are not comfortable with how they speak in every situation. The issue here seems to be that when we talk to someone we do not know well (or who has some power over us, as in an interview), we use a 'standard' or neutral language variety to shield ourselves from potential disapproval. The counterpart to the use of the standard in formal situations is that we use more casual styles of speech with people we know well, whose attitudes to language and other social questions we have learnt and whom we can therefore trust. As we said above, the split between the two halves of this dual system seems starker in French than in comparable languages like English. We do see the same attitude in English – for example strange statements like 'foreigners speak better English than we do' – but the French seem to have been subjected to a longer and bitterer process of standardization, reflecting the French centralizing tendency of state interference with the lives of its citizens. We can see the ambiguous attitude to non-standard French as one more manifestation of the average French person's attitude towards the state. From this point of view, non-standard French is a sort of linguistic *système D*, where 'D' stands for *débrouille* or *démerde* – the kind of resourceful short-cut used by the French when they pit their wits against the nanny state.

The situation we have just described is of course grossly simplified. Although the gulf between formal and informal French, both spoken and written, is probably greater than in English, the image of a 'gulf' is not suitable because intermediate between the formal and informal extremes lies a continuum of varieties, shading the one into the other and differentiated by a smaller or greater number of in/formal features. In other words, the differences between formal and informal varieties are often a matter of degree, not of kind. For example, we mentioned above that omitting the negative word *ne* in speech is a feature of *français populaire*. This is true, but only in the sense that *ne* will be omitted very frequently indeed in *français populaire* – about 90 per cent of the time. In other informal registers of French, like *le français familier, ne* will still be dropped very frequently.

When we compare non-standard French and *français standard*, we are implicitly looking at how social class influences language use, as we suggested in our discussion of the term *populaire*. We said above that the term *populaire* is not very suitable, since features of *français populaire* are not the exclusive preserve of working-class speakers, but are used by all classes to greater or lesser degrees. This is also true of UK and US English, but what seems to distinguish the French situation from the UK and USA is the linguistic level on which 'working-class' language is sharply apparent. This is especially true if we compare the French and UK situations. In the UK, accent is very important: it is hard to separate out regional origin from social class, such that regional origin is increasingly detectable in speech as one goes down the social-class continuum, and vice versa – the higher the speaker's social class, the more subtle the regional accent.

Is the same true of France? We need to distinguish firstly between northern and southern France. There is of course a considerable difference between the broad accent groups of these two large regions. There is however some evidence that the pronunciation of 'northern' or 'standard' French is quite highly 'levelled' compared to the UK situation. By levelling we mean the reduction of features that distinguish speaker groups: young–old, male–female, middle-class–working-class, speakers from different cities. What distinguishes French speakers most noticeably is the grammar and vocabulary they use. Reproduced in Table 2.1 is a sample of the 50 pairs selected by a researcher conducting a study of non-standard French vocabulary (Lodge *et al.*, 1997: 27). They were chosen to avoid specialist slang and so can be used by all speakers. The table shows that this non-standard vocabulary includes nouns and verbs, but adjectives like *rigolo* ('funny') could also be added to the list.

Table 2.1 *Sample of lexical pairs* (Lodge et al., 1997)

Non-standard	Standard	Translation
baffe (pop.)	gifle	'slap'
bagnole (fam./pop.)	automobile	'car'
bahut (arg. des écoles)	lycée	'secondary school'
se balader (fam.)	se promener	'walk'
baratin (pop.)	discours abondant	'spiel'
blague (fam.)	farce	'joke'
bosser (pop.)	travailler	'work'
bouffer (fam.)	manger	'eat'
boulot (fam.)	travail	'work'
bouquin (fam.)	livre	'book'

A comparison between English and French highlights the fact that, although there are of course plenty of slang terms in English, the extent of the phenomenon seems wider in French, both in the number of casual or informal terms used and in the number of people who use them. Very many French speakers will refer to their car as their *bagnole* when talking to family and friends. Is there an equivalent term in English that is so widespread socially? Similarly, is there a non-standard synonym in English for 'eat'? The point here is that although the commonly used French word *bouffer* is of course a more casual term than *manger*, it seems to mean exactly the same thing. Instead of 'eat' we might say 'scoff', but this seems to add something as well as casualness – 'scoff' implies greed of the eater as well as informality of the speaker. Table 2.1 shows a small sample only of the sets of non/standard words that speakers can use; one researcher (Armstrong, 2001, ch. 7) counted 237 pairs of this kind in a corpus of spoken French.

One result of this situation is a steady outpouring of books about non-standard French vocabulary, referred to variously as *argot*, *français branché* ('trendy French'), *français non conventionnel*, *tchatche*, etc. Attitudes to the phenomenon range from friendly to hostile; the latter type of response is reminiscent of the official attitude that we discuss below.

We now look briefly at some grammatical features of non-standard French, considering difference with the English situation and assessing the criticism made by elite groups that non-standard French is 'simple'.

THE GRAMMAR OF NON-STANDARD FRENCH

A striking difference between French and English is that variation in grammar seems more prominent in English. Earlier, we used the example of the negative word *ne* to illustrate this. Non-standard grammar is used by all French speakers to greater or lesser degrees, while in English its use polarizes groups of speakers. This seems to be because some non-standard grammatical constructions are perceived in English as betraying lack of education, and even of the capacity to think straight. So speakers who use non-standard multiple negation, as in 'I can't get no satisfaction', often attract adverse comment, expressed in this case through the argument that multiple negation is illogical on the analogy of mathematical formulae, where two negatives express a positive. This is of course inapplicable to natural languages, and multiple negation is frequent in Shakespeare, for example. What has happened is that the standardizing process has fastened on features like multiple negation and put them beyond the pale of the standard language. French differs sharply from English in this respect, tolerating a good deal of variation in its grammar.

A striking example is so-called 'WH interrogation', that is the formulation of questions using a 'WH word' like 'who', 'what', etc. (*qui, quoi*, etc. in French). As Gadet (1997, ch. 12) points out, French speakers potentially have available a considerable range of WH-interrogative structures, although not all speakers use all of the variants available. The four most common are listed below under (a)–(d), in descending order of sociostylistic value.

(2) (a)   quand venez-vous?

    (b)   quand est-ce que vous venez?

    (c)   vous venez quand?

    (d)   quand vous venez?

Some variants are surprisingly convoluted, like the following:

(3) (e)   c'est quand que c'est que vous venez?

    (f)   quand que c'est que c'est que vous venez?

Variant (a), realized through inversion of subject pronoun and verb, is now rather formal in everyday French, although still the standard construction in formal writing. Variants (b) and (c) might be called more or less 'neutral' in their sociostylistic value, while (d) is rather colloquial. Variants (e) and (f) illustrate again the point that socially coded language is influenced by several social factors: sex, age and social class or prestige are the most frequently studied in sociolinguistics, but other factors like region and ethnicity can also influence language use. The examples in (3) seem to convey somewhat of a rural flavour, hard to render in English without resorting to exaggerated 'peasant' stereotypes like Cletus the slack-jawed yokel in *The Simpsons*.

Alongside this greater participation in the use of non-standard grammar, there is the usual double-think that condemns some constructions, and by implication some speakers, as 'simple', as for example:

(4) *y'en a j'aime pas le rythme*

   'there's some where I don't like the rhythm' (of rock songs)

The 'problem' with this French sentence is that it lacks a relative pronoun: *dont* would be needed to make it more standard. The argument is sometimes heard that a sentence like this is simpler because it merely places two elements side by side, instead of relating them more explicitly. The underlying argument relates to the people who use language like this. This is another form of the quite common statement of the type: 'I think the Yorkshire accent is so sloppy'. Language in itself cannot be simple, sloppy, etc., although it can be used in a simple or sloppy way. Judgements on language of this type are really social judgements. We see them perhaps in a sharper form when applied to grammar, because grammar is perceived as being in some way connected to reasoning. The French context certainly does not lack criticism of non-standard grammar and vocabulary by social elites who prize 'high' culture, and who therefore condemn popular culture for its linguistic expression as well as for its cultural 'poverty'.

   There are practical benefits in being aware of the grammatical and lexical features we have discussed above – most obviously, because when speaking or writing French it is important to tailor the language register to suit the person addressed. But these features are very often used in popular-cultural products like films, songs, BDs, novels, TV shows, internet chat and so forth. Awareness of the social and stylistic value of these language features is crucial to full understanding of the cultural products.

   Below is a fragment from a French novel that illustrates this point, taken from Queneau's *Zazie dans le Métro* (Zazie in the Metro, 1959: 47):

(5) Le type paie et ils s'immergent dans la foule. Zazie se faufile, négligeant les graveurs de plaques de vélo, les souffleurs de verre, les démonstrateurs de nœuds de cravate, les Arabes qui proposent des montres, les manouches qui proposent n'importe quoi. Le type est sur ses talons, il est aussi subtil que Zazie. Pour le moment, elle a pas envie de le semer, mais elle se prévient que ce sera pas commode. Y a pas de doute, c'est un spécialiste.

   Elle s'arrête pile devant un achalandage de surplus. Du coup, a boujplu. A boujpludutou. Le type freine sec, juste derrière elle. Le commerçant engage la conversation.

   [The guy pays and they immerse themselves in the crowd. Zazie weaves in and out, neglecting the engravers of name-plates for bicycles, the glass-blowers, the stallholders hawking ready-made ties, the Arabs pushing watches, the Gypsies pushing anything at all. The guy's tight on her heels, he's as clever at it as Zazie herself. Just for the minute she doesn't wanna lose him, but she warns herself that it'll be no pushover. No doubt about it, he's a specialist.

She stops dead in front of a stall of Army surplus clothing. And doesn't budgeaninch. She doesn'tbudgeatall. The guy stamps on the brakes, just behind her. The stallholder engages the conversation.]

One notable feature of *Zazie* is its importation into the narrative of some non-standard features of spoken French, which are found throughout the dialogue and narrative of the novel. Queneau was by no means the first to use this device; it can be found in Céline, Zola, Hugo and Balzac. Queneau seems here to be playing a sophisticated literary game, deploying both popular- and high-cultural resources to provide diversion for the reader who shares the resources. One way of analysing this is to suggest that the amusement deriving from the quite frequent infusion in the book of dialogue into narrative depends on a tension, here between expectation and literary practice. Queneau's practice goes against the convention used in most novels, where narrative and dialogue are demarcated, so that in the passage cited above colloquial elements like *y a pas de doute* contrast with carefully chosen literary words such as *s'immerger*. This is most vividly apparent in the sequence *Du coup, a boujplu. A boujpludutou* in the above passage. In a more standard register of French this is: *Du coup, elle (ne) bouge plus. Elle (ne) bouge plus du tout*. Here the words written solid evoke the stream of speech, where there are no gaps between words, while the semi-phonetic spelling seems to have been triggered by the author's decision to represent *elle* as *a*, an old working-class Parisian feature.

THE SOCIAL FUNCTION OF NON-STANDARD FRENCH

The terms in the right-hand column in Table 2.1 can be referred to as *argot*, which translates fairly straightforwardly into English as 'slang'. Mainstream dictionaries are usually behind the game when they define non-standard language, and this reflects the difficulty of those who operate in standard French in keeping in touch with every-day usage. For example, as late as 1995 the *Petit Robert* had as the first definition of *argot: langage secret des malfaiteurs, du milieu* ('secret language of criminals, of the underworld'). The linguist Jean-Louis Calvet has criticized this definition (1994, referring to the 1987 *Petit Robert*):

It is in fact difficult today to accept as 'criminals' all users of what is commonly called 'slang' [...] the same 'slang' word can be used by a petty criminal or a government minister, for different reasons naturally, for slang is no longer the secret language it originally was; it has become a sort of emblem, a way of situating oneself in relation to the linguistic norm and therefore in relation to society.

This expresses very clearly one of the major functions of non-standard language. The term 'linguistic norm' is here more or less interchangeable with 'standard language'. As we pointed out above, many speakers have ambivalent attitudes towards the standard language, and beyond this towards what we might very broadly call 'authority', or 'society' as Calvet expresses it. As Calvet's quotation implies, *argot* was at one time chiefly a secret language, used by criminals to conceal their activities from outsiders. An obvious English counterpart is Cockney rhyming slang. We shall see below that French *verlan* or backslang can have a similar purpose, but the main function of *argot* is now symbolic. We said above that language varies according to the social groups who use it, and groups are usually defined by age, sex and social class. A fourth category important in France is ethnicity, and we discuss this in connection with *verlan* below.

Criminals need to conceal their activities, partly by encrypting their speech in slang (French films like *Touchez pas au grisbi!* and *Les Ripoux* famously illustrate this). In contrast, the symbolic function of contemporary slang indicates in-group membership, which implies the exclusion of outsiders. We see this function most vividly in the speech of young people, who are commonly regarded as the most copious creators and users of slang, and this is motivated at least in part by the wish to proclaim membership of a group that has very clear visibility, because of its difference from the mainstream. The age example also points up the contrast between what we can call the 'long-term' and 'short-term', or 'social' and 'stylistic', uses of *argot*. French adolescents in general, or *Beurs* (French people of second- or third-generation Arab origin), find themselves in a situation of more or less permanent exclusion from mainstream society. Most young people will of course join it sooner or later, but from an adolescent point of view this can seem a long way off. For many *Beurs* living in the *cités*, the low-quality housing projects surrounding French cities, the exclusion is permanent. Their use of slang is therefore 'long-term' or 'social', serving to symbolize their membership of a group that has little to do with 'straight' society. This is perhaps most famously illustrated in *La Haine* (1995), a film portraying a day in the life of some inhabitants of the *cités*.

Calvet's example of a politician who uses slang provides a sharp contrast, since here we see someone who is fully integrated into mainstream values, to the extent of being in a position of helping to maintain them. When someone belonging to an elite group like this uses slang, the motivation is clearly quite different from our previous examples of young people and *Beurs*. Government ministers are far from being at odds with mainstream values, so that when they use slang it will be to achieve a local, temporary effect – what we called above a 'stylistic' effect. Speakers tailor their language to the situation in which they are speaking, and we cited above the example of formal language used to speak to strangers, as in a job interview. But the opposite principle obviously applies, and our government minister will be quite capable of using slang when talking to family and friends, or when wishing to lend informality to discussions with colleagues. Another way of looking at this is to say that the minister is using French as it is informally acquired, not formally taught. This shows how it is possible to use non-standard language to produce a 'short-term' effect: the government minister has no real commitment to the subversive ideology behind the slang that s/he uses, but understands, like all native speakers, that slang can be used temporarily to redefine the tone of a conversation. These then are two of the 'very different reasons' for using slang that Calvet refers to. Both share the expression of an attitude to the standard language. One is permanent or at least long-term: at its most extreme, the expression of a predicament. The other is a stylistic device that subverts the tone of a conversation to induce greater intimacy. As we suggested above, the French situation is distinctive in using vocabulary more than pronunciation or grammatical features.

STATE RESPONSES TO NON-STANDARD FRENCH

So far we have looked at individual responses to the tension between everyday language and standardizing pressures. A further important aspect of popular language in France is how the state responds to it. Elsewhere in this book, attention is paid to the attitude of the French state to other manifestations of popular culture like music, radio and film. Although we emphasized at the outset some important differences between language and other types of cultural behaviour, there are also similarities when we consider responses at this official level.

Students of French and France soon meet the notion of French *étatisme*: interference by the state in the lives of individual citizens. This goes back a long way, although the Revolution was a catalyst that intensified the process and increased its efficiency through the apparatus set up by Napoleon. A key date in the history of French government intervention in language is 1635, when Cardinal Richelieu, Louis XIII's chief minister, established the Académie Française, the body that was later given the task of creating an official dictionary and grammar. The general point here is obviously that France has a long history of state initiatives to regulate language, and parallels in the UK and the USA are notably absent. The French tradition of laying down the law about language is true not only figuratively, but also literally.

It makes sense to consider contemporary French state responses to non-standard French from the viewpoint of how French people perceive the role of their country in the wider world. In France and in other countries having a highly developed sense of being a nation-state, where political and cultural boundaries are expected to coincide, much stress is laid on the relationship that citizens have to the centralizing state as well as to their fellow citizens. This dual relationship is in turn connected with outward- and inward-looking aspects of nationhood; in its outward-looking aspect, a nation defines itself in contradistinction to other nations, and this can call for a patriotic or nationalistic response from its citizens. The inward-looking aspect implies a concern with internal cohesion and the diminution of difference, the counterpart of external distinction. In times of crisis, external distinction can turn into external threat: a state of war is the most obvious example. At these times internal cohesion is also of paramount importance, and anyone who dissents from this cohesion is likely to be thought of as an 'enemy within'.

The odd thing about France is that in linguistic matters, the state, or at least some of its representatives, quite often shows this wartime mentality, as if the very existence of the French language were being threatened. This is odd because France is a mature, autonomous, prestigious nation-state, and its language is a *langue de culture* with a rich literature. One obvious explanation is the French sense of having been relegated to the second rank of nations during the twentieth century. But this is true of the UK also, and does not in the UK find expression in official alarm about an Apocalypse threatening to engulf the language through external threat and internal perfidy. The real issue here is of course not linguistic, but sociocultural and political, and the debate reflects the sense of cultural uniqueness that is prevalent in France at the political level and elsewhere, and is summed up in the phrase *l'exception française*. The French response can also be explained in part by the nation's sense of itself as a beacon of culture and civilization – phrases like *le rayonnement de la culture française* ('the world-wide influence of French culture') are still common. The counterpart to this is that the perceived invasion of France by Anglo-American popular culture – and language – is regarded by some French people as humiliating; this invasion is summed up in the phrase *la coca-colonisation*. What is only sometimes mentioned in debates about the so-called 'exportation' of Anglo-American popular culture is that many French people are enthusiastic importers of it – and these are the enemy within.

This issue is relevant here because French popular language makes copious use of Anglicisms, referred to by those who disapprove of them by the term *le franglais*. The most recent hostile official response to the perceived flood of Anglicisms into French was the Loi Toubon of 1994, which obliged French state employees to use, when composing state documents, officially approved alternatives to English terms. Once one has got used to the idea of the French state using the law to regulate language in this way, this does not seem too bizarre, but an earlier version of the law was rejected by the Conseil Constitutionnel, the body responsible for making sure that legislation conforms to the Constitution. The first version of the Loi Toubon sought to ban the use of all Anglicisms in advertising, media and business, and this would have affected radio stations broadcasting to young people, for example. The Conseil Constitutionnel ruled that this first draft limited the freedom of expression enshrined in the Constitution, since it concerned private citizens as well as state employees.

As Thody points out (1995: 82), ' "la querelle du franglais" can sometimes be seen as an example of what the French themselves call "les guerres franco-françaises", quarrels among themselves about what kind of society they ought to have'. As Thody remarks, what is distinctive in the French situation is the ferocious and polarized nature of these quarrels, with battle-lines drawn up on predictable ideological grounds. In contrast to the political centre, which seemed fairly indifferent to the *franglais* issue and which no doubt includes most French people, the reactionary right and the *étatiste* left expressed strongly favourable views when the Loi Toubon was debated in parliament. One Gaullist senator declared: 'when I see all these American words on the walls of Paris, I want to join the resistance'.

It would be going too far to say that the debate over *le franglais*, which is found in technical, commercial and other types of French as well as in non-standard French, inspires debate about the really fundamental question of French national identity. It is rather that French unease about 'what kind of society they ought to have' tends to infuse many debates about issues like *le franglais*. This unease reflects the relatively recent establishment in France of a stable, consensual system of democracy, which purely symbolic threats from within and without seem to awaken in a fashion that can surprise the outside observer.

FORMATION OF NON-STANDARD FRENCH

Thus far, we have looked at how non-standard French functions from various sociological viewpoints. In contrast to proposing theories about why French people use slang, and how they react to it, it is refreshing to look at how slang terms are formed. This is because we gain an insight into how ordinary people add to the resources of their language in a culturally creative way, in what has been called *la culture de l'éloquence*. When considering how slang is formed, it is useful to make a distinction between modifications of words themselves on the one hand, and on the other the concepts expressed. We will see below however that these processes can change both aspects of the word.

Looking at the way words are modified, we can say first that simple reduction is a common process, and this is of course understandable in French, a language with words that on average are quite long, since they derive from Latin and Greek. So *sensationnel* becomes *sensass*, *conversation* becomes *conversass*, and so on. Speakers simply wish to save time and effort by taking short-cuts.

Against this, reduction + expansion is also common, as when *directeur* becomes *dirlo.* The reduction here is obvious, but what happens next is that a suffix is attached to the shortened form to give it further slang value. Not any suffix will do, of course: they are drawn from a non-standard stock that includes *–lo*, *–lingue* and *–loche*.

Slang systems also depend on the transposition and addition of syllables and letters, as in the cases of *verlan* and *loucherbem*. We look at *verlan* in more detail below, but it is worth looking briefly at *loucherbem*, which might be translated as 'butchers' slang'. The term itself represents an example of what is involved, whereby *boucher* transforms to *loucherbem*. The first letter of the source word transfers to the end, the suffix *–em* is added, then 'l' is attached to the front of the new word. These processes respond, at least in part, to the playful functions of language; people simply like playing around with words. They also enjoy playing around with the concepts behind them, as shown immediately below.

When we look at the processes that speakers use to change concepts, we are in the realm of rhetoric. This term generally suggests the dishonest use of language – the 'rhetoric of politicians'. But rhetoric in its original sense means the figures of speech used to make language more vivid and varied, and hence more memorable and persuasive. Two very common rhetorical devices are metaphor and metonymy. A metaphor is an implicit comparison, most often using imagery. An explicit comparison (a simile) will obviously use a word such as 'like' or 'as': 'My love is like a red, red rose'. Metaphor either suppresses the comparison: 'My love is a red rose'; or simply substitutes the image for what it is being compared to: *pépin* (a 'pip') for *problème*. Metaphor is so common that we cease to notice it; people prefer the concrete, as expressed through an image, to the abstract.

Metonymy, again a common device, substitutes the whole for the part, or the part for the whole. So, 'the hall' can be used to stand for the audience contained in it (as can *la salle* in French); a further example is *verre* ('glass') representing the drink it contains: *si on prenait un verre?* Substituting the part for whole, the second subtype of metonymy, seems more frequent. An English example is 'the Crown', which frequently represents its wearer. A less stuffy example is the US English use of 'ass' to refer to its possessor: 'your ass is mine'. A slightly different type of metonymy substitutes a quality of the thing for the thing itself, as in the recent slang term *nuit grave* for 'cigarette', from the warning on the cigarette packet: *nuit gravement à la santé* 'seriously damages health'.

Three examples (from Wise, 1997: 217) show operations on the concept using metaphor and metonymy, and then an operation on the concept and the word:

(6)   *mansarde* = 'head'

      faire le trottoir = 'to solicit'

      beu-beu = 'cannabis'

The first example shows one of the numerous non-standard synonyms for the head. Clearly, a metaphor will be selected because it bears a resemblance to what it refers to, and a mansard roof has a vaguely head-like shape. The second example shows metonymy; in this case, the location of the activity is substituted for the activity itself. The third example shows metaphor plus shortening: *herbe* ('grass') is substituted for cannabis, then the word is shortened (after preliminary lengthening to *herb-euh*; we discuss this process in more detail in the next section). In this example shortening is achieved through omitting the first syllable. Reduplication, another quite common device, then takes place.

FORMATION OF *VERLAN*

No account of non-standard French would be complete without a mention of *verlan*. The more recent bilingual dictionaries (Collins-Robert and Oxford-Hachette) explain *verlan* quite fully, so recognizing its prominence and cultural distinctiveness. Earlier dictionaries referred to it simply as 'backslang'. But, unlike English backslang, which relies on spelling and gives for instance 'yob' for 'boy' and 'wonk' for '(those who make it their business to) know', *verlan* is syllable-based. The basic rule to form verlan is to invert a two-syllable word, and indeed this is how the word *verlan* was formed: *l'envers* ('backwards') is switched round to give *verlan*, so the rule of the game is shown in the name of the game, *l'envers à l'envers* or 'backwards backwards'. Other examples:

(7) métro → tromé   pascal → scalpa   café → féca

The game becomes a bit more complicated when applied to one-syllable words, since two syllables are required before anything can happen. In this case a single syllable, an 'euh' sound, is added to the end of the word to supply the second syllable. This 'euh' sound ('schwa' in the linguistic jargon) is quite often heard in colloquial speech anyway, when people say *tu m'énerve-euh!* or *à la fac-euh*; or as in the example of *herb-euh* in the previous section. Inversion then takes place as before, with an extra rule to shorten the end of the resulting word if need be:

(8) mec → me-keuh → keu-meuh → keum

flic → fli-keuh → keu-fli → keuf

femme → fa-meuh → meu-fa → meuf

Because one of the functions of *verlan* is to baffle the straight people, the initiated have to keep ahead of the game, since the point is lost if everyone knows what a *verlan* word means. One way of keeping ahead is through *reverlan*, where an existing word goes through the process again:

(9) meuf → meuh-feuh → feu-meuh → feum

    keuf → keuh-feuh → feuh-keuh → feuk

At this point, of course, the word can only spin endlessly between two combinations.

FUNCTION OF *VERLAN*

Our remarks made above on the social functions of *argot* apply also to *verlan*, with some modifications. Much *verlan* still relates to illegal activity, and this reflects its heavy use by *Beurs*, or at least those who lead a marginalized life in the high-rise council estates. It has been suggested that the frequent use of *verlan* by some *Beurs*, in the context of other linguistic features that differ considerably even from colloquial French, let alone standard French, reflects the *Beurs'* intermediate status; not yet fully French, no longer Arab. This illustrates a more general point to do with social differentiation; highly visible distinctions between social groups (ethnic in this case) will be reflected in sharp linguistic differences. In the case of *Beurs*, this is seen not only in *verlan*, but also in grammar and pronunciation. *Beur* French can look and sound very different from mainstream French, as the following example shows:

(10) *on a bien chafrav, maintenant c'est en teboi qu'on va*

    'we've worked well, now we're going to a club'

This sentence looks very alien from a mainstream French viewpoint, mainly because the verb *chafrav* (borrowed from Romany) is not conjugated like any native French verb. It is non-standard French of this kind that caused one French linguist (Duneton, in Merle, 1996) to say: 'we are in the presence of a gulf [between standard and non-standard French], and only the future will reveal if it is going to threaten our language as it now exists, or simply amount to an amusing phenomenon'.

Conclusion

When considering variation in any language, linguists tend to look at change too, since change arises from variation. Our last quotation above implies that momentous changes are afoot in French, but in reality the French language is broadly stable, especially in its pronunciation and grammar, since these are the structural levels of language that change very slowly. It is on the open-ended lexical level that variation and change are mostly seen, and much of this variation is any case ephemeral, as it does not lead to permanent change. For this reason, there is little point in trying to keep up with the latest fashions in slang: *verlan* today, Anglicisms and Arabisms tomorrow. And yet, as we suggested above, it is important to develop a sense of how French varies according to style and social group. For this is needed extensive study of the classics as well as the popular texts.

SUGGESTIONS FOR FURTHER THINKING AND STUDY

1. It is often said that slang refers to areas of activity that attract respectable disapproval: sex, drugs, crime. But other areas are body parts, bodily functions and money. How many different areas of activity can you think of? Are there any areas that provide exceptions to this generalization? What do money and sex have in common that make them such rich producers of slang?
2. Look at a novel by a writer like Queneau, San Antonio or Djian, or a film like *La Haine*, where non-standard French is used extensively, and try to work out why non-standard French is being used in each case.
3. Compare the variety of French used on a high-culture radio station like *France-Culture* with a contrasting one like *Radio NRJ*. Are the language differences most notable in vocabulary, grammar or pronunciation?
4. Consider a French 'reality TV' show like *Audience privée*, where two people engaged in a legal dispute try to resolve their differences in front of a studio audience. The two people are often of quite different social background; how are these social differences expressed in French in the very public setting of a TV studio?
5. What are the features of what must now be some of the commonest forms of written French – emails, internet chat and text messages? How much does this kind of written French differ from its nearest equivalent, correspondence written using paper and pen?

BIBLIOGRAPHY

Armstrong, N. (2001) *Social and Stylistic Variation in Spoken French: A Comparative Approach* (Amsterdam and Philadelphia: John Benjamins).

Calvet, L.-J. (1994) *L'Argot* (Paris: Presses Universitaires de France).

Gadet, F. (1997) *Le Français ordinaire* (Paris: Armand Colin).

Lodge, R. A., N. Armstrong, Y. Ellis and J. Shelton (1997) *Exploring the French Language* (London: Arnold).

Merle, P. (1996) *Dico de l'Argot fin-de-siècle* (New York: French and European Publications).

Queneau, R. (1959) *Zazie dans le Métro* (Paris: Gallimard).

Thody, P. (1995) *Le Franglais: Forbidden English, Forbidden American* (London: Athlone).

Wise, H. (1997) *The Vocabulary of Modern French: Origins, Structure and Function* (London: Routledge).

CHAPTER 3

Press

Denis Provencher

We understand the contemporary press as a communicative tool that informs us about a variety of local, national and international topics. It is a media form that reflects the world we live in. Yet, many scholars have convincingly argued that the press not only describes the world, but actually shapes and defines it. They contend that various forms of print media (newspapers, magazines and popular fiction) serve as vehicles for nations, regions and other groups to successfully build identity through an 'imagined community' of readers. For example, they claim the individual reader both experiences and understands the world simultaneously with other literate neighbors by reading a common news story that provides a particular version or 'narration' of reality (Bhabha, 1990, and Anderson, 1991). In this sense, the press is a powerful print medium that predetermines the world order for its readers and shapes their opinions about it. Newspapers and magazines can become political actors: '[they] are both the main arteries of a sophisticated system of political communication and major players within that system' (Kuhn, 1995: 1). Hence, this chapter introduces us to a number of French newspapers and magazines that have become important actors in the post-war era. Our case-study analysis of a recent event, as it appeared in some of the more 'popular' and 'specialized' titles, also helps us better understand how the French press both reflects and shapes contemporary French attitudes and mentalities on a variety of issues.

THE FRENCH PRESS: BRIEF HISTORY AND BACKGROUND

Although the first daily newspaper (*Journal de Paris*) appeared in 1777, the French press did not fully emerge until the Third Republic. In 1870, 36 Paris-based (national) newspapers and 100 provincial (regional) papers circulated daily, including the mass publications *Le Petit Journal*, *Le Petit Parisien*, *Le Matin* and *Le Journal*. 'Special-interest' or 'popular' titles also circulated, such as *Le Chasseur français* for the avid French hunter. By 1914, the number of 'national' and regional papers had reached 80 and 242 respectively with a combined print run of 9.5 million (Pedley,

1993: 149; Kuhn, 1995: 17). Many scholars now refer to this period (1870–1914) as the golden age of the French press.

The French press experienced great decline however during both world wars. In 1914 the state set page limits and censored newspapers from dealing with war-related events. Consequently, many publishers folded as they lost readers and revenue; only the largest mass publications could survive these economically hard times. The French press of the inter-war period faced such challenges as the press baron (i.e. Jean Prouvost), the quasi-monopoly on news distribution by large press groups (Hachette), and the control of news coverage and advertising by the international agency Havas. During the Second World War, both German and Vichy authorities intervened to censor and ban French dailies that did not support their respective agendas. For example, the Vichy government formed the Office Français de l'Information (OFI) in the unoccupied zone to produce its own version of official news and required newspapers to adhere to this source. Again, newspapers experienced loss of revenue as readers turned to the clandestine newspapers of the French Resistance and regional dailies that published information about food prices and rationings.

Following the Liberation, French authorities outlawed all newspapers that had supported the Nazis or Vichy and only 28 newspapers (out of 206 dailies) that appeared before the war resumed operation after 1945. The state replaced OFI with the national news agency Agence-France-Presse (AFP) and promoted new titles by providing new forms of financial assistance to newspapers through tax reduction or exemption. France experienced a wave of new daily papers (two to four pages in length on average) with a print run of 15 million dailies in 1946 in comparison with only 11 million in 1939. The French legislature also passed a new press ordinance in 1944 to guarantee the pluralism of the French press by preventing the concentration of press ownership in the form of the press baron. It also aimed to secure the pluralism of the 1881 'freedom of the press' law by removing the economic threat of the large press companies. However, such legislation did not prove economically realistic, nor did it guarantee the long-term success of all publications created in the immediate post-war era.

It is important to note that several large press groups continue to dominate the contemporary French press market, including Hachette, Prisma Presse and Hersant. The latter group incited legislation (known as the anti-Hersant laws) in the 1980s to further combat the monopolization of the press. Current French laws require that press groups control no more than 30 per cent of total daily newspaper circulations. The contemporary French press remains both pluralistic (based on the 1944 law) and controlled (anti-Hersant laws) because of such legislation. This minimally regulated system contributes at least in part to the persistent bureaucratic and 'status quo' nature of many French publications, which tend to lack entrepreneurial spirit and any taste for investigative journalism.

THE PRESS IN THE POST-WAR ERA

Since 1945, the number of both French 'national' and regional dailies has continued to drop, from 28 to 11 and 175 to 62 respectively (Kuhn, 1995: 24), while the total print run has dropped from 15 million to between 10 and 11 million. The French read fewer newspapers today than they did 50 years ago. In fact, the French read only half as many daily newspapers as the British and Germans and only one quarter of the number read by the Swedish and Finnish (Moores, 1998a: 389). Several trends have taken place since 1945 that help us understand this decline.

First, the *national* dailies have lost readers to the regional newspapers as well as news weeklies and specialty titles. In the early 1940s, regional dailies represented about 50 per cent of the total print run. Today they represent approximately 75 per cent with a total of 7 million copies printed every day in comparison to 3 to 4 million national dailies. As mentioned above, many French citizens living in the regions turned to the local press for reliable news during the Second World War. Indeed, the local press still represents a dependable news source for many French citizens. In addition to these regional titles, several news weeklies (magazines) and hundreds of specialty titles have appeared since 1945 to compete with the dailies in a dwindling market.

The French in the post-war era also spend less time reading overall than doing other activities. For example, in the 1980s, approximately 55 per cent of the population read a daily in comparison with 72 per cent who listened to radio and 70 per cent who watched television (Kuhn, 1995: 2). The advent of other media (i.e. radio and television) has created an additional source of competition for the French national daily. To a certain degree, these newer media represent an overlap in news coverage and faster access to the same information for an on-the-go citizenry.

Advertising (see Chapter 15) also plays an important role in this context. In 1967 the French press accounted for 80 per cent of advertising. However, in 1968 the French government legalized advertising on French television and it has since continued to encourage the creation of new commercial and privatized television and radio stations. Consequently, advertising revenue for the French press has dropped sharply as electronic media draw advertisers away from the print forms. Between 1979 and 1998, the advertising revenue of the French press was cut in half; it currently represents only 14.5 per cent of the total advertising spent on the media (Sergeant, 2000: 232–3). This has affected newspaper and magazine prices, which in turn discourages some readers from buying increasingly expensive publications. Today, national dailies are priced at about €1.20 and their cost has grown more than twice as fast as the cost of living. Regional papers are slightly cheaper at less than €1.00 while weekly and specialty magazines are more expensive and range between €3.00 and €5.00).

Most recently, the internet (see Chapter 6) has contributed to the decline of the

French press. Although the internet has not replaced print media, this newest electronic format has affected the success of French .newspapers and magazines. Indeed, most French press titles are now available online and the French government has assisted with this effort. Nonetheless, newspapers and magazines do not publish full-text versions of what appears in print form and readers must still pay a subscription price if they want to read the publication from cover to cover. Hence, readers may now have a tendency to consult only the free information available to them on these and other sites. All of these factors contribute to the current state of the French daily and the French press in general.

CONTEMPORARY NEWSPAPERS AND MAGAZINES

In this section, we present a number of the most widely distributed and read French newspapers, news weeklies and specialty magazines currently available, with particular attention to some of the more 'popular' titles that will figure in our case study at the end of the chapter. The number of French titles currently available makes it impossible to include all of them here. However, this section should serve as an initiation for the reader. We have also included the websites for many of the titles to help facilitate further investigation.

Paris-based daily newspapers

Currently, only a dozen Paris-based or 'national' dailies circulate in contemporary France. These include: *Le Figaro, France-Soir, Le Monde, Libération, Aujourd'hui en France, Le Parisien, L'Equipe, La Croix, L'Humanité, Les Echos, La Tribune* and *Paris-Turf*. According to the website of the National Federation of the French Press (www.portail-presse.com), the five most widely distributed of these titles in 2001 included: *L'Equipe* (359,598), *Le Figaro* (358,977), *Le Monde* (352,956), *Libération* (163,084) and *Aujourd'hui en France* (143,786).

The top-selling 'national' daily *L'Equipe* (www.lequipe.fr) was founded in 1946 and is both the oldest and the best-known national sports magazine. Like most other French 'national' titles, it appears daily except Sunday and has a Saturday supplement, *L'Equipe-magazine*, which is also devoted to sports. However, due to its scope, we could certainly consider it a specialty newspaper as it does not offer national/international news coverage like the other four leading national dailies. In fact, the term 'national' is misleading in this context as our list of Paris-based dailies includes four 'specialty' (sports and finance) and two 'popular' titles. Along with *L'Equipe*, these include *Paris-Turf, Les Echos, La Tribune, Le Parisien* and *France-Soir* (see the discussion of these below). Press scholars do not agree on the classification of these titles, but the fact that this list of 12 'Paris-based' dailies includes a total of six 'specialty' and 'popular' titles suggests that contemporary French reading practices have become more 'popularized' in terms of subject matter. This becomes particularly relevant as we consider the number of specialty titles that have emerged to compete with 'national' and regional dailies.

Le Figaro (www.lefigaro.fr) is France's oldest newspaper; it started as a weekly in 1854 and became a daily in 1866. Although *Le Figaro* ceased publication during the Second World War, it is one of only two right-of-center papers (along with *Le Parisien*) that reappeared after the Liberation. Today, *Le Figaro* is the leading title for the Hersant group and covers a variety of news topics including financial and business information for readers who come mostly from the professional middle and upper classes. In 1976 Hersant also purchased *France-Soir* (no website available; 149,000 circulation) from Hachette and this title represents a down-market Gaullist daily to complement *Le Figaro*. *France-Soir* began as an evening paper after the Second World War, but is now a morning daily that competes with *Le Parisien*. *France-Soir* relies largely on photographs and tends to publish more human-interest stories (*fait divers*); for this reason, some scholars consider *France-Soir* to be a 'popular' daily (Albert, 1990: 211). Since the late 1970s, the Hersant group has also launched other 'specialty' titles including the women's luxury magazine *Madame Figaro*, the television guide *Le Figaro TV*, and the Paris guide to weekly events *Figaroscope*.

Le Monde (www.lemonde.fr) began in 1944 as the post-war equivalent of the widely read *Le Temps* (banned after the Second World War) and represents France's most comprehensive national daily (published by Hachette) to compete with *Le Figaro*. *Le Monde* has an international reputation and it deals with both national and world news events. It publishes very few photographs and is perhaps the most sober newspaper in both tone and appearance. Nonetheless, it is a socially progressive, left-of-center publication that demonstrates a commitment to justice and human rights for a highly educated readership. Although Hachette does not publish a 'popularized' down-market equivalent to compete with *France-Soir*, this group does publish the special-interest supplement *Le Monde philathéliste* for stamp collectors.

Libération (www.libération.fr) began in 1973 as a radical Maoist daily paper and is the only national daily created in the post-war era still in existence. The paper continues the spirit of 1968 and tries to speak for marginal groups traditionally left out of mainstream debates. It regularly came under attack in the 1970s and 1980s for its polemic tone and use of investigative journalism. Since 1981, however, it has abandoned much of its counter-culture edge and has moved more toward center left. Today, *Libération* aims to survive as a quality publication that competes with other national titles. It tends to attract a readership that is younger than that of *Le Figaro* or *Le Monde* (aged 25 to 34 on average) and is drawn more to its tone and style than to any political viewpoint.

Aujourd'hui en France (no available website) began approximately ten years ago as the national version of *Le Parisien* (www.leparisien.fr; 361,000) and these two dailies publish much of the same national news information. Together, the two papers have a total circulation of over 500,000 and compete successfully with other 'national' dailies like *Le Figaro*. *Le Parisien* appeared in conjunction with the Resistance (of the right) in 1944 as *Le Parisien libéré* and became simply *Le Parisien* in 1986. Although *Le Parisien* started on the political right, it has moved more to the center. Today, it represents more of a local paper for Paris and the Ile-de-France region than a national daily. The National Federation of the French Press considers it a 'regional' title for this reason. It publishes short accessible articles as well as information on local events and was the first newspaper to use full color (in 1986). It is also the only Paris-based daily to document a rise in sales in the 1990s. *Le Parisien* serves more of a 'popular' audience with its tabloid and human-interest stories and sports coverage.

Along with these best-selling titles, several other Paris-based dailies continue with relative success. These include the Catholic daily *La Croix* (no website; 83,000); the French Communist party daily *L'Humanité* (www.humanite.fr/journal; 51,000); as well as the financial paper *Les Echos* (www.lesechos.fr; 111,000); its competitor *La Tribune* (www.latribune.fr; 81,000), and the horse-racing daily *Paris-Turf* (www.turf.fr; 97,000). Again, we could certainly classify these final three 'national' dailies as specialty titles.

Regional dailies

As mentioned above, the regional newspapers have greatly succeeded in the post-war era and represent approximately 75 per cent of the total print run. The popularity of the provincial or regional press seems to run counter to a largely hierarchical and centralized French system that privileges the capital. In fact, the dominance of regional papers in contemporary France resembles the success of US city-based dailies (*New York Times, Washington Post, Chicago Tribune*, etc.) and differs from the success of British national dailies (*Sun, Times*, etc.). Interestingly, while more men (60 per cent) read French national dailies, virtually equal numbers of men and women (51 and 49 per cent respectively) read their regional counterparts. Furthermore, a certain regional loyalty exists among regional readers, who are often older (average age of 67). Regional papers also tend to be cheaper and little competition exists between the regional markets. In addition, the regional publishers tend to have the most up-to-date printing technologies available and use more color than the Paris-based papers. Finally, they rely less heavily on national advertisers and news providers (AFP).

The most successful regional daily is *Ouest-France* (www.ouestfrance.fr; circulation 773,470), published in Rennes in the Brittany region. It began in 1944 and has outsold all regional and national dailies since 1976. This is a colorful newspaper that tends to cater to a middle-brow audience. Interestingly, the Bretons seem to read the highest number of newspapers with approximately 60 per cent of households read-ing the local paper. Other very successful regional titles include the Bordeaux-based *Sud-Ouest* (www.sudouest.com; 336,424); Lille's *La Voix du Nord* (www.lavoix-dunord.fr; 319,635), and Lyons' *Le Progrès-La Tribune* (www.leprogres.fr; 264,702). Other regional publications with circulations exceeding 200,000 include: *Le Dauphiné libéré* (Grenoble); *Nouvelle république du centre quest* (Tours); *La Montagne* (Clermont-Ferrand); *La Dépêche du Midi* (Toulouse); *L'Est républicain* (Nancy); and *Les Dernières Nouvelles d'Alsace* (Strasbourg). Among the many other regional titles are: *Le Républicain Lorrain* (Metz); *Le Midi libre* (Montpellier); *Le Télégramme* (Morlaix); *Le Provençal* (Marseille); *L'Alsace* (Mulhouse); *Paris-Normandie* (Rouen); *L'Union* (Reims); *Le Courrier de l'ouest* (Anger); *Nice-Matin* (Nice); *La République du centre* (Orléans); and *La Nouvelle République* (Loiret). Of course, a list of regional titles would not be complete without mention of dailies published in France's overseas departments and territories (DOM-TOMs) such as *France-Antilles*, *La Dépêche de Tahiti* and *Le Journal de l'île de la Réunion*. Nonetheless, the sales of regional titles have followed trends similar to the Paris-based dailies and we can partially attribute this decline to the competition from news weeklies and specialty magazines.

Weekly news magazines

Although news magazines first appeared under the July Monarchy (1830–48), most magazines emerged after the Second World War. For example, the right-of-center *L'Express* (www.lexpress.fr) began in 1953 as a left-wing weekly to supplement *Les Echos*. In the early years it was politically controversial as it commented on peace and decolonization issues, especially during the Algerian War; in the 1970s it was sold and moved further to the right. In 1972 many of its journalists left to start the new right-of-center weekly *Le Point* (www.lepoint.fr). Today, both *L'Express* and *Le Point* offer a clear synthesis of weekly news events for a readership comprised most-ly of conservative male city dwellers in middle and senior management with above-average incomes. *Le Point* in particular tends to deal with many moral and philosophical issues, though both magazines practice an American-style investigative journalism (inspired by *Time*) based more on solid factual reporting and less on political commentary.

Le Nouvel Observateur (permanent.nouvelobs.fr) began in 1964 and is the pri-mary left-of-center news weekly that competes with *L'Express* and *Le Point*. It is the descendant of *L'Observateur*, which was launched in 1950 and renamed *France-Observateur* in 1954. In the 1960s and 1970s *Le Nouvel Observateur* defended stu-dent causes and played a central role in several civil rights movements including women's rights, sexual liberation and the defense of immigrants. Like most current press titles, it now downplays party politics and has launched its own television supplement, *TéléObs*.

Le Canard Enchaîné (www.chez.com/lecanard/canard.htm) began in 1915 as a satirical news weekly in reaction to wartime propaganda. The 'chained duck' refers to rebellion against censorship and falsehoods published in the mainstream press. This leftist news weekly has called into question many political careers over the years and does not restrict its humor or coverage of issues. It is an independent newspaper owned by its journalists and it refuses advertising. It also maintains a minimalist website that satirizes politics, the press and the internet. Although published in Paris, it does not reflect dominant thought and could be considered a specialty title for this reason.

Perhaps the most successful publishing venture of the post-war era is Paris-Match (www.parismatch.com), which was created in 1949 by the press baron Jean Prouvost. It is the direct descendant of the 1930s sports magazine Match that ceased publication during the Second World War and reemerged as Paris-Match in 1949. It began as a general-interest glossy magazine following the format of the American publication Life. During the 1950s it shed its 'sports' identity, adopted a Gaullist (right-of-center) approach and became known for its use of dramatic color and photographs and included stories on political events as well as science, cinema, fashion and the private lives of celebrities. In 1976 Daniel Filipacchi purchased it and the magazine began to rely increasingly on sensational journalism and photoreportage to compete with television. It also adopted a new slogan: 'Paris-Match – Le poids des mots, le choc des photos' (Moores, 1998b: 409). As we will see in our case study below, photographs, catchy wording and dramatic photographs greatly contribute to the success of this publication. Circulation numbers peaked at 1.5 million copies in 1960 and have often topped 1 million copies; today's sales average around 800,000 copies.

There are many other weeklies that concentrate less on news reporting and more on leisure-time activities and special interests. For example, L'Evénement du jeudi is a left-of-center iconoclastic newspaper that publishes sensational headlines and incorporates investigative journalism to deal with politics, philosophy, music and television. Vendredi Samedi Dimanche (VSD) is a leisure magazine that deals with news stories, tourism, cars, TV, cooking, health, daily life and celebrities. Ici-Paris is a weekly scandal sheet that publishes horoscopes, cartoons, society gossip and love intrigues. France-Dimanche is a sensational Sunday publication created at the end of the Second World War to cheer up the population with escapist entertainment based on the lives of celebrities and public figures. Finally, Charlie-Hebdo is a descendant of the Mai '68 generation and publishes satirical cartoons that have provoked regular difficulty with French authorities.

Special-interest titles

'Special-interest' publications have existed as long as national dailies. For example, women's magazines began in the eighteenth and the nineteenth centuries with such titles as *Le Courrier de la nouveauté* (1758), *Le Journal des dames* (1759) and *Le Petit Echo de la mode* (1878). Specialty titles for farming date back to the Napoleonic era and hunting magazines date back to the end of the nineteenth century. Similar to the weekly news magazine, most specialty titles and 'popular' magazines have emerged since the Second World War with relative success. In fact, many new popular and specialty magazines appear each year, although very few titles succeed for more than several months. As mentioned above, some of the best-selling Paris-based papers are in fact special-interest papers devoted to sports. *L'Equipe* remains the only generalist sports daily in France and *Paris-Turf* is devoted to horse racing. Other sports weeklies include *France Football*, *Vélo* (biking) and *Midi olympique* (rugby). Of course, the best-selling specialty magazines of the post-war era are devoted to television programming (see Chapter 5). According to the National Federation of the French Press, these include: *TV magazine*, *Plus magazine de canal +*, *Canal satellite magazine*, *Télé -7 jours*, *Télé Z*, *Télé loisirs*, *Télé star* and *Télé 7 jeux*.

Publications targeted to women also represent another top-selling special-interest market. Important women's magazines from the post-war market include such luxury titles as *Elle*, *Marie-Claire*, *Vogue* and *Madame Figaro*. For example, *Elle* was launched in 1945 as a weekly *haut de gamme* (luxury) women's magazine by Hélène Gordon-Lazareff. It was considered a key reference for French women of the 1950s. Following 1968, it published many articles dealing with 'less radical' women's rights related to abortion, contraception, extended maternity leave and public child care. It continues to succeed relatively well today, especially thanks to its overseas editions. Similarly, *Marie-Claire* began as a luxury women's monthly in 1937 under press baron Jean Provoust. It ceased publication during the Second World War and was not allowed to reappear in 1945 because it had continued publication during the Vichy regime. However, it was relaunched in 1954 and had relative success throughout the 1950s and 1960s. Along with *Elle*, it also adopted many of the feminist ideas born out of the women's movements of the 1960s and 1970s in order to increase sales and promote a new image. Like most women's titles, it also experienced a period of crisis and redevelopment in the 1980s as it shifted focus. Today magazines such as these appeal to young, style-conscious women who have been able to reconcile feminism and femininity.

The more 'radical' women's magazines or French 'feminist' publications were associated with the Mouvement de Libération des Femmes (MLF) of the 1970s. These included such titles as *Le Torchon brûle*, *Les Pétroleuses* and *Les Cahiers du féminisme*. In turn, these publications affected the content of more mainstream specialty women's magazines such as *Elle* and *Marie-Claire*. Nonetheless, by 1975, the luxury women's magazines experienced more competition from other specialty press titles. These *haut de gamme* publications have survived mainly due to high advertising revenue and the number of overseas editions. Today, many more 'popular' women's titles exist that compete with these luxury women's magazines. These include *Prima* and *Femme actuelle* published by the Prisma group, which began in the 1980s. In fact, the 1990s women's press market was dominated by a mix of luxury and popular weeklies/monthlies as each one sold over half a million copies. These include *Modes et travaux, Marie-Claire, Prima, Femme actuelle, Madame Figaro, Maxi* and *Femme d'aujourd'hui* (Cayrol, 1991: 234). Nonetheless, there are many other successful titles to consider, including *Cosmopolitain, Biba* and *Mixte* to name just a few.

The gay and lesbian movement, like the women's movement, emerged in the 1960s and 1970s and prompted its own series of specialty titles. Earlier publications circulated in the 1950s, including the newsletter *Futur* and André Baudry's long-running magazine *Arcadie* (1954–82). More recently, Jean LeBitoux and Gérard Vappereau introduced *Gai-Pied* to news stands in April 1979. From 1979 to 1991, this left-of-center weekly provided a forum where gay men could speak their minds, defend their rights and forge their own identity through writing. Since *Gai-Pied* ceased publication in 1991, many other titles have emerged to carry on its tradition. The current generation of French gay and lesbian magazines published in Paris includes *Têtu, Lesbia* and a series of magazines published by Groupe Illico.

Têtu (www.tetu.fr) was launched as a monthly in 1995 under the direction of Didier Lestrade, former director of ACT-Up Paris and former contributor to *Gai-Pied*. The magazine began with the financial support of Yves Saint-Laurent and Pierre Bergé; however, it continues today largely by subscription. The inaugural issue called upon French readers to subscribe to a magazine that represents a French gay community of readers in the Anglo-American model of identity politics. *Têtu*'s slogan is 'Le magazine des gays et des lesbiennes' and it aims to offer something for everyone, but the content clearly appeals more to middle-class male readers. Many female readers turn instead to *Lesbia*, which was created in 1982 by Christiane Jouve and Catherine Marjollet. This is the best-known lesbian publication in post-war France. Other free or inexpensive titles are published by Groupe Illico, including *Illico* and *Double Face*. While *Têtu* and *Lesbia* deal with local, national and international events, Illico publications tend to focus more on regional/Paris-based happenings.

There are specialty weekly and monthly magazines for virtually every interest. These include publications for families (*Dossier familial*), children (*Enfant magazine, Phosphore, Babar, Youpi, Le Journal de Mickey, Spirou*), retired folks (*Notre temps, Les Jeux de notre temps, Vermeil*), health and fitness fans (*Top santé* and *Santé magazine*), gourmets (*Guide cuisine, Cuisine actuelle, Cuisine gourmande*), interior designers (*Art et décoration*), nature admirers and travelers (*Géo* and *Guide bel air*), science enthusiasts (*Science et vie, Science et vie découvertes*), ecologists (*Le Nouveau Politis*), detective fans (*Le Nouveau Détective*) and car enthusiasts (*L'Auto journal, L'Action automobile et touristique, Auto-moto, Automobiles classiques, L'Auto magazine*). The list of specialty titles is much too long to address all of them here and we have focused on some of the titles that figure prominently in our case study below.

CASE STUDY

OCTOBER 2002 ATTACK ON PARIS MAYOR BERTRAND DELANOË

In this section, we examine the popular news reporting of the October 2002 attack on the Paris mayor Bertrand Delanoë. We analyze the media coverage in the right-of-center *Paris-Match* and the left-of-center *Têtu*, and include supporting examples from other French publications to underscore the differences in reporting styles and ideologies. With this approach we hope to gain a better understanding of French attitudes and mentalities as they relate to certain social-political and cultural issues as depicted in popular press titles. We begin with a brief synopsis of the event based on information provided by Agence-France-Presse and published in the national dailies. In sum, the openly gay Paris mayor Bertrand Delanoë organizes an all-night gala (*la nuit blanche*; 'sleepless night') on 5 October 2002 for Paris residents. An aggressor (Azedine Berkane) enters City Hall during the festivities and stabs the mayor in the abdomen. Delanoë is seriously wounded and is transported to a nearby hospital. French officials apprehend Berkane, who has a police record and expresses a dislike for politicians and homosexuals.

The print version of *Paris-Match* (17 October 2002) devotes the first two pages of the article to a photograph of Delanoë enjoying *la nuit blanche* while standing in front of an *écorché* (human display/cutaway) at the National Museum of Natural History. The headline reads: 'Quand les hommes politiques risquent leur peau' ('When politicians risk their skin'). *Paris-Match* links the opening photo (a human display without skin) with a play on words ('risk their skin') to produce a foreshadowing and dramatic storyline that attracts the reader. The article then situates this attack as part of a larger *série noire* ('chain of disasters' or series of attacks) in 2002 on political officials including Jacques Chirac (14 July 2002) and eight Nanterre city-council members (26 March 2002). This narrative is supported visually by the initial two-page photograph that depicts the Paris mayor, which is followed by a two-page image of the Nanterre council meeting and another two-page image of the attempted shooting of Chirac. These six pages are primarily devoted to images, with a smaller section on each page devoted to a narrative of the events.

In this article, *Paris-Match* staff writers rely heavily on dramatic wordplay to make sense of the event by associating such unrelated ideas as *la nuit blanche*, *cauchemar* (nightmare) and *série noire*. Through such word associations, the magazine crafts a sensationalized story that appears natural, without serious regard for the facts or the actual relations between events. The article is replete with language that does not carefully synthesize the news from AFP. It continues with a statement that implies that Delanoë has been 'savagely' attacked by a man who is 'perhaps' associated with Islamist fundamentalism, homophobia and anti-republicanism. This sensational article could appeal to a number of readers as it strings together many 'isms' and perpetuates stereotypes about the Muslim fundamentalists who criticize the mayor's republican ideas. All in all, *Paris-Match* transmits racial stereotypes and provides incomplete information by using circumspection and suggestive wording.

Only the last two pages of the article (pages 7 and 8) address the attack; the rest high-lights preparation for the gala, the build-up to the event and the mayor's 'miraculous' recovery. Interestingly, the article minimizes coverage of Delanoë's homosexuality, mak-ing only a few vague references to a 'clique of homosexuals' who accompany him during the gala and his 'entourage' and 'family' who visit him in the hospital. On the last page, *Paris-Match* also publishes a short article devoted to the agressor: 'Azedine Berkane, proie idéale pour les prêches islamistes homophobes' ('Azedine Berkane, ideal prey for homophobic Islamic teachings'). However, neither the headline nor the article ever direct-ly relates homophobia to the mayor's sexuality. It is no accident that a right-of-center paper employs conservative republican rhetoric that erases the mayor's homosexuality or leaves it ambiguous. This short article presents Berkane as a 'marginal' character and potential 'assassin' who lives with his parents in a Parisian suburb where he leads a poor and shameful life plagued by drugs. It makes no attempt to downplay Berkane's back-ground when it depicts him as an impressionable Muslim fundamentalist who hates homo-sexuals. Hence, *Paris-Match* does not decline Arab or Maghrebian stereotypes that circulate in contemporary France. While most national dailies are more neutral on this issue (see *L'Express*, *Le Figaro* and *Le Nouvel Observateur*), *Paris-Match* preys on French readers with sensationalistic journalism that perpetuates stereotypes and draws its own conclusions.

The online edition of *Têtu* (7 October 2002) published the following headline: 'Bertrand Delanoë poignardé lors de la Nuit Blanche' ('Bertrand Delanoë stabbed during La Nuit Blanche'). The first line of this article describes Delanoë as 'openly homosexual' and this is one of the only French publications (besides *Libération*) to use a direct statement relat-ed to the mayor's sexuality. Most French newspapers avoid any mention of the private lives of elected officials; in this instance, they concentrate on Delanoë's political status and make sense of the event by situating it alongside other recent attacks. This is unlike the *New York Times* coverage (7 October 2002), which described Delanoë as 'one of France's openly gay mayors.'

It is not surprising that a *Têtu* journalist (Judith Silberfeld) should view this as a homo-phobic act. What is interesting is that this point of view provides the basis for the entire coverage of this event. Silberfeld briefly describes Berkane as a recluse who does not like politicians or homosexuals and who lives with his parents in Bobigny, but the news story does not concentrate on the aggressor. It continues by offering Delanoë several statements of solidarity and sympathy from various organizations such as L'Interassociative LGBT, Homosexualités et Socialisme and SOS Homophobie. The article ends with a statement that calls the reader to remain vigilant against hate crimes and to write an email message of sympathy or support to the mayor. This magazine constructs Delanoë and its readership as part of an imagined community of citizens who believe in a different set of republican values than those put forth in *Paris-Match*. While *Paris-Match* explains the October 2002 event as part of a series of attacks against politicians, *Têtu* situates this event as part of a larger, historical series of acts and debates related to homophobia, hate crimes and the recognition of less visible groups in contemporary France. The journalist makes it clear that this is a homophobic act and calls gay and les-bian readers to take action.

This brief analysis illustrates how two French popular magazines recount the same events with varying emphasis related to Delanoë's sexual identity and Berkane's motives as well as his ethnic and religious backgrounds. These newspapers tell us much about their philosophies and missions as well as various French attitudes related to private life, sexual identity, ethnicity and notions of 'Frenchness'. Several other daily newspapers depicted this event and we encourage the reader to explore and compare their narratives with those presented here. In some cases, the French publications present a range of information and leave it up to the reader to construct a sense of coherence. Other publications sell their own definitive version of the story. The reader will see that newspapers and magazines represent the same events in slightly different ways that lead the careful reader to different conclusions.

Conclusion

In this chapter, we have offered an introduction to the French popular press and its relevance in contemporary France. We have presented a number of French newspapers, magazines and specialty titles that emerged in the post-war era and have situated many of these titles in their larger historical and sociopolitical contexts. Throughout the chapter we have also taken into account issues particular to the French press, including press laws, readership and the resistance to and adoption of an American-style investigative journalism. Finally, in our analysis of the press coverage of the October 2002 attack on Paris mayor Bertrand Delanoë we have begun to map out a range of reporting styles and points of view related to such issues as race, sexual identity and 'Frenchness' as they appear in this popular-culture form. We encourage you to continue to develop your reading and analytical skills through further investigation of these various titles that work as important political actors in contemporary France.

SUGGESTIONS FOR FURTHER READING, THINKING AND STUDY

Many useful introductory chapters related to French newspapers and magazines are cited in the references listed below. A few key examples will help the reader get started: Albert's *La Presse française* is an excellent introduction to national, regional and specialty French press titles and is a rich resource in terms of quantitative figures; Kuhn's *The Media in France* offers a well-written historical and political introduction to French press, television and radio; the first two chapters deal specifically with the press. Thogmartin's *The National Daily Press of France* is a historical and cultural introduction to the French press with particular chapters devoted to *Le Monde* and investigative journalism. The website of La Fédération Nationale de la Presse Française (www.portail-presse.com) offers the most up-to-date information on the production, distribution and ranking of a wide range of French newspapers and magazines as well as useful information about the history of the press and press laws.

Possible case-study analyses for a number of media events include such topics as: the disappearance of Charles de Gaulle during the events of 1968; the lack of media coverage concerning François Mitterrand's illness or the existence of his natural daughter Mazarine; the death of the Princess of Wales in 1997; the introduction of the euro in France and the CEE; representations of mad cow disease (*la vache folle*) and foot and mouth disease (*la fièvre aptheuse*) as they relate to 'foreign invaders' and French–British relations; the first round of the 2002 French presidential elections and the close margin between Lionel Jospin and Jean-Marie Le Pen; the French news coverage of the events of 11 September 2001; and the continued French opposition to US-led military intervention in Iraq. Other interesting themes are the resistance to an Anglo-American cultural and linguistic presence as well as anti-American and anti-British sentiment.

BIBLIOGRAPHY

Albert, Pierre (1990) *La Presse française* (Paris: La Documentation Française).

Anderson, Benedict (1991) *Imagined Communities* (New York: Verso).

Bhabha, Homi (1990) *Nation and Narration* (London/New York: Routledge).

Cayrol, Raymond (1991) *Les Médias: Presse écrite, radio, télévision* (Paris: Presses Universitaires de France).

Charon, Jean-Marie (1991) *La Presse en France de 1945 à nos jours* (Paris: Editions du Seuil).

Kuhn, Raymond (1995) *The Media in France* (London: Routledge).

Moores, Pam (1998a) 'National press in France', pp. 388–90 in Alex Hughes and Keith Reader (eds), *Encyclopedia of Contemporary French Culture* (London: Routledge).

Moores, Pam (1998b) 'Paris-Match', pp. 408–9 in Hughes and Reader (eds), *Encyclopedia of Contemporary French Culture*.

Pedley, Alan (1993) 'The Media' in Malcolm Cook (ed.), *French Culture Since 1945* (London: Longman).

Sergeant, Jean-Claude (2000) 'From Press Barons to Digital TV: Changing Media in France' in William Kidd and Siân Reynolds (eds), *Contemporary French Cultural Studies* (London, Arnold).

Thogmartin, Clyde (1998) *The National Daily Press of France* (Birmingham, AL: Summa Publications).

CHAPTER 4

Radio

Geoff Hare

RADIO AND POPULAR CULTURE

Radio, like television, has a different relationship to popular culture than, say, music, sport or holidays. Radio listening is a habit or activity engaged in by an overwhelming majority of French people every day (86.5 per cent for three hours a day at the end of 2002), and 98.8 per cent of French people own a radio receiver, indeed several (the average is 6.3 per household: radio alarm, car radio, kitchen transistor or radio cassette player, radio tuner in a hi-fi, walkman, and increasingly access to radio on the net via personal computer or cable/satellite TV). To this extent radio listening is a cultural practice similar to, if more frequent than, going on holiday. Compared to music and sport, very popular interests, radio has an added dimension, since it is one of the media through which people are able to engage in other cultural phenomena like listening to music or sports commentary or results. In other words radio is a mediator of popular culture, as well as being a cultural phenomenon in its own right. There is radio listening as a cultural practice (meaning part of everyday culture as a way of life) and there is radio, or more precisely radio programmes, which can be seen as cultural productions, culture as a form of art.

Radio is now a major factor giving shape or pattern to people's daily lives. Many people wake up to it, reestablish contact with the wider world or at least with France's place within it over their breakfast coffee, use it to get into the mood for the day during their drive to work, have it as company in the background during the day at home or at work, reestablish contact with the wider world through the news on their way home from work or once back home in the early evening, and some, especially younger people, use it at night to tune in to how their peers are coping with sex, love and death by listening to talk-show phone-ins. Increasing numbers of *ados* (adolescents) are in fact also actively participating in these intimate discussions as a means of self-expression or to seek advice about their personal anxieties. Radio, then, has become an important part of 'youth culture'.

After a brief historical sketch showing how French broadcasting evolved to its current state, this chapter deals with the broadcasting system as it exists in 2003. It looks at who listeners are in France, and how and to what end their listening habits are measured, at issues of supply and demand, at popular radio genres in France, the extent and effects of state regulation on music radio, and the position of radio within key debates in French public life, in particular in relation to the issues of globalization and national identity.

ISSUES OF SUPPLY: RADIO BEFORE AND AFTER THE CHANGES OF THE 1980S

Radio and television in Britain and France began life, in their respective societies, in eras that were still dominated by the elitist view that these new media should be used to uplift popular culture. As part of the Radiodiffusion-Télévision Française (RTF) and then the Office de Radiodiffusion-Télévision Française in the post-war period up to and including the 1970s, French state radio was heavily influenced by the BBC model of broadcasting developed pre-war under Lord Reith's earnest values, where the mission was to inform, educate and entertain. Gaullist values and policy were equally elitist and 'improving'. In the 1960s there was close supervision of political coverage (a distinct lack of satire) and banning of anti-establishment songs (such as Boris Vian's 'Le Déserteur') from the airwaves, and little reflection of life in the regions, or programmes aimed specifically at powerless groups like young people or immigrant communities. Until the 1980s French radio was limited in supply – there were very few stations (the generalist, mass-audience France Inter, and two minority stations France Culture and France Musique, the latter covering little other than classical music). Entertainment certainly featured on France Inter, along with news, while the other two stations were giving transmission time mainly to the national (high) culture.

Unlike television, however, most of France was also able to tune in to at least one and usually two of what were called the *périphériques* stations, commercial radios broadcasting in French from long-wave transmitters just across the border in Luxembourg (RTL), Monaco (RMC), West Germany (Europe 1) and Andorra (Sud-Radio). Commercial radio, whose livelihood depended on using radio programmes as a vehicle to put advertisers in contact with an audience of consumers, had no high-cultural project like that of the French ruling elites. Indeed, they challenged French state radio by concentrating on popular programming: entertainment (variety, game shows), popular music and extensive news.

Kuhn (1995) describes the reasons and the process by which the French state under the new socialist government of François Mitterrand from 1981 onwards dismantled this central control, under pressure from technological and economic forces that made change inevitable in radio and television. Radio broadcasting was given much more commercial autonomy within a new regulatory and licensing system, over the period of the 1980s, when small new radios on the FM waveband (called *radios libres*) brought lungfuls of fresh air to listeners over the airwaves. Then, in the 1990s, most, but not all, local independent commercial music stations were bought up by large media companies and consolidated into nine or ten national commercial networks to create what is by and large the radio broadcasting system of the early twenty-first century.

State radio, or more properly nowadays public-sector radio, is run by Radio France and has a variety of stations catering for different groups and needs: the generalist mass-audience France Inter; the 24-hour rolling news station France Info; the 'serious music' station France Musiques (the recently acquired plural reflects the ambition to broaden its repertoire); France Culture, talk radio providing in-depth coverage of news, culture and discussion of scientific, philosophical, political and artistic ideas; Le Mouv', a young people's station (in ten large towns); FIP (soothing music and traffic reports in Paris and three major cities); and the network of over 40 local or regional stations called France Bleue ('généraliste, populaire, adulte, de proximité'), aimed at the 40–60-year-olds.

Radios in the commercial sector are owned by three major media groups: Le Groupe Europe 1 (itself part of the Lagardère Matra Hachette group of companies) runs Europe 1, Europe 2 and RFM; the other major old périphérique RTL (part of the Luxembourg-based European Bertelsmann group CLT-UFA, now part of Audiofina) runs RTL, RTL2 and Fun Radio; and the newest but the most powerful player is Jean-Paul Baudecroux's group, which controls NRJ, Cherie FM, Rire et Chansons and Nostalgie. The pattern of ownership of existing commercial networks broadcasting to the nation on FM has led, for reasons of competition and the search for niche audiences, to a structuring of music radios in particular into formats which target different age groups. Each commercial group tends to have a station that targets an audience of jeunes, jeunes adultes, adultes and seniors. The latter tends to be the generalist radios (RTL, Europe 1, RMC Info and some of the public-sector radios) which are broadcasting more and more news and discussion programmes and appeal to the adult audience in general.

Over 80 regional or local commercial radios operate independently of the large national networks, for instance Wit FM in the south-west, Alouette in the west, or Radio Scoop in Lyon. A few of these could be called community radios (or radios de proximité) in so far as they target communities defined by ethnic origins (Beur FM and Radio Alfa – aimed at the Franco-Algerian and Franco-Portuguese communities respectively) or by sexual orientation (Radio FG – formerly Fréquence Gaie). A number of community radios properly speaking are not classified as commercial but as radios associatives and have access to public funds to help them survive; Fréquence Protestante, Radio Notre-Dame, Radio Shalom are quite big Paris-based ones. Others abound in the regions and small towns, from Radio Arverne in the Auvergne to Radio Zinzine in the Hautes Alpes, which has a special weekly programme for Romanies. Such community radios could be regarded as outside the scope of this chapter, since they target geographical, ethnic or cultural minorities. However, this should not be taken to mean that those who listen to such a radio do not also listen to one of the national radios. More and more listeners are using a range of radios to satisfy various needs. It remains true however that only 4 per cent of overall volume of listening is to the non-commercial *radios associatives*.

LISTENERS AND LISTENING HABITS

We know a lot about radio listening habits in France, especially since advertising has become the key source of income for commercial radio stations, particularly since 1984. Commercial motives have led radio stations and TV channels (alongside advertisers) to develop sophisticated instruments to measure audiences' consumption of their output. They are all the better able to justify the rates they charge for advertisements, and to adjust their output to attract audiences and therefore advertisers. Detailed profiling helps advertisers to promote their products/services to particular media audiences. The French audience research companies are Médiamétrie (jointly owned by TV and radio companies and advertisers) and the private market-research firm IPSOS (see p. 61 for their websites). Figures are regularly available for each radio station for *audience moyenne* (average of each quarter-hour measurement of the audience, for a given time slot), *audience cumulée* ('reach' in English, total number of listeners who have listened at least once in a given day), *durée d'écoute* (average listening time per listener) and *part de marché* or *part d'audience* (market share or audience share, the percentage of the total listening audience for a given day or a given time slot).

The daily rhythms of radio listening reflect French daily life: on weekdays radio prime time is traditionally between 7 a.m. and 8.30 a.m. Then the audience falls gradually up to mid-day, but retains relatively high levels, flattens out, then starts to rise again from 2 p.m. to 6 p.m. without catching up the morning highs. There is a sharp drop from 7 p.m. to 8.30 p.m., and a slower fall up to midnight. Traditional high TV viewing in the evening depresses the radio listening figures, except among the under-20s. The major news radios see their peaks during the morning prime time, at lunchtime and in late afternoon/early evening drive time. Radio listening is ahead of television in the morning up to 12.30 p.m. and also from 2.30 p.m. to 6 p.m. on weekdays. At weekends television comes more into its own (see Cheval, 1997: 203–4). Listening shows an obvious correlation with the daily routine, reflecting, for example, the numbers of French workers who still manage to go home for lunch, and the numbers who listen to the radio while driving to and from work. Despite the increasing importance of car radios, radio listening in the home still accounts for 60 per cent of the total, with 20 per cent in the car and 18 per cent at work. In the home it is the kitchen that accounts for 40 per cent of all listening, the living room/sitting room/dining room for 27 per cent and the bedroom 22 per cent.

An increasing amount of listening is happening on digital television and the internet. What is suggested in these figures, and what becomes clear when we consider the diversity of radio equipment at the disposal of listeners, is that radio listening has become an increasingly individual activity, whereas historically it was much more a collective activity. This is also linked to the multiplication of targeted stations.

There is significant differentiation by region: the south listens less than the north. The regions listening the most are Alsace, Ile-de-France and the Pays de la Loire, whereas the ones who listen least are Provence-Alpes-Côte-d'Azur, Auvergne and, least of all, Corsica. Regarding the south-east and Corsica one could speculate about the effects of the warmer climate and the accompanying outdoor conversational culture. Inverse regional figures obtain for television, which suggests strongly that the two are in competition in overall terms. Geographical differences must however be seen too in social terms. Médiamétrie figures show that differences can operate between neighbouring towns such as Aix (85 per cent reach) and Marseille (74 per cent), which is put down to the larger student population in Aix, and in general to the different socioeconomic and cultural identities of the two cities. Radio listening, as a cultural activity, does reflect the social and cultural realities of France.

RADIO GENRES

It is useful first to come back to the now traditional splitting of radio in France into the categories of *généralistes* and *thématiques* (or niche) radios. The former are what is left over from the small number of stations that competed for the mass national audience before 1981, offering something to everyone at different times of day. The *niche* radios are those targeting a segment of the national audience – these segments being differentiated either by age and hence musical taste or by content, e.g. news radio, or a particular type of music. Like all niche radio stations they constantly monitor their format in terms of the target audience through market research and 'panels'. One consequence of targeting in a commercial system is that audiences with a less commercially attractive profile might be less well served by programme schedulers (the unemployed and the very old, for example, may have less disposable income than average, but more time in which to listen to the radio).

Another way of dividing up radio is between talk radio and music radio. The first new all-talk radio was the public-sector radio France Info, founded as a 24-hour rolling news service in 1987. It has become enormously successful, as the third top radio in terms of reach, behind NRJ and RTL. The *généralistes* have traditionally offered both talk and music, although there is a trend for them to become dominated by talk; for instance, RMC has changed its name to RMC Info, and Europe 1 is equally concentrating on news and interactivity, as phone-ins, talk shows, discussion programmes, personal advice and *libre antenne* programming are being called. The

following sections deal with particular genres within talk radio and music radio, starting with talk radio.

Talk radio

A significant development in French radio from the 1990s has been the talk show for
a youth audience. The type of phone-in programme that first caught the attention of
the wider public and indeed that of the regulator in the 1990s for its offensiveness
was based on satirical and provocative discussion of news events. The genre is not
entirely new in the sense that there is a tradition on French radio of topical or even
satirical debate, starting in the early days of radio in the pre-war *chansonnier* tradition, although it was limited in the Gaullist years. One well-remembered programme,
L'Oreille en coin dimanche matin, which began in 1968 on France Inter, set a high
standard of wit without a particularly malevolent tone. An even less controversial
entertainment programme in its witty content was the long-running *Les Grosses
Têtes*, hosted by Philippe Bouvard, on RTL. The tradition on public-service radio has
been continued by Laurent Ruquier in the 1990s. An earlier programme occupying
the same France Inter lunchtime slot as Ruquier was *Le Tribunal des flagrants délires*
(1980–3) with Pierre Desproges, who was much more ferocious with his political
guests. While there was satirical content in programmes produced by public-service
radio, their political debate was in the hands of professionals, and if they occasionally went over the top these *dérapages* were calculated. More recent youth radio
phone-in talk shows could much more easily go off the rails when inexperienced
young presenters misjudge comments or find it difficult to prevent callers from doing
so. Both Fun and Skyrock found themselves in trouble with the regulator for jokes
about the Auschwitz concentration camp and the killing of a *flic*. The Parisian radio
Ici et Maintenant was taken off the air by the Conseil Supérieur de l'Audiovisuel (CSA)
in 1995 after complaints from the French anti-racist league (LICRA) concerning
repeated airings of racist, anti-semitic and revisionist views by phone-in callers.

The most popular type of talk show for young people in the twenty-first century,
the youth sex phone-in (the subject of the case study at the end of the chapter), may
also be seen as a genre that has its historical antecedents, such as those programmes of personal advice and sympathy hosted in the afternoon on RTL for 14
years from 1967 by the celebrated Ménie Grégoire. Hers was an older audience (up
to 3 million listeners), dominated by women whose sackfuls of letters she responded to on air. She used her listeners' letters to raise issues related to work and health,
and questions to do with relationships and sex. She has said she was not handing
down advice in the way a magazine 'agony column' might have, but giving a voice to
her listeners' everyday anxieties at a time of rapid social change and changing values. It was in the 1970s that the great debates about contraception and abortion
were at their height.

In the category of talk radio that can be characterized as entertainment fall some iconic programmes from France Inter. While they are popular, they do not descend to lowest-common-denominator radio. A game show where the questions still demand a certain 'culture' is *Le Jeu des mille francs* (now *euros*), broadcast every weekday lunchtime. This programme has been travelling from town to town since it began in 1958 and is still going strong in the new century. Other programmes that began in the 1950s are the history programme *La Tribune de l'histoire* and the arts discussion programme *Le Masque et la plume*. The interview genre had its iconic exponent also on France Inter, for two decades: Jacques Chancel. From 1968 his hour-long live daily interview *Radioscopies* brought out the intelligence and humanity in his guests from the world of politics, culture and the arts.

Music radio: the search for the *ménagère de moins de 50 ans*

It is difficult to talk about individual programmes on much of current music radio, since it is now dominated by formats – all of the type 'music and news'. The news bulletins are however brief and the music is aimed at mythical creatures that sum up a socially and demographically defined target audience. Since the dawn of commercial radio in France advertisers have wanted to attract and keep the attention of people with high disposable income. One such is the *ménagère de moins de 50 ans* – the housewife and mother (below 50) responsible for spending on a range of domestic consumer products. Since RTL and Europe 1 were born in the era prior to the massive entry of the French female into the paid workforce from the 1970s onwards, generalist-radio day-time programming (including the public-sector France Inter) has long tried to attract this mythical creature. Tools have included the serial *La Famille Duraton* (RTL in the 1950s) and games offering chances to win money or consumer items by phoning in on or being telephoned by the presenter (*La Valise*, RTL). It was Europe No. 1 (as it was originally called) that changed the position of music on French radio. From its birth in 1955 it brought an American feel to its radio: in addition to devoting significant morning, lunchtime and early-evening slots to news and current affairs, it programmed much more music in the morning and afternoon, with new-style, mainly male presenters (like Pierre Bellemare) whose main job was to establish and keep up a friendly, more intimate relationship with the listener for whom they provided company.

In the current era it is a number of *adultes* music radios, in particular Cherie FM and RFM, that are targeting this social-demographic profile. The canned music in the smaller supermarkets which do not have their own-produced background music is likely to be from one of these two stations. This choice of format by Cherie and RFM is for commercial and opportunistic reasons. RFM has changed its format and target audience at least twice since it was an early pioneer of the *radios libres*. Initially, it sought a viable audience through an American west coast sound. Having been taken over by a British commercial company, Crown Communications, it adopted a new format to target a segment of the market identified as being hitherto under-exploited in France: the 25–40-year-old *actifs* living in towns of over 100,000 people, more male than female, from the cadre categories. They could sell this audience of 'French yuppies' particularly to advertisers in the automotive industries (70 per cent of their advertising income was motor-car related), and to advertisers of certain other new products. RFM's *animateurs* (who included the nationally known singer Eddy Mitchell and the ubiquitous Antoine de Caunes) were individualized much more than, say, those on NRJ where the music was all important. RFM's tone was also more insolent and caustic than other stations.

Having failed to win a viable audience with this format, RFM, under its new owners, Europe 1, as *Le Monde* (7–8 April 1996) put it, 'is targeting the 35–50 year-olds, with a predominance of women'. The format and tone of both RFM and Cherie FM is now 'soft'. Cherie, described by *Le Monde* as 'la plus féminine des radios' and as the best example of a radio entirely designed according to the laws of the market, carefully avoids rock guitar and dance or hip-hop. The play list, carefully tested by telephone polls, is an eclectic selection of popular recent and older hits, with a number of new releases. Presenters are mainly male, with female voices for *chroniques* (health and beauty) and news. RFM concentrates on hits from the mid-1950s to the mid-1980s, golden oldies, plus a quota of new releases. It has built its image around the notion of 'gold', with its slogan 'la radio en or' and various *rubriques* such as a gastronomy feature entitled 'L'or du terroir'. Like Cherie FM, it has female *chroniqueuses* (sounding like 'friends giving tips').

The recent success of Cherie, RFM and other stations shows us that 'adult music radios' have listeners that advertisers are seeking, that the old *périphériques* that were thought to be losing out to the new FM *radios libres* have literally bought into the market by taking over smaller networks along with their audience and their publicity income, and that radios now build their programme schedules on a niche audience easily identifiable by advertisers. However, even if the techniques and the concepts are imported from the USA, the radio market is a national one not a local one. The exception is the Paris region where the density of population allows some specialist music niche radios (Ouï-FM for rock music, Voltage-FM for dance music, FG for Techno, Radio Latina for Latino rhythms). In terms of the specific niche that RFM has targeted, it argues that it is following its *auditeurs historiques*, the 20–30-year-olds of the 1980s, 'pour les retrouver 15 ans plus tard'. Another way of looking at it is that there is less room for manoeuvre at the lower age range, since the French demographic pyramid is shrinking at the bottom (the 13–25-year-olds), whereas the late 30s to 50-year-olds are a solid reservoir of potential audience with high spending power.

VALUES AND DEBATES: MUSIC RADIO AND NATIONAL CULTURAL IDENTITY

Concentration of ownership of music stations in the late 1980s and competition for listeners led the major national commercial youth music networks to play less French popular music. By 1992 figures showed 13 per cent of plays for French music on NRJ, 8 per cent on Skyrock, and 7 per cent on Fun. New or relatively unknown French artists were being passed over in favour of already successful British and American music. The conservative press encouraged a reaction of 'moral panic' in the French cultural establishment about the loss of national identity if French popular song disappeared; the French music industry saw it more in terms of a commercial issue; and the political classes opted for protectionism, with legally enforceable linguistic quotas on popular song programmed on French radio. The so-called 'Pelchat amendment', passed into French law as part of a wider Broadcasting Reform Act on 1 February 1994, imposed on all French radio stations a compulsory minimum of 40 per cent of French-language songs in their popular music programming at times of day when there is a significant listening audience (6.30 a.m. to 10.30 p.m.). Within this 40 per cent minimum there was a further requirement for radios to give airtime, for at least half of the quota, to new talent or new issues.

The CSA was given powers of enforcement, and in 1998 found itself giving final warnings to ten national and regional networks and banning one regional radio from broadcasting for a day following persistent flouting of the quotas. But within two years up to full implementation of the law, 1,300 independent radios had their licensing agreements either simply renewed by the CSA or modified so that they would progressively come into line with the new law.

As implied above, in addition to the highly publicized cultural and linguistic motivation behind this legislation, there was also the issue of commercial and economic protection of the French music industry, since the music industry depends on radio's capacity to disseminate and market its products (and to pay for the privilege through royalties). In the 1990s sales of French-produced music recordings had fallen behind non-French sales on the internal French market by 10 percentage points, the reverse of a few years earlier. Since there was an accepted link between sales and radio play lists, the music industry blamed radio programmers.

More potent politically were the cultural and linguistic concerns that had long been a part of French cultural policy, concerns about the status of the French language in the modern world and its links to national identity. The ultimate fear was that French might be relegated to the status of a second-class language, and with it French culture and France itself. (See Chapter 2.) What is particular about the French cultural scene is that popular song in the shape of *chanson* sits quite happily within the French establishment's definition of culture. It has not been seen as divorced from high culture (unlike in Britain), and has been a very productive area of French artistic creativity ever since the birth of radio and the record industry. Therefore new concerns about the dwindling influence of the French language within youth music radio and the loss of creativity in French popular music put radio programming of French song on the agenda of traditional French cultural protectionism.

Youth radio stations had the most problems with the regulation. The most popular national networks targeting the under-25-year-olds, such as NRJ, Skyrock or Fun Radio, had built their audiences on a diet of music containing a high proportion of American rock and pop. NRJ claimed that whereas the French repertoire for an *adult* audience was very rich, the youth radios were stuck between rap and boy bands and there was very little to play. Fun Radio reacted by introducing more phone-ins at evening prime times, partly as a way of stretching the limited amount of playable French music to the 40 per cent of remaining programming. Skyrock, seeing the difficulty it would have in reaching the 40 per cent quota, changed its format radically in 1995, banking its future on French rap music. Its percentage of rap went from 35 in 1995 to 50 in 1996, and to 75 in the late 1990s. Its audience increased and it contributed to a remarkable flowering of French rap which was in a phase of development that coincided with the quotas. After one year of quotas, French record sales went up from 45 per cent to 52 per cent of total music sales.

The quotas issue tells us that while the interests of the music industry and of music radio are symbiotically interlinked, they are not automatically identical. In the late 1990s disagreements between the music industry and the radio sector led to an amendment to the law in the direction of greater flexibility. Greater specialization of radios had led to formats being differentiated both by age of listeners and by musical style – dictated by highly competitive conditions. In order to take account of the diversification of French radio, and to avoid the risk of standardization of radio in general through more and more uniform play lists, the CSA and parliament (in 2000) accepted an amendment to the law that favoured the exposure of new performers on radio, but without penalizing radios that concentrate on the musical heritage ('adult' radios). A radio can now either drop to 35 per cent of French records provided the percentage of new talent reaches 25 per cent of the total, or play only 10 per cent of new talent if it reaches 60 per cent of French song overall.

Figures for 2002 show that, from the point of view of listener, half the songs heard on French radio are French, and that the most popular French singer with radio stations is Jean-Jacques Goldman. They also show the importance of the Top 40 chart which accounts for two-thirds of plays on youth radios like Skyrock and NRJ.

Cultural-imperialism theories and models are behind the quotas issue, which may reflect the dominance of an older generation of French decision-makers rather than the mass of the younger generation of listeners. Radio quotas are part of a much wider anxiety among French elites about national identity and merely one of a number of policy instruments putting into effect a defence of the French language and ultimately of national identity. However, whereas French elites readily apply notions of cultural imperialism to the relations of the USA to Western Europe, French youth has been fascinated by American culture in the post-war era. Music radio has been a prime site of the debate over the relationship of French culture and Anglo-American culture.

YOUTH TALK RADIO – THE CASE OF LOVIN' FUN

The vast majority of talk programmes in the 1990s were intended for a different audience to Ménie Grégoire's, but one that has been equally in need of a voice in their era. Adolescents and pre-adolescents in the under-20 age range or under-25s were the audience of the youth sex phone-in genre that has proved the longest lasting and has caused most controversy. Fun Radio and Skyrock are the two radio stations which have developed interactive youth talk radio most notably, although other youth stations have from the turn of the new century also essayed this format of programme. The presenters of the various shows on Fun and Skyrock have become media celebrities, with large followings of listeners. Competition between *animateurs* to increase listener ratings has produced increasingly salacious topics of discussion. While it is not surprising that the subject of sex should interest young people, it needs to be pointed out that radio phone-ins in France have been used by young people not only for showing off or 'talking dirty' but more seriously as a source of information, advice and education about their own sexual development and the ethics and health implications of sexual practices in general.

The most memorable example of sex on the radio is Fun Radio's infamous programme *Lovin' Fun*, presented jointly by Doc Spitz and Difool, who, against copycat competition, remained the champions of sex talk radio until Difool's departure in August 1996. Other programmes on a range of radios have since imitated this model. While Doc was the serious sex therapist and medic, Difool was there to add spice and humour. First broadcast in October 1992, *Lovin' Fun* achieved maximum publicity when in 1994, as a result of what were seen by the regulator as excesses of vocabulary and over-explicitness, the CSA intervened to request that the show should no longer be aired live, and that its principal presenter Difool should leave comments on sex and health matters exclusively to the supposedly better-qualified Doc Spitz. At the time, *Lovin' Fun* was the most popular radio show in its weekday 9–11 p.m. evening slot, reaching an average 1.3 million listeners. The *affaire Lovin' Fun* developed rapidly as an issue of freedom of speech versus attempted censorship, requiring the CSA to give an involved explanation of its actions and presenting Fun Radio with free publicity and a forum for justifying the format, style and functions of *Lovin' Fun*.

The programme was certainly offensive to some people, but it did clearly fulfil a need for personal sexual and emotional advice among rather disoriented young people torn between the sexual values and explicitness of advertisements and television culture and

the censoriousness of their parents' generation, who had grown up at a time when contraception was not freely available and abortion was illegal, and neither were acceptable
topics of public conversation. One sociological justification that is often aired for this highly popular type of *libre antenne* show is that it gives airtime to private individuals to
express their own views, giving a voice to young people – part of radio's democratic function. However, critics have stressed the commercial factors in the FM radio industry of
the 1980s and 1990s. The niche marketing of programme formulae developed particularly by Pierre Bellanger, the director of Skyrock, created a spiral of competition and rival-
ry in which quality provision was replaced by lowest-common-denominator broadcasts in
a quest for audience ratings and advertising revenue. The fact that Fun Radio's *Lovin' Fun*
was initially denounced to the CSA by Skyrock, who provided the regulators with cas-
settes of offending extracts, underlines both the competitiveness of the sector and its bit-
terness. The regulator moved from a position of declaring that 'free speech was not the
freedom to make money through being vulgar' to increasingly stressing the need for the
radio stations themselves to develop their own professional ethos and exercise editorial
control over offensive topics and language. The CSA has accepted that there is a 'strong
demand from young listeners for such programmes that deal humorously with questions
that concern them directly, such as sex and their place in society'.

By 2003, in addition to Fun Radio, NRJ was running a nightly programme at 8 p.m.
called *Accord parental indispensable*, a provocative title suggesting a range of X-rated
subjects, but where programme policy is to avoid topics such as incest and paedophilia
and vulgarity for its own sake. The young presenter, Maurad, has become the listeners'
favourite in a short time. In addition to chatting to callers about sex, there is a nightly trick
phone call, for example having a presenter ring a caller's unsuspecting partner to subject
him to an on-air (un)faithfulness test, and humour in poor taste that is not universally
appreciated. On Europe 2's similar programme, questions about family, love and sex are
on the nightly agenda, plus, for its slightly older audience, social and political issues.
However, now on Skyrock, the unshockable Difool, who lost 90,000 listeners to Maurad,
runs his own show where no subject is off-limits and the language is often crude. The CSA
is keeping an attentive ear on these programmes.

Conclusion

Radio should not be seen as a poor cousin of television – television without the pic-
tures. It fulfils different cultural functions. It is of course in competition with television,
since it is difficult to pay attention to both at the same time. But the older medium
has kept its place in French people's cultural life. Indeed in a Sofres survey published
in 2003, of the three main mass media French radio retains clearly more trust and
credibility than television and newspapers. Radio accompanies practically all French
people in their day-to-day existence, punctuating the key periods of their daily lives,
bringing information, news and background music to some, emotional reassurance
and a link with a lifestyle to others. Radio listening has become a more and more

individual and solitary activity, perhaps making the solitude of modern life more bearable. It reflects the values of modern society, for example talk radio in the way sex has become the explicit centre of life, particularly for young people.

Radio escaped the constraints of state control rather later in France than in other Western European countries. Supply of radio programming was highly restricted until the 1980s. Then, as supply and demand made radio a vector of the dominance of Anglo-American musical culture, radio stations were subjected to quotas in defence of French identity, at least as defined by the older French political elite. Despite the commercial pressures to standardize radio into formats, a visitor is struck by the variety of radio on offer at least in the major urban centres, but also in the vivacity of local radio. Radio seems well placed to use the new digital media and the internet to maintain its position as an important medium in French popular culture.

SUGGESTIONS FOR FURTHER STUDY

Even from outside France, it has become fairly easy to listen to French radio. Long-wave access to France Inter, Europe 1 and RTL is feasible. Listening on the internet has also become quite straightforward. Studying the categorization and number of listeners for various types of music radio and talk radio can be done on the Médiamétrie website (see below). The CSA site gives definitions of the official categories of radio. An examination of stations' own websites will show what new content and new or extra uses the internet and digitization are allowing radio to make available to its listeners, in the form of downloads. The style of a site also reflects a station's particular format and target audience. Play lists of competing music stations can be assessed for their overlap and similarity, and for the extent to which they appear to be respecting the linguistic quotas.

Once in France it will be easier to investigate the range of provision of radio stations, for example by looking at radio/TV guides. For provision of local radio in specific towns and beyond the Paris region, local visits may be necessary. Whereas a certain amount of quantitative date on listening habits is available via the web, for qualitative data students could interview acquaintances of all ages in France on which stations they listen to and when they listen and why.

Space has not permitted coverage of the historical range of entertainment and news programmes. An excellent source of material is the Jeanneney-Chauveau historical dictionary, for example on major figures like Jean-Christophe Averty (and his contribution to bringing the history of the music hall to the modern listener) or Alain Duhamel (the major political commentator on Europe 1).

BIBLIOGRAPHY

Barnard, Stephen (2000) *Studying Radio* (London: Arnold).

Cheval, Jean-Jacques (1997) *Les radios en France. Histoire, état et enjeux* (Rennes: Apogée).

Jeanneney, Jean-Noël and Agnès Chauveau (1999) *L'Écho du siècle. Dictionnaire historique de la radio et de la télévision en France* (Paris: Hachette/Arte/La 5e, rev. edn 2001).

Kuhn, Raymond (1995) *The Media in France* (London: Routledge).

Prot, Robert (1997) *Dictionnaire de la radio* (Grenoble: Presses Universitaires de Grenoble).

Remonté, J.-F. and S. Depoux (1989) *Les Années radio* (Paris: Gallimard/L'Arpenteur).

Com.fm: http://www.comfm.com/ (links to all radio internet sites and streamed live radio).

CSA: http://www.csa.fr/ (the broadcasting regulator).

French Links (broadcasting): http://frenchlinks.org.uk/ (links to many professional and academic broadcasting sites).

IPSOS: http://www.ipsos.com (for audience measures).

Médiamétrie: http://www.mediametrie.fr/ (for audience measures).

CHAPTER 5

Television

Hugh Dauncey

Television is a medium which interacts with a variety of expressions and forms of popular culture and national self-awareness. Television broadcasts programmes on music, sport, literature, leisure, food and fashion. Television screens (often repeatedly) popular films and provides a vehicle for advertising commercials. Television provides programmes which present and analyse developments in the press, radio (to a lesser extent) and new forms of media such as Minitel and the internet. Television broadcasts to the general public events of national significance – presidential addresses, Bastille Day, elections, funerals of public figures and commemorations of national events – which, although they are not forms of popular culture in themselves, do contribute to creating and maintaining aspects of national identity. Increasingly, in recent years, television has begun to show programmes which reflect upon itself, by investigating its own past and role in society.

As with so much else in France, television – in all its aspects – has been heavily marked by the hand of the state, and much of the story of television's relevance as popular culture concerns either the breaking free of television from state monopoly, or public-service channels' attempts to reinterpret their provision of culture and popular culture in reaction to changes in government cultural policy. Television in France has always been a subject of much discussion and debate – more so, arguably, than in Britain or the USA, because of French awareness of the scale and rapidity of sociocultural changes that France has seen since 1945, and because television, as a popular medium, has had to negotiate its place vis-à-vis traditionally accepted views of culture. In France, partly because of the prestige of the state, the governance of TV – its autonomy or lack of it – has long been a controversial issue. But socioeconomically, as Hervé Bourges, who was director general of the public-service France-Télévision organization during the mid-1990s, has stated: 'Television has witnessed and accompanied this changing France which has gradually learned to wear off-the-peg clothes and to lose its local accents. To a certain extent, television has also dug the grave of traditional France' (Bourges, 1993: 11).

Hayward has suggested that television is a 'transparence' on modern France, in the way the images of this form of mass communication and popular cultural medium reflect society. Written at the start of a decade which saw the working through of many major structural changes to the French television industry (the liberalization and commercialization of broadcasting and the growth of new channels), Hayward's insightful analysis suggests that in French TV 'the commodification of the dominant ideology falls into four categories of representation: the state institutions and elites that control society (mostly seen in news and current affairs programmes), the middle-class, heterosexuality [...] and the family' (Hayward, 1990). So French television programmes – produced by industrial and commercial structures and institutions – reflect the politics of power, class and gender in France. This chapter provides some background to understanding just how it is that programmes on French TV 'show' the realities of life in France.

INSTITUTIONS: FROM STATE-CONTROLLED PENURY TO A MIX OF CHANNELS

One of the first things necessary to an understanding of French television is an awareness of what the choice of television viewing actually is in France. How many channels are there, and what are their specialisms? The French use the expression *paysage audiovisuel français* (French audiovisual landscape) when talking about TV, radio and new media, and the array of TV channels available to viewers is a starting point for an initial picture of the 'televisual landscape'. The television listings in any newspaper show that there are seven main (terrestrial) channels available to anyone with a standard set and aerial and a huge variety (100+) of 'thematic' channels (music, film, sport, etc.) for those with cable and satellite subscriptions. The seven main TV channels are TF1 (Télévision Française 1), F2 (France 2), F3 (France 3), C+ (Canal Plus), F5 (France 5), Arte and M6. Four of these channels are public-sector/public-service broadcasters (F2, F3, F5 and Arte – part of France-Télévision, the national public-sector TV company), and the remaining three (TF1, Canal Plus and M6) are private-sector.

Compared with Britain, for example, where the standard choice of viewing for those without digital, cable or satellite is restricted to five terrestrial TV channels, the 'supply' of television in France seems generous and pluralist (to the extent that viewers have a choice between a variety of channels). It is only relatively recently, however, that French television has acquired this plurality, because, from the beginnings of television in France until the mid-1980s, the sector was subject to stifling state control which limited the number of channels as well as the content of their programmes. The current TF1, Canal Plus, F5 and M6 channels are essentially the fruit of the liberalization of broadcasting which began in the mid-1970s under President Giscard d'Estaing and produced its first real effects under the socialist administration in the mid-1980s when Canal Plus (1984) and La Cinq (1986) were launched, and – under the right-wing Chirac government – when the public-sector state television channel TF1 was privatized (1987) and as M6 (1987) successfully replaced the short-lived TV6 (1986). An understanding of the institutional background to television in France is also necessary to explain how the medium contributes to disseminating and creating popular culture. This is why we now turn to a brief discussion of the development of French television from the 1960s until today's 'televisual landscape'. In this discussion, the key issues concern state ownership, government control and public-service broadcasting.

It was only in the late 1950s and 1960s that television in France really began to emerge as a significant cultural phenomenon, as increasing prosperity, the developing French electronics industry and growing interest within the state broadcasting services (who held the monopoly of television provision) led consumers to purchase sets and tune in to the restricted menu of programming available on the single national channel. Whereas in the 1950s broadcasts only reached the few households with sets in the five major urban areas (in 1954, only 1 per cent of French homes had a set and even in 1960 there were only 2 million sets, representing about 10 per cent of households), after the creation of the second national channel (1964), the introduction of colour broadcasts (1967) and the expansion of programming, by 1969 two-thirds of households possessed a television. The development of television in France lagged behind other European countries such as the UK (where a third of households had a set in 1958) and West Germany. This was partly because of socioeconomic, industrial and geographical factors such as the relatively low standard of living of many French people in both rural and urban areas, France's late industrialization and high-tech weaknesses and the difficulties of providing reception in a country of the size of France, but was exacerbated by negative cultural attitudes towards the new medium held by the country's intellectual and governing elites. The traditional attachment of these elites to France's 'high-cultural' heritage and vocation in the world made state television channels concentrate on information and dissemination of high culture to the masses, rather than acting as relay and creator of mass or popular culture. We return to these issues in a following section.

Thus during the 1960s, French television was really only just beginning its development, and it was the presidency of Charles de Gaulle (1958–69) and Gaullist uses of broadcasting – for both political and cultural ends – which set practices and structures in the television sector until the liberalization of the state monopoly in the mid-1980s produced the contemporary situation where state television and private-sector channels co-exist and compete for audiences. The Gaullist years represented the heyday of the state monopoly. As Kuhn points out, during this period the state enjoyed a monopoly of ownership, was policy maker and regulator, financial controller, primary definer of television's political agenda, censor of news and formulator of industrial policy (Kuhn, 1995: 112–13). And, as we shall see below, the Gaullist state made television an instrument of its cultural policy. The inseparability of state and television during the 1960s, and the subordination of television to the purposes of government and president – both in terms of everyday news and information and culture, and during elections and moments of national crisis such as the Algerian War or May '68 – helped create dissatisfaction with television among the French public. Gaullist politics and the inability of de Gaulle's governments to manage France's socioeconomic modernization gave rise to the social, political and cultural protests of May '68, which included demands for more liberal and pluralist audiovisual media.

The institution which embodied the state's broadcasting monopoly, television as government servant and (public-service) tool for disseminating elite culture was the Office de Radiodiffusion-Télévision Française (ORTF) created in 1964 to replace the previous Radiodiffusion-Télévision Française (1949). Described by Gaullist president Pompidou (1969–74) as the 'official voice of France', the ORTF – challenged by those tired of television as the state's poodle – was abolished, being split into seven separate companies engaging in regulated competition. Between 1974 and the socialist reforms of broadcasting post-1982, the audiovisual landscape was thus made up of three television channels (Télévision Française 1 (TF1), Antenne 2 and France Régions 3 (FR3)), the national radio company Radio France, an archive and research organization (l'Institut National de l'Audiovisuel (INA)), the transmission company Télédiffusion de France (TDF) and a company producing programmes (la Société Française de Production (SFP)).

Whereas the break-up of the ORTF really only rearranged the furniture of the state broadcasting monopoly, the reforms introduced in the 1980s by the socialist governments of 1981–6 and the right-wing government of 1986–8 rapidly introduced new channels and real competition between public and private sectors. TF1 (until 1987), Antenne 2 and FR3 remained as the public-sector channels but were joined by Canal Plus (1984), the short-lived La Cinq (1986–92) and TV6 (1986, succeeded by M6 in 1987). In 1987, TF1 was privatized, breaking the triumvirate of public-sector channels, and creating a major competitor for the renamed France 2 and France 3, merged in 1989 in a joint organization called France-Télévision. The defunct La Cinq's frequency was reallocated in 1992 to the Franco-German cultural channel Arte, which now shares it with the public-sector France 5 (F5, formerly La Cinquième), which specializes in educational programmes.

VALUES AND DEBATES: TELEVISION AS PURVEYOR OF HIGH CULTURE TO THE MASSES?

In a study of debates surrounding the public-sector Franco-German cultural TV channel Arte, Susan Emanuel has suggested that 'On both left and right of the political spectrum, as within Marxist and liberal intellectual *milieux* alike, there is an ingrained suspicion of mass culture, and a belief that State television – even if not part of the national culture, like the cinema – can be used, at best, to shore up the *patrimoine'*. She goes on to explain:

> Among the dimensions of the crisis confronting the public service in all industrial-
> ized cultures over the last decade is the problem of the mediation of classical and
> modernist culture. Uncertainty about the cultural role of television in France goes
> back to the 1960s, when there were already confidential studies into the low level
> of viewing of cultural programs. Was it the fault of scheduling or an outmoded style
> of presentation? Since the 1980s the villain has been commercialization: money
> chases out art, even at the heart of the state channels.
>
> (Emanuel, 1994: 140)

Focusing on a channel which aims to provide French and German viewers with high-cultural television (feature and TV films, documentaries and magazines) this analysis rehearses the issues discussed in debates on the place of popular, mass cultural programmes on French television. The fundamental value at issue is that of public-service broadcasting and what – in an industrial and commercial context where state- and private-sector television channels compete for viewers and advertising – the public-sector channels should provide.

For its creators, state television and broadcasting in general (see Chapter 4) had the three-fold mission of educating, informing and entertaining. Under the state monopoly until the mid-1980s, the state channels did their best to provide these services, but were more successful in educating and informing the French public (and there was much protest at the nature of such education and information) than they were in entertaining it. In the serious-minded approach of the Gaullist state towards the role of broadcasting in its wider cultural policy, entertainment was often conflat-ed with the 'democratization' of high culture in the form of television productions of classical French drama and literature. The traditional weakness of television produc-tion in France – for various industrial reasons, as well as because of the perceived low status of programmes of contemporary fiction and popular entertainment in gen-eral, along the lines of UK soap operas for instance – meant that state television con-centrated on news and documentary programming. When advertising was introduced for the public-service channels in 1968 (TF1) and 1971 (Antenne 2) in order to com-plement the funding from the *redevance* (licence fee) the need for healthy audience figures – measured by the Audimat ratings – and the attractiveness of programming as entertainment became more important. And when the state monopoly was reformed in the 1980s, and private-sector channels competed with Antenne 2 and FR3, the phrase *dictature de l'Audimat* was coined to express the influence of ratings on scheduling and audiovisual production.

In the value systems of French governing elites it has always been 'high culture' (over-simplistically: art, literature, theatre, classical music and so on) which is impor-tant, both in its own right, and as the proper concern of the French state in its role as guarantor of citizens' well-being, and of France as the safe-keeper of an incomparable legacy (the French term is *patrimoine*) of art, literature and philosophy from French genius throughout the centuries. During the 1960s – perhaps the heyday of public-service broadcasting – the ministry of culture under André Malraux implemented policies of cultural democratization intended to bring high culture to the masses through museums, *maisons de la culture* and tools of the state such as television. In such a vision of culture little importance was attached to entertainment on television and even less place was given to coverage by television of 'popular culture' in general, equated with forms of activity of low cultural importance. Some critics such as Thibaud (1970) maintained that television should have no educational role in purveying 'official culture' because of the divorce between such a traditionally defined elitist culture and the everyday life of viewers, but the place of 'popular' programmes on television remained challenged, even if fiction and light entertainment – variety programmes, series, serials, game shows – reflected television's increasingly mass audience.

As David Looseley has documented (1995), under the socialist administrations of the 1980s and 1990s and Culture Minister Jack Lang in particular, cultural policy changed to become more inclusive and pluralist in its definition of cultural value, moving away from the previous concentration on *beaux-arts* towards 'a politics of fun'. Such a reconsidering of what could and should be seen as culture – Rachmaninov or rap, Balzac or *bande dessinée* – and what the state should do to facilitate citizens' access to it fed into developing thinking on what television should provide for viewers to watch. At the same time as the liberalization of broadcasting created private-sector television channels obsessed with attracting the largest possible audiences to prime-time viewing, fixed French preconceptions about the cultural validity of 'popular' entertainment were shaken away from the culturally elitist assumptions of the state monopoly and its faith that, of information, entertainment and education, education was the strongest duty of television.

Cultural commentary on television seems almost everywhere to operate on the basis of concerns over declining quality and 'falling standards', postulating a largely imaginary past where programmes were irreproachable, and a present where (essentially under the dual influence of the mass audience and commercial competition) standards have fallen and children, language, morals, culture, civic values – one takes one's pick – are in danger. Ethics, civics and children can be protected by regulation in the form of successive watchdogs, of which the latest is the Conseil Supérieur de l'Audiovisuel. Language and culture (increasingly broadly defined) can be safeguarded by France's attachment to her *exception culturelle* and consequent right to protect French-language and French-produced programmes in television scheduling. Such filters on the influence of coca-colonization through (for example) *Kojak* and the doubly pernicious effects of Japanese cartoons reflect the debates over the 'content' of French television, but the principal underlying concern – vividly illustrated by a polemical and much-discussed analysis by Pierre Bourdieu (1996) – revolves around the commercial imperatives which drive contemporary channels and the perceived pressure this must have towards 'lowest-common-denominator TV', exemplified by early reality programming in the 1990s, and more recently TF1's *Loft Story* (the French version of the UK C4's *Big Brother*).

One example of high (but also 'popular', in that they attract high ratings) culture on French television are the – usually annual – dictation competitions, the finals of which are screened at prime time, reminding viewers of the glorious difficulties of French grammar. The star presenter of such spectacles (and evergreen host of higher-brow literary discussion programmes) is Bernard Pivot, who has been an unofficial champion of broadcasting standards. Early in the debate over the ethics and cultural value of reality programming (RP) in the 1990s, Pivot castigated the genre in a curious mix of scatology and existentialism: 'The more I learn that my neighbours are up shit creek, the more I see them undressing, arguing, being shouted at, crying or calling for help, the more I'm content with my own lot in life: Hell is other people' (Garcin, 1992: 92).

It has sometimes been suggested that 'the new media' can help free people from norms of cultural oppression and intimidation, and we can indeed see that Pivot's polemicking advertised RP's challenge to received ideas of what was culturally legitimate on television. The duel between the watchdog of the 'educated and cultivated classes' and the major proponent of reality programming (producer Pascale Breugnot) showed how the 'new media' of television in the 1990s – in the form of RP – had begun to present the viewing public, if not with pleasure and fun, at least with new choices of programmes.

GENRES AND PROGRAMMES: TRENDS TOWARDS LOWEST-COMMON-DENOMINATOR TV?

Of the seven current terrestrial channels, TF1, F2, F3 and M6 are arguably now broadly similar in terms of their programming content, providing an essentially generalist menu of genres. Canal Plus, F5 and Arte occupy niche positions partly defined by their specialisms in cinema and football (C+), educational programmes (F5) and cultural documentary programmes (Arte), although each also purveys more general material. The main genres of programming identified by analysts of French television are: *fiction*; *divertissement* (entertainment); *information*; *magazines* and *documentaires*; *sport*; *jeunesse* (youth programmes). In what follows, we will concentrate on showing how the genres of 'fiction', 'entertainment' and 'magazines and documentaires' illustrate debates and issues in French television as (popular) culture.

Television fiction has always been a category of programming which has focused debate on questions of cultural values. The category covers essentially *films de ciné-ma* or *cinéfilms* (feature films), *téléfilms* (TV film or film made for TV), *feuilletons* or *séries* (TV soaps and serials). One basic opposition which runs through such debate is that between 'classic' fiction on the one hand and on the other hand 'popular' fiction. Thus is the old division in literature between the works of the established canon and those outside the canon replicated in television's representations of culture. Another fundamental opposition is that between French fiction and fiction from other origins, dubbed into French.

During the 1950s and 1960s, under the dual influence of the state monopoly on broadcasting and Gaullist cultural policy, television drama was dominated by adaptations of classics of French theatre and by prestigious productions of new, socially conscious drama exemplified by the work of Marcel Bluwal. From the 1960s and 1970s, television drama was often live or recorded stagings of classical drama, adaptations of historical novels or historical dramas, but, increasingly, 'high-cultural' literary drama was competed with by cinema and imported popular series and soaps from the USA and UK. In the 1980s and 1990s, the French television industry tried to produce home-grown drama series and soaps, but these met with limited success.

The feature films screened by the different channels vary in nature and in the cultural and artistic category into which they can be classified. In general, the requirement for both private- and public-sector channels to attract viewing audiences sufficient to provide advertising revenues means that films have to be of significant mass/popular appeal. Only the Franco-German cultural channel Arte screens films of a more restricted appeal with any degree of regularity, although Canal Plus, because of its close links with the cinema industry, can offer films (through its pay-per-view subscription) which escape the 'blockbuster' or family-viewing' nature of the majority of cinema found on French television. Canal Plus focuses principally, however, on the first showing on TV of new cinema films.

Films made for television are an interesting category, since they can be either adaptations of works of literature (of differing kinds) or original works of television drama. The programming of adaptations of works of literature naturally involves choices about the appeal of the literature in question to the viewing audiences. Different kinds of literature appeal to larger or smaller sections of the French public, depending on their degree of difficulty. Thus, in 2002, F3 and Arte collaborated in the filming of *Ruy Blas* – the Victor Hugo classic play set in the seventeenth century – starring Gérard Depardieu and other top-drawer actors, screened in November (FR3) and December (Arte). During the same period, F2 chose to reschedule – at prime time after the evening news – a three-part telefilm adaptation of Marcel Pagnol's famous Marseille trilogy *Marius-Fanny-César*. The contrast between the different scheduling choices was clear: although F3 has to compete for audience with commercial channels, it is still invested with the brief of encouraging the dissemination of high culture (here in collaboration with the unambiguously informative and high-culture Arte), whereas F2 has to concentrate single-mindedly on its ratings battle with TF1, and thus programmes fiction/drama of the widest possible appeal.

The category 'fiction' also includes soaps, serials and situation comedy. Here again, discussion of television in France has tended to focus on the perceived (low) 'intellectual quality' of the programmes and on their origin. American and British viewers of French TV tend to be shocked at both the sheer volume of US and UK serials screened and rescreened by all channels and by the amateur nature and quality of much of the French-produced material. For every successful French drama – yet another adaptation of either Simenon's Maigret detective or Pagnol's romantic novels – there appear to be dozens of repeats of *Columbo*, *Kojak*, *The Avengers* (translated as *Chapeau melon et bottes de cuir* – Bowler Hat and Leather Boots), *Dallas*, *Dynasty*, *Miami Vice* (*Deux flics à Miami*) and the *Cosby Show* from the 1970s and 1980s (to mention but a few) and *ER* (*Urgences*), *Midsomer Murders* (*L'inspecteur Barnaby*), *NYPD Blue*, *Dawson's Creek*, *Heartbreak High* and a host of others from the 1990s. This can be explained both culturally – by the French public's fascination for all things 'Anglo-Saxon' – and by the long-term weakness of French television production, the development of which was stifled by the state monopoly and which is now unable to compete on cost and quality with imported fiction. The drama series and soaps which have been French-produced – *Chateauvallon*, *Premiers baisers* (First Kisses), *Hélène et les garçons* (Helen and the Boys) – have generally struggled, both critically and in terms of ratings (although, of course, Helen and the Boys had good ratings among the young audience it targeted, even if it was derided by 'serious' TV viewers). *Chateauvallon* (Antenne 2, 1985) was generally perceived as 'a French Dallas' and its significance as an object (work of art) and practice (product of the organization of mass media industry) of fiction/drama/soap in the context of popular (television) culture has been unpacked by Marshall (1990). Marshall concludes that *Chateauvallon* reflected France's late espousal of industrialized television and mass television culture and was a response to the 'difficulties of creating a space for fiction that speaks to contemporary French realities' (Marshall, 1990: 148). Analysing the third true French soap opera (after *Chateauvallon* and TF1's *En cas de bonheur*) as it started to run – *Riviera* (TF1, 1991) – Susan Hayward suggested that, if it failed (as it did), it should be seen as 'another nail in the coffin of French TV's efforts at *la creation française* – a policy so dear to Jack Lang and yet so remote from the television screens' (Hayward, 1992: 59). Hayward's interesting study of *Riviera* considers it as a blend of US and French traditions of drama (Parisian *théâtre de boulevard*) and soap opera (Hollywood production practices) which, although it questions assumptions about class, caste and sex in France, ultimately lacked enough French cultural specificity to succeed.

The genre of *divertissement* (entertainment) covers *jeux* (game shows), talk shows, *humour* (comedy) and *variétés* (variety shows). Entertainment – along with information and education – is, as we have seen, one of the briefs of public-service television. Entertainment programmes of traditional formats have seen their place in scheduling squeezed since the 1970s, as television production in general has moved more and more towards genres which are all 'entertaining' in one way or another. The traditional programme format which has perhaps been most challenged by television's overall drift towards info- and 'edu-tainment' has been *variétés*, but – space being at a premium – we must briefly consider talk shows. Talk shows appear very frequently on French TV; discussing talk shows of the 1990s as an instrument for the redrawing of boundaries between private and public spheres and for a new conceptualization of citizenship, one analyst has described them as a 'staple feature of the televisual landscape' (Mazdon, 1999: 51). As Mazdon points out, contemporary talkshows such as *Ça se discute* (You Could Argue About That, F2, Jean-Luc Delarue) are genealogically linked to the (political and social) debate shows of the earlier years of French television, but the current format of these shows has abandoned the pedagogically informative approach (presenter/expert/politician talks to viewing public) of public-service state monopoly in favour of the 'hybrid provocation' of shows such as *Ciel mon mardi* (Heavens my Tuesday, TF1, 1988–92, Christophe Dechavanne). Animated by 'star' presenters such as Dechavanne, Nagui and Delarue, these immensely popular shows mix discussion between the (non-expert) presenters and members of the general public invited onto the show because of various personal experiences, and entertainment in the form of music, celebrity guests, comedy and video-clips. Unlike the stilted debate programmes of earlier periods – and unlike the discussion show which is arguably their direct forerunner, the controversial *Droit de réponse* (Right to Reply, Antenne 2, 1981–7, presented by Michel Polac) – such shows are non-political and non-ideological; in some ways, through their presentation of 'real-life' and 'every-day culture' they legitimate individual identities and experience and provide a new mediation between state and citizens and popular culture.

Magazines et documentaries is the genre – somewhat surprisingly – into which the Institut National de l'Audiovisuel (INA) puts arguably the most controversial of all French television trends of the 1990s, namely the 'reality show'. One of the most infamous of French reality programmes – *Témoin No. 1* – is the subject of detailed discussion in the case study below, so here we merely provide some background to this programming format. Dauncey (1996) provides a detailed discussion of French reality programming in the 1990s. Alongside 'fiction', 'magazines and documentaries' is the category which increased its share of broadcasting the most during the 1990s. The rise of this genre was principally a result of the reality shows produced by TF1 and other new light-hearted programmes of a presenter-meets-guests format (such as *Ciel mon mardi*, *Frou-frou* and *Coucou c'est nous!)* rather than serious investigative or informative documentaries.

Defining reality programming (RP) can be complicated. According to Kilborn, RP must include 'recording "on the wing" [...] events in the lives of individuals or groups', and the simulation of such real-life events in dramatized reconstructions in 'an attractively packaged television programme which can be promoted on the strength of its "reality" credentials' (1994: 423). This is a useful working definition of the format's basic features, and Kilborn also interestingly suggests that in Britain and France resistance to US models of reality shows has led to 'styles and forms of RP [...] more in tune with national and cultural priorities' and characterizes French RP in particular as concentrating on topics of 'love, sex and family relationships'. Thematically, French reality programming presents three main types: 'everyday dramas of courage', 'talking about feelings' and 'civic action'. This common-sense classification of the variants of the genre helps us focus on the cultural and political issues they have raised in France. 'Everyday dramas of courage' deal typically with rescues and the work of emergency services, as in *La Nuit des Héros* (Night of Heroes, Antenne 2, 1991). 'Talking about feelings' covers programmes which Kilborn has rightly suggested are most typical of French reality television and which are concerned with love, sex and family relationships – such concerns are not exclusively French, but, nevertheless, the success of these programmes arguably reflects French interest in forms of 'psychotherapeutic discourse'. It is 'civic action' reality shows which have focused attention on television's potential to create parallel structures of policing, justice and arbitration and raised concerns over the 'exhibitionism' encouraged in citizens participating in these reality shows, and consequent audience 'voyeurism'.

Supporters of reality shows claim they are healthy examples of French television's modernization and a sign of a praiseworthy new attention being paid to the demands of the viewing public. For their critics, reality shows represent the worst excesses of lowest-common-denominator programming policy governed by viewing ratings (the dictature de l'Audimat), and the channels' constant need to reduce production costs.

CASE STUDY

REALITY TELEVISION – *TÉMOIN NO. 1*

Témoin No. 1 is the French version of the British programme *Crimewatch UK*. The French word *témoin* means 'witness', so the title of the show could be translated as 'Prime Witness'. The programme is directly inspired by its UK forerunner. To place *Témoin No. 1* in the context of American television (and as an illustration of the American origins of many 'reality shows') it suffices to say that it is the French version of crime programmes such as *Rescue 911* (CBS) or *Unsolved Mysteries* (ABC). In Britain, concerns raised by programmes such as *Crimewatch UK* were addressed in official reports and academic studies, but in France debate was more heartfelt – sometimes reaching proportions of 'moral panic' – because of traditional French unease (there was a lot of it during the German Occupation) at 'informing'.

Témoin No. 1 was created and produced by Pascale Breugnot for TF1, the commercial channel arguably most concerned with viewing ratings and advertising revenues. The programme was vital to TF1's ratings strategy, occupying the mid-evening prime-time slot after the main 40-minute news programme which commences at 8 p.m. Lasting for a full two hours, *Témoin No. 1* filled the evening schedule, frequently competing with popular feature films on all the other channels. The greatest popularity of the show was reached in February 1996, with an audience of 8.5 million viewers, representing 16.3 per cent of the viewing public. Breugnot was the principal exponent of reality programming in France. Coming from the TF1 reality-show production line, this show combined all the features of the genre which had led to the cancellation of the still-born *La Trace* crime show in 1990. In fact, the threat of *Témoin No. 1* to moral standards went further than that of *La Trace* through its appeal for viewer-participation and the possibility of discrediting existing traditional mechanisms of law and order. The principle of *Témoin No. 1* was simple: unsolved crimes were presented to the viewing public in the form of filmed reconstructions, and viewers were encouraged to telephone the studio where the presenter of the programme animated a discussion between police, examining magistrates, witnesses and victims.

From the beginning of its first series in 1993, *Témoin No. 1* purportedly aimed to present its investigations as soberly as possible. The monthly scheduling of the show represented TF1's desire to distinguish the programme from other (weekly) reality shows and game programmes. Despite the care expended by its creators to make the content acceptable, *Témoin No. 1* attracted criticism with the first programme (1 March 1993), which covered the difficulties experienced by police and investigating magistrates in a number of unresolved child murders. Many critics and analysts of French television considered this topic unnecessarily emotional for a reality show claiming seriousness and public-service motivations. As well as unease at the topics, there was criticism of filmed reconstructions of events (confusingly mixing actors and real witnesses), extravagant camera work, melodramatic music and studio decors. As with US TV crime shows, filming, mise-en-scène and music were designed to heighten 'spectacle'.

Criticisms of *Témoin No. 1* arose despite efforts to deal only with unsolved cases in which there was no suspect, and to refrain from screening identikit photos or broadcasting live phone calls. The producers promised to obtain approval from the victims' families and legal authorities before showing reconstructions, and to transmit phone leads immediately to examining magistrates. *Témoin No. 1* found itself undermining its own validity through concessions to police and legal authorities: as TF1 accepted modifications to the programme format, *Témoin No. 1* caused increasing confusion in viewers' minds. The presence of police and magistrates 'live in studio', for example, seemed to blur the lines between mere reality television (however ostensibly careful) and official procedures of policing and justice.

Témoin No. 1 was withdrawn in December 1996. During its four years, arguably it acquired a certain respectability as the flagship of French reality shows. Its popularity with viewers, however, never prevented criticism from the legal establishment and television regulators. A succession of scandals arose as *Témoin No. 1* overstepped its own limits, or contravened CSA guidelines on acceptable TV. In October 1993, at the start of the second series, an apparent breakdown of safeguards intended to ensure close collaboration

between journalists and examining magistrates occurred as the show's presenters directly called for witnesses to come forward, instead of leaving such appeals to be made only
by legal officials. In March 1994 *Témoin No. 1* diverged from working in partnership with
the police and legal system when a murder case was brought to TF1 by the lawyer of the
victim's parents and was broadcast against the advice and without the participation of
magistrates.

The programme's producers and presenters claimed such slips were minor errors of
organization, or could otherwise be justified. But analysts of French RP tend to believe
that reality shows, by their nature, must increasingly sensationalize in order to maintain
audience figures. It also seems that this kind of crime show must inherently enjoy an
ambiguous relationship with the official structures of justice and the police. There were
claims in 1994 that, after only six months, *Témoin No. 1* was already abandoning its 'safe'
formula of collaboration with examining magistrates and was pursuing a 'freedom of
action' intended to maintain its notoriety and viewing ratings.

The producers repeatedly rebutted accusations that their programme sensationalized
human suffering. Although doubts over the altruism of TF1 persist, Breugnot and presenter Jacques Pradel professed to believe that *Témoin No. 1* provided a service for citizens
for whom traditional methods of criminal investigation had failed. They argued that the
occasional freedom the programme allowed itself from safeguards imposed by the CSA
regulatory body and the legal system were justified by its good intentions. This belief
served to condone occasional ethical-legal slips and facilitated a split between the programme and judicial system, as *Témoin No. 1* exploited cases where police and legal
investigations had failed but TF1 produced both results and audiences. Much of the
French debate over *Témoin No. 1* and RP in general focused on fear that, like pornography, they trap viewers and channels in a vicious circle of ever more ethically unacceptable
thrills.

The last word on reality shows should perhaps lie with Hervé Bourges, former director
general of France-Télévision, who as poacher-turned-gamekeeper president of the
regulatory Conseil Supérieur de l'Audiovisuel declared: 'Despite ratings successes –
which may change – I refuse to believe that this hotchpotch of greed-TV, sleaze-TV and
sex-TV is really the future of our television' (Bourges, 1993: 220). Bourges, among others,
campaigned for a true 'state commercial television' merging private-sector financial
efficiency with the 'quality' and responsibility of *le service public*.

SUGGESTIONS FOR FURTHER THINKING, READING AND STUDY

This chapter has tried to cover the basic features of television in France for those
who want to come to a better understanding of it as a manifestation of popular culture and of people's everyday lives. What we have discussed should provide a basis
for looking at programmes and seeing their place in TV and culture. Although a variety of programmes have been mentioned, there are many iconic television pro-

grammes which have here been ignored. We could have discussed satirical programmes of the 1980s and 1990s such as Canal Plus' *Les guignols de l'info* (The News Clowns, from August 1988) or TF1's *Le Bébête Show* (The Silly Show, from October 1982) and assessed their cultural and political significance. We could have considered programmes on music, cookery, sport, gardening, and compared them with their US and British counterparts.

The first thing anyone interested in thinking further about these questions should do is to spend some time studying the programme schedules of the main channels – what kinds of programmes are broadcast by each channel? Do there seem to be any programming omissions compared with the menu you are used to in the USA or UK? What proportion of the programming is French in origin? How does the proportion of 'high cultural' and 'entertainment' or 'popular culture' programmes vary between the channels? Convenient sources of schedules are daily newspapers or the websites of the main weekly TV magazines *Télé 7 jours* and *Télérama*. Studying these newspapers' coverage of television and how the specialist magazines present television can show a lot about how TV is perceived in France.

The next stage involves actually looking at the programmes themselves, and getting a feel for how – say – the presentation of news differs between the different channels, or how politicians are treated by different programmes. If you are interested in how French television has adapted programmes and genres from abroad, you could perhaps study how your favourite UK or US programme-format (game show, reality show, etc.) has fared in its transfer to France. In terms of the popular memory of television, it would be interesting to conduct a survey of programmes which have marked different generations of viewers: what are the iconic programmes of French television? In terms of the role of television in creating a shared national identity, who regularly watches – say – the president's New Year address?

BIBLIOGRAPHY

Bourdieu, Pierre (1996) *Sur la télévision* (Paris: Liber-Raisons d'Agir).

Bourges, Hervé (1993) *La Télévision du public* (Paris: Flammarion).

Chapman, R. and N. Hewitt (eds) (1992) *Popular Culture and Mass Communication in Contemporary France* (Lewiston, NY: Mellen).

Dauncey, Hugh (1996) 'French "Reality Television": More than a Matter of Taste?', *European Journal of Communication*, 11 (1) March, pp. 83–106.

Emanuel, Susan (1994) 'Cultural Television: Current French Critiques', *French Cultural Studies*, v, pp. 139–50.

Garcin, Jérôme (1992) 'Putain de part de marché', *L'Evénement du jeudi*, 20 February.

Hayward, Susan (1990) 'Television: A Transparence on Modern France' in Martyn Cornick (ed.), *Beliefs and Identities in Modern France* (Loughborough: ASMCF/ERC), pp. 97–105.

Hayward, Susan (1992) 'Riviera or Bust – French Soap: Third Time Lucky?', *French Cultural Studies*, iii, pp. 43–59.

Kilborn, Richard (1994) ' "How Real Can You Get?": Recent Developments in "Reality" Television', *European Journal of Communication*, 9 (4) December, pp. 421–39.

Kuhn, Raymond (1995) *The Media in France* (London: Routledge).

Looseley, David (1995) *The Politics of Fun: Cultural Policy and Debate in Contemporary France* (Oxford: Berg).

Marshall, Bill (1990) '*Chateauvallon*: Discourse and Television in 1980s France', *French Cultural Studies*, i, pp. 129–48.

Mazdon, Lucy (1999) 'The Television Talk-show in France: Constructing Audiences, Constructing Identities', *French Cultural Studies*, x, pp. 51–65.

Rigby, Brian (1991) *Popular Culture in Modern France: A Study of Cultural Discourse* (London and New York: Routledge).

Thibaud, Jacques (1970) *Une télévision pour tous les Français* (Paris: Seuil).

CHAPTER 6

Cyberculture

Gabriel Jacobs

The year 1980 was a momentous one in France, although it was not immediately recognized as such. It marked the beginning of a development which was to have an even deeper effect on French life than the left's dramatic return to power a year later. It was to open people's minds to new ways of communicating and obtaining information, and in doing so to generate an online culture which was peculiar to France for more than a decade. In order fully to appreciate its impact, it is necessary to know something of the circumstances which brought it about.

THE FRENCH ELECTRONIC REVOLUTION: MINITEL

In the summer of 1980, French government officials first saw a working version of an online digital communications system called Télétel, developed by the Direction Générale des Télécommunications (the DGT – the National Telecommunications Administration), later to become France Télécom. The project had its origins in a report which had been commissioned by the then French president, Valéry Giscard d'Estaing: the Nora-Minc Report (Nora and Minc, 1978). The report expanded on an idea first propounded by Gérard Théry, then head of the DGT, for a *plan télématique* (a telecommunications plan, *télématique* being an amalgam of *télécommunications* and *informatique*, 'information technology'). The authors of the report contended that if France were to compete successfully in a world about to be radically modified by the advent of the information society, and thus dominated by the USA, it would have to mount a full-blown effort in the area of data communications. They predicted that a substantial social change was about to take place in which personal computers capable of communicating with each other might well lead to a decentralized social chaos, the result of interactive lateral communication replacing the one-way, vertical communication of the existing media. Since, in the view of the authors of the report, the social change was inevitable, the state would be able to retain at least a measure of control if it took the lead in its development. Proof of the significance of the report came in the unsympathetic reactions of newspaper proprietors and editors: France's leading daily newspaper, *Le Monde*, for example, predicted that a telecommunications initiative on the scale being suggested would dig the grave of the written press (*Le Monde*, 1980).

The French government nevertheless decided to act decisively on the report's suggestions, particularly in view of the fact that the telephone infrastructure in France was in the process of being modernized and the time was therefore plainly right to ensure that the new system's technical features would allow for compatibility with online communications.

From a technological standpoint, however, Télétel was neither new nor specifically French. It was an American idea which had been imported into Britain in the late 1970s by British Telecom (as it then was) in the form of a service known as Prestel, a 'videotex' (or 'videotext') system based on the 'block graphics' still seen on present-day TV Teletext services – that is, the letters of the alphabet, the digits 0 to 9, punctuation, and rudimentary images all composed of so-called alpha-mosaics on the screen, and based on 'pages' of information with neither scrolling nor hyperlink capabilities. Germany had also implemented a similar system. But, whereas in the USA, Britain and Germany a critical mass of videotex users was never reached, in France a number of innovative measures ensured the success of Télétel. These included differential tariffs based on the estimated value of the information offered, public access to the system throughout France with only a local telephone call, and – above all – the decision to give away a free communications terminal, called the Minitel, to every French telephone subscriber. The expectation was that the increased use of the telephone would in the long term pay for the investment (Housel and Davidson, 1991). This ultimately turned out to be the case, although France Télécom struggled for years to make Télétel profitable, and ironically succeeded in doing so only as the internet was spelling its demise. Meanwhile, wide public acceptance came very quickly after its launch, Minitel or *la boîte* ('the box') soon becoming the words commonly used to refer to the whole system.

The Minitel terminal itself was in some ways ground-breaking: it consisted of a customized keyboard and integral screen (most home computers at the time had to be attached to a TV set). Inside were communications electronics requiring no set-up procedures, and this at a time when installing a modem was beyond the capabilities of many a non-technical person. Simplicity had been the main driver behind the design of the Minitel terminal so that it would be usable by even the least computer-literate. There were no facilities beyond its intended use as a 'dumb' terminal, not even for saving information. All that was required to use it was to plug it into a telephone wall-socket. And accessing a Télétel service was as uncomplicated as it could be (as it still is today): you keyed a four-digit code representing a particular tariff band plus an appropriate word. For instance, typing '36 15 MARIECLAIR' would take you to the Minitel site of the magazine *Marie Claire*. Other types of service were soon added, the numbers 36 14 and 36 15 being associated with general public sites, 36 16 and 36 17 with business-oriented sites, and with a range of bands for research databases and other high-value services.

A further trigger for the success of Minitel was the introduction, from the start, of an online national telephone directory (*l'annuaire électronique*). The costs of printing and distributing the printed directory were becoming prohibitive. The Minitel directory, free for the first three minutes of use, and searchable nationally or within defined regions by name, address, telephone number or profession, replaced the printed version. This proved a crucial factor in encouraging mass usage, and the online directory was consistently to remain the most widely used Minitel service (DECD, 1998: 14).

After a few trials in selected geographical areas with just a handful of services, Télétel was officially launched nationwide in 1982, and within a couple of years had come to dwarf any online network anywhere in the world. By 1986, over 1,000 different services were available. By 1987, the number of terminals in regular use ran into the millions. By 1989, over a third of French citizens had a Minitel terminal at home or at work, and were able to access more than 12,000 services, from news of the current depth of snow at ski resorts to job-seeking sites, from online games to online banking, from travel reservations to mail order. Business-to-consumer e-commerce was a flourishing reality in France well before other developed countries had even heard of the idea. By the peak of Minitel's success in the early to mid-1990s, there were over 25,000 services, and the vast majority of the French population had at some time made use of one or more of them (DECD, 1998: 10–11). It has to be remembered that this success was in the days before the internet explosion, when comparatively few people, even in the USA, had an online connection of any kind. Britain's Prestel peaked in the mid-1980s at around 75,000 subscribers (Mayne, 1987: 22); if the Minitel of that time had lost that many it would have made only a minor dent in its user-base.

It would be hard to underestimate the effect of this on French daily life. Within just a few years of its introduction, the French were turning naturally to Minitel whenever information was required. In May 1968, the streets had been the locus of the popular voice; a couple of decades later, it had manifestly moved in the direction of Minitel. Such was Minitel's penetration into both the national psyche and official thinking that it became the sole means of performing certain operations or accessing certain important pieces of information; students wishing to register at university, for example, or to get exam results, might well be obliged do so via Minitel.

What, then, is beginning to happen today with the internet world-wide happened in France more than a decade ago. Yet even at the height of Minitel's success, when almost every French citizen was familiar with the system, few people outside France had even heard of it. Despite concerted efforts on the part of France Télécom to create and support gateways to it in a number of countries, the attempted internationalization of Minitel failed miserably, mostly as a result, it has to be said, of French parochialism. In the 1980s, the French stood a chance of founding a global telematic network: the opportunity was wasted. The Minitel phenomenon was, and was to remain, uncompromisingly French, and this in good measure because of the lack of any concerted effort to encourage services offered in the world's *lingua franca*, English. The international dimension of Minitel was perceived by the state as a means of defending and promoting French culture abroad rather than of establishing the system as a world standard. In the 1990s, Italy, with the lion's share of international Minitel usage, never reached connect time amounting to more than an insignificant fraction of the French total, while Britain, Germany and the USA combined did not account for even a small portion of Italian usage (France Télécom, 1994). It was inevitable that sooner or later some other system would provide a global network. As we now know, this was to be the internet, which, as it happens, had been defined by the Americans in the same year as the launch of Minitel, and which, as we shall see, was eventually to deliver a body-blow to Minitel from which it could not recover.

POPULAR INTERCHANGE: MINITEL MESSAGING

Minitel began as an information-delivery service, but was also to become an important vehicle for person-to-person communication termed *messagerie conviviale* ('user-friendly messaging'), mostly via electronic bulletin boards and text chatlines.

We have seen that the newspaper industry had raised early objections to a publicly funded telecommunications project. In order to counteract the effect of negative publicity, shortly after the launch of Minitel the DGT concluded an agreement with newspaper proprietors in which it partly financed Minitel press services in return for supportive publicity (a decision which was to give rise to an ironic state of affairs when, in 1986, a national student strike was organized via the Minitel site of the newspaper *Libération*). Partly as a result of this accommodation between the DGT and the written press, and with potential revenue in sight, a number of newspapers started to offer their own *messagerie* services, beginning in 1981 with Grétel, the service run by the Strasbourg newspaper *Dernières nouvelles d'Alsace*. According to Minitel mythology (though the story may well be true), some computer enthusiasts hacked into Grétel's interactive Help system and altered the program code in such a way that they could communicate online with each other. When the administrators of Grétel discovered what was happening, they legitimized the facility and made it available to all those accessing their site, a move resulting in a massive increase in users' connect time, and, so the story goes, making Grétel for a short while the most used Minitel service apart from the telephone directory.

Other organizations followed Grétel's lead, and within a year or two several dedicated systems were up and running which now allowed users to communicate with sites other than the one to which they were connected. France Télécom joined in with its official, and soon quite heavily used, email service called Minicom. A network of interconnected communities had been created, and real-time Minitel messaging and chatlines became a widely accepted form of communication, giving rise to an online subculture seen nowhere else in the world at the time. *Messagerie* usage grew at such a rate that in 1985 Télétel suffered a system crash due to information overload, caused mostly by heavy usage of the most notorious among the chatlines, those forming part of what is known as *messagerie rose*, literally 'pink messaging' – although in English-speaking countries the colour blue is associated with what it offers, that is, adult chatlines.

Sex chat took off on Minitel almost as soon as the system had established itself as a popular mass medium; indeed, it became so well known as a Minitel activity that the term *messagerie* alone came to be almost synonymous with it. That supposed nubile women making lewd suggestions to male Minitel users were (and still are) in reality more often than not young male actors paid to keep users online for as long as possible, and that many of the users were (and are) actually aware of this, did nothing to slow down the growth of the *minitel rose*. Before long, it had become one of the main forces behind Minitel's success, especially between about 1983 and 1987, by which year 'pink' sites were clocking up staggeringly high usage figures (Périer: 1988: 122). Some of these sites (such as 36 15 CUM or 36 15 GAY) were effectively dating services; others, such as 36 15 DOMINA or 36 15 EROS, were aimed principally at *fantasmeurs* (fantasizers), and their content knew few bounds of what we might call decency.

The trend was studied in universities by psychologists and sociologists, and the media gave it very wide coverage. Most of the newspapers denounced it as a discreditable use of a development which had put France at the forefront of information technology, while at the same time titillating their readers with lurid details: *minitel rose* stories, very much the stuff of modern myths in French popular culture, were an endless source of material for tabloid journalists. The FFF (Fédération des Familles de France) vigorously campaigned for draconian regulation of the *minitel rose*; several members of the French parliament made speeches calling for the closure of sites promoting debauchery, bestiality, paedophilia and prostitution; the police complained about the ease with which drugs and sex businesses could use Minitel to expand their markets; the public was outraged when a Parisian call-girl was brutally murdered after a meeting arranged on a sex chatline (Périer, 1988: 190 ff.; Jay, 1991: 52–5).

The wave of adverse publicity led to a dramatic fall in connect time on 36 15 sites as a whole, in good part as a result of many businesses barring calls to them. Such a fall was a blow to France Télécom's forecasts for revenue, which were already beginning to prove insufficient to ensure a return on the original huge investment (France Télécom, 1997a). It is tempting to assume that, if such a fall in usage had not occurred, France Télécom would have retained its initial laissez-faire attitude towards sex-chat services. But public opinion was very strong. The revelation of the existence of AIDS had suddenly changed the discourse about sex, and the *minitel rose*, a prime target for moral outrage, was painted black as a consequence. The result was a somewhat half-hearted official attempt at regulating *messagerie rose*. A Minitel code of conduct was drawn up and circulated, higher charges were introduced for services deemed to be degrading, and a few services causing particular offence were disconnected from the system.

In tandem with the clamp-down on *messagerie rose*, and in an attempt to counter the damage being done to Minitel's reputation, there was also a new official focus on its promotion as a tool for commerce and industry, with advertising slogans such as 'Taper Télétel c'est taper fort en affaires' ('Key Télétel, the key to business success'), and for its educational potential in delivering courses and practice for examinations. Business and educational use of Minitel did increase, but sex-chat services continued to hold on to their position as second only to the online telephone directory, many of them having dodged the regulations by mixing their sex-chat with horoscopes and the like, thus creating services which were, at least, not exclusively pornographic. As late as 1992–3, and even after a long, resolute denunciation of the *minitel rose* in the media and in official statements, sex-chat and other 'personals' still accounted for nearly a quarter of total Minitel connect time (France Télécom, 1995). The coming of the internet has recently shifted the attention of the guardians of French public morals towards pornographic websites. But the *minitel rose* continues apace, even if now competing with many similar internet services.

Sex chatlines, together with online games, have also been held largely responsible for the widely publicized evidence of Minitel addiction. Especially in the late 1980s and early 1990s, the popular press, and even its high-brow counterpart, abounded with stories of marriages breaking up when wives discovered that their husbands had for years been living secret lives on the *minitel rose* and, even when found out, were unable to get shot of the addiction, or of formerly happy families thrown into turmoil as parents raged against their children wasting hours online in fantasy worlds at both financial and social cost as well as damage to eyesight. There was no doubt some exaggeration of the extent of the problem, but addiction to online services was certainly an appreciable social phenomenon in France before it also became one in other parts of the world, and there is plenty of reliable evidence of the compulsive attraction of Minitel – addicts regularly spending over 100 hours on chatlines each week (out of a possible 168 hours), even logging up over 70 continuous hours apparently without sleep, and parents facing gigantic phone bills as a result of their teenage children's fixation (Le Roux, 1995).

A CULTURAL CONVERSION BY POPULAR DEMAND: THE INTERNET IN FRANCE

Given France's ferocious pride in its cultural identity, it was perhaps to be anticipated that, when extended abroad, Minitel should be considered primarily a vehicle for the dissemination of French civilization, society and customs. Hardly surprising too, therefore, was the unfavourable reaction during the 1990s within French government circles to the global spread and attraction of the internet, the result of a belief that this signified the most recent, and most pernicious, potential increase in the saturation of French society with American popular culture and its English-language medium. The internet was seen by many in France (and is still seen today, not without some justification) as a tool of American cultural imperialism, and accordingly the protection of France's 'Frenchness' was used as sufficient reason for attempts, in the main unsuccessful, to set restrictions on internet usage. President Jacques Chirac has on several occasions expressed his concerns about the fact that the vast majority of internet traffic world-wide is in English, and the laws passed in France aimed at protecting the French language have been intended to apply as much to online activity as to other media. But the decentralized nature of the internet makes it virtually uncontainable. The French government may have been able in some measure to police Minitel, but it is difficult to conceive of the internet being subject in practice to national restrictions in a democracy. The 1978 Nora-Minc report rightly foresaw the general effect of lateral communication on the control of information, and Minitel has been unable to fend off the global community spirit of the internet which has appealed to the popular imagination in France no less than in countries where official paranoia about American cultural imperialism is not so prevalent.

From 1999 onwards the switch from Minitel to the internet, in both households and businesses, became something of a fever (ART, 2001: 11–12). It would seem – reliable demographic information is hard to come by – that the profile of the current typical French internet user (young, male, middle-class) is not quite that of the Minitel user (male or female of almost any age, though still middle-class). Be that as it may, internet usage figures for the last three or four years have shown exponential growth, especially between 1999 and 2001 (ART, 2001: 8–9), and the number of French internet domain names has simply skyrocketed (STATS, 2003).

The change has come about, however, not only by popular demand, but also as a result of commercial and political pressures on the French government. By the mid-1990s, it was abundantly clear that unless there was a change in French online practice, specifically that unless internet usage in France increased to the detriment of the outdated and insular Minitel, the country was in danger of becoming isolated, a Have Not of the global online community trapped in its own restricted shell. The onslaught of American popular culture was consistently deplored, but there was a reluctant acceptance that, as far as the internet was concerned, blows could be parried only at the cost of undesirable economic and social consequences. And, more so than any other country, France was in a position to appreciate the commercial and social importance of the information society, having experienced it at first hand for so long.

Thus, in 1997, Prime Minister Lionel Jospin urged the French to join the global information revolution. He warned that Minitel was hindering the development of new applications of information technology, which could have dire economic repercussions, and pledged financial support for a campaign effectively to kill off Minitel (Jospin, 1997; France Télécom, 1997b). Much of the money was used to fund a *Fête de l'internet* (an Internet Celebration) in which schools throughout France were used as examples of how it was possible to kick the 'Minitel habit', Minitel being (rightly) seen as the major obstacle to the mass adoption of the internet. A new telecommunications regulatory authority was set up (ART – Autorité de Régulation des Télécommunications), with the particular brief of promoting the internet in France. France Télécom, with its profits in peril and (again rightly) seeing that the spectre of Minitel would not easily be exorcised, deployed new terminals able to access both Minitel and the internet, and aggressively marketed its PC- and Apple Macintosh-based Minitel emulation systems (DECD, 1998: 20, 28–9, 31). The French media strongly backed such moves (see, for example, Alberganti, 1997; *Le Monde*, 1999).

The problem with these hybrid solutions was that they encouraged users to continue thinking 'Minitel' rather than 'internet'. However, in the face of intense popular demand that way of thinking is now rapidly fading: whereas only three or four years ago the word 'Minitel' was to be heard and read with extraordinarily high frequency in the French media, 'internet' and 'web' have replaced it to a large extent. Some advertisements still urge you to type 36 15 for more information or to order goods, but 'www' is now much more widely accepted as the natural online alternative. Newspapers occasionally carry articles unfavourably comparing the internet with Minitel (for example, Alberganti, 1998; Piliu, 2001), but they are becoming increasingly rare. And, while Minitel email still functions, its internet counterpart has eroded it to the point of its impending disappearance, and the Anglicisms *email* or simply *mail* (or *mel*) are now much more commonly used than *messagerie,* or *courrier électronique* (electronic post) or its contraction to *courriel.*

One other point should be mentioned in the context of Minitel's battle with the internet. Almost immediately after the internet became widely available in the West, it spawned communities of enthusiasts served by their own astonishingly wide range of both online and offline sources of information, notably internet forums where the use of the internet itself was the subject of discussion, and many specialist newsstand magazines (which continue to proliferate today – proof, if that were needed, of the enduring nature of printed material even in a specifically online sphere). Minitel did not generate such a subculture to any significant degree (except as manifested in the proliferation of advertisements for sex-chat sites in the press and as street posters), the main reason doubtless lying in its ease of use. Minitel did not lend itself to tweaking in order to improve performance, nor did new products to be evaluated and argued about often come on the market. Especially during the late 1980s and into the 1990s, there was a fervour in industrialized countries for the use of computers in the home, a fervour which grew dramatically as networking and data communications became the order of the day, replacing the stand-alone use of home computers which had characterized the preceding years. This enthusiasm was less vigorous in France, a fact certainly in part due to the use of Minitel being almost as natural to the French as picking up the telephone to speak to somebody.

Paradoxically, then, the very success of Minitel in terms of its deep penetration of French life prevented the French from sharing fully in the dynamism being experienced elsewhere. There is no doubt that Minitel seriously held back sales of personal computers in France for a number of years, and dampened enthusiasm for their use, while the same enthusiasm was elsewhere rapidly increasing, fired as it was by a flourishing market in peripheral publications. A 'computer nerd' culture it may have been called by some, but the zeal displayed by that culture, not seen in France to the same extent as, for example, in Britain or the USA, helped to energize – was perhaps even the origin of – the internet revolution and its cyberculture.

CASE STUDY

THE CLAUDE GUBLER AFFAIR

The limited success of the French government's attempt to place restrictions on the *minitel rose* was due to the conflicting pressures of public demand and the maintenance of revenue: France Télécom had certain powers to crack down on sex chatlines but chose not to use them to the full in the face of a lucrative source of income. Such powers of control are, for practical purposes, absent with respect to the internet, an illustrative case in point being the skirmish between French officialdom and Dr Claude Gubler, the personal physician of former French president François Mitterrand, one in which the popular voice simply could not be silenced.

A few days after Mitterrand's death in 1996, Gubler published a book entitled *Le Grand Secret* (*The Great Secret*) (Gubler, 1996) in which he recounted the history of the president's eventually terminal prostate cancer which had been kept secret from the French public for many years. He included in the book a number of damaging allegations (and spicy anecdotes) about Mitterrand's personal life. Mitterrand's family sought an injunction. The book was banned, and unsold copies were removed from booksellers' shelves. Gubler was struck off the medical register, stripped of all national honours, fined and sentenced to four months in prison. But the full text of the book, which the owner of an internet café in the town of Besançon had scanned, appeared on the café's website.

Again, the state moved in, and France Télécom was able to use its then monopolistic control of telecommunications to close down the offending website (and ultimately the café), ostensibly for reasons of non-payment of telephone bills (even as early as 1996, it was recognized that the use of regulatory powers over the internet in France might well provoke an unwelcome popular reaction, especially when the only real justification for using such powers seemed to be a political one).

The debate which took place at the time within official circles about how, in future, to control online content is revealing of a lack of understanding of the ways of the internet and a deeply engrained *dirigiste* attitude towards the manipulation of information. A working group from the ministries of justice, culture and telecommunications was formed. Measures proposed ranged from cutting phone lines to servers thought of as being hostile to the state, to the (ludicrous) idea of encrypting entire portions of the French web. But it was soon realized that attempts at such national control were futile, as was very soon to be proved when the text of *Le Grand Secret* reappeared on an American website, and was almost instantly mirrored on other foreign sites (they are no longer active). The only saving grace for the French authorities was that in 1996 the internet had not yet taken off in France to the extent it has today, so that comparatively few French people would access the text. But the writing was, so to speak, on the wall.

It would be going too far to suggest that the Gubler affair was ultimately responsible for the change in attitude towards the internet which was to be officially promoted just one year later. But it is an important case not only because of the lengthy and extensive coverage it received in the media, especially on both Minitel and the internet, but also because it represented the first significant manifestation of the emerging French involvement in what had become by 1996 a powerful international cyberculture which did not necessarily respect national prescriptions. As such, it was influential in making the French government fully aware that accepting the advantages of global online activity entailed a galling but unavoidable side-effect, namely the force of popular lateral communication predicted in the Nora-Minc report of 18 years before.

Conclusion

There can be no denying that the internet has posed in the last few years, and continues to pose, a threat to the Frenchness of France's popular culture. Whether the French like it or not, not only the English language but also American ways of thinking are at the core of the World Wide Web, and it is difficult to see how their influence in France can be avoided. Neither chauvinistic appeals, nor do-or-die initiatives to salvage Minitel, can in the long run stem the tide. As we have seen, French officialdom has grudgingly recognized this state of affairs, and this despite the bleating of certain French intellectuals such as Pierre Bourdieu who, in an often-quoted speech tangentially bemoaning the official change of mind as a shameful capitulation, set out in no uncertain terms the view that American culture represents nothing but a vulgar homogenization which threatens to dilute the hallowed purity of French cultural identity (Bourdieu, 1999).

But Bourdieu makes no mention of the fact that, after initial rejection, France has in the past found value in numerous forms of American mass culture, from jazz to detective novels. In any event, the very character of the internet in point of fact may offer France its strongest shield against the seemingly overwhelming might of Anglo-

Saxon culture. In France, Minitel is often referred to in the media as a kind of proto-internet of which France can be justly proud, but this is true only in a restricted sense. Despite Minitel's messaging capabilities, the system has always been flood-ed with information and ideas emanating from official and commercial sources, whereas with the internet, and despite the huge official and commercial interest in it, there is no obvious location of power. Anyone with access to the web is not only a receiver of information but also a potential publisher – the notion of a site on which any individual or group of individuals can immediately broadcast ideas at minimal financial cost and with, in practice, little or no constraint on content is exclusive to the web, and doubtless its most durable quality. Linguistic and cultural uniformity are thus not the inevitable consequences of the rise of the internet; indeed, it is the most powerful tool ever seen for the dissemination of a culture beyond its own national boundaries. Rather than necessarily being a medium for the advancement of American culture, it can be – in fact perhaps inevitably is – a potent force for multi-culturalism. The recent dramatic rise in the number of French websites and search engines has resulted in a palpable French internet presence. Internet users in France need no longer be saturated with American culture each time they log on, even if some of that culture inexorably seeps through. And the new French internet presence has already done far more for the promotion of French culture outside France than Minitel ever did during all its years of national success.

A process of intercultural exchange, the inevitable result of the advent of a glob-al cyberculture (which, curiously enough, perfectly embodies the French ideals of Liberty, Equality and Fraternity) therefore appears set to characterize future French online communications. The long-term challenge for those desperate to avoid the dilution of the French identity is to ensure that the outflow is sufficiently strong to counteract some of the power of the inflow, a power whose cultural significance entails considerable political consequences (Arendt, 1993), in other words to foster an acceptable balance between local use of French websites on the model of what was once almost universal Minitel usage, and the use of the internet as a global, outward-looking system.

SUGGESTIONS FOR FURTHER READING

Most of the dependable information with respect to Minitel is in French. The best introduction to its history and social impact up to its peak years is J.-Y. Rincé, *Le Minitel* (1994).

Relevant printed publications in English tend to be chapters in books dealing with the general history of telecommunications. One worth reading is H. Reingold, *The Virtual Community: Homesteading on the Electronic Frontier* (2000). Chapter 8 covers Minitel in a somewhat anecdotal but informative way.

The World Wide Web offers an incalculable amount of information concerning both Minitel and the internet in France, but it tends to be fickle both in content and in the fact that web pages can disappear without notice. One reliable website, however, is that of the Autorité de Régulation des Télécommunications (ART). It produces regular detailed reports on the state of French telecommunications which can be found at: www.art-telecom.fr/dossiers/index.htm. *Le Dossier noir du minitel rose* by Denis Périer (1988) makes fascinating reading for those interested in the *minitel rose* subculture.

A penetrating analysis of French attitudes towards the threat of Americanization via new technologies can be found in the final chapter of R. Kroes, *If You've Seen One, You've Seen the Mall: Europeans and American Mass Culture* (1996). A historical survey of French attitudes towards American popular culture, including the new threat posed by the internet, is presented in Chapter 9 of Kroes's later excellent book *Them and Us: Questions of Citizenship in a Globalizing World* (2000).

SUGGESTIONS FOR FURTHER INVESTIGATION

1. Get a (limited) feel for Minitel by accessing it free of charge via the internet at www.minitel.fr, from where the necessary emulation software can be downloaded. No registration is required for the *répertoire des services* (full list of services) and France Télécom's information site.
2. Log on to some specifically French internet search engines which give preference to Francophone sites, whether based in France or elsewhere, thus differentiating themselves from global search engines which generally allow searches to be limited only to broad domains (for example, .fr for France). Worth trying are:

http://ctrouve.com
http://kartoo.com
www.nomade.tiscali.fr
http://fr.yahoo.com

BIBLIOGRAPHY

Alberganti, M. (1997) 'Les fournisseurs de services réclament la modernisation du Minitel', *Le Monde*, 28 August.

Alberganti, M. (1998) 'A quoi sert Internet si on ne peut pas y acheter un billet de train?' *Le Monde*, 14 March.

Arendt, H. (1993) *La Crise de la culture* (Paris: Gallimard (Folio)), p. 285.

ART (2001) *Internet, premier bilan* (Paris: Autorité de Régulation des Télécommunications).

Bourdieu, P. (1999) 'Questions aux vrais maîtres du monde', *Le Monde*, 23 October.

DECD (1998) *France's Experience with the Minitel: Lessons for Electronic Commerce over the Internet* (Paris: Directorate for Science, Technology and Industry) (OECD report of 20 October).

France Télécom (1994) *La Lettre des services en ligne* (annual report) (Paris: France Télécom).

France Télécom (1995) *La Lettre de Télétel et de l'Audiotel, Bilan 1994* (Paris: France Télécom).

France Télécom (1997a) *La Lettre des services en ligne* (annual report) (Paris: France Télécom).

France Télécom (1997b) 'Le Minitel face à la montée en puissance du multimédia', *La Lettre de Télétel et de l'Audiotel*, 42 (2) (Paris: France Télécom).

Gubler, C. (1996) *Le Grand Secret* (Paris: Plon).

Housel, T. and W. Davidson (1991) 'The Development of Information Services in France: The Case of Public Videotex', *International Journal of Information Management*, 11, pp. 35–54.

Jay, A.-M. (1991) *Les Messageries télématiques* (Paris: Eyrolles).

Jospin, L. (1997) 'Préparer l'entrée de la France dans la société de l'information', speech by PM Lionel Jospin at the Université de la Communication, Hourtin, 25 August. www.premier-ministre.gouv.fr

Kroes, R. (1996) *If You've Seen One, You've Seen the Mall: Europeans and American Mass Culture* (Chicago: University of Illinois Press).

Kroes, R. (2000). *Them and Us: Questions of Citizenship in a Globalizing World* (Chicago: University of Illinois Press).

Le Monde (1980) leading article, 27 September.

Le Monde (1999) 'Quand l'Internet deviendra Net', *Le Monde Interactif*, 3 March.

Le Roux, P. (1995) 'Virtual Intimacy – Tales from the Minitel and More', In J. R. Levine and C. Baroudi (eds), *Internet Secrets* (New York: IDG Books), Ch. 1.

Mayne, A. (1987) *The Videotext Revolution* (London: Marathon).

Nora, S. and A. Minc (1978) *Rapport sur l'informatisation de la société* (Paris: La Documentation Française). In English as *The Computerisation of Society* (Cambridge, MA: MIT Press, 1980).

Périer, D. D. (1988) *Le Dossier noir du minitel rose* (Paris: Albin Michel).

Piliu, F. (2001) 'Le Minitel surfe sur la vague Internet', *L'Express International*, 8–14 March.

Reingold, H. (2000) *The Virtual Community: Homesteading on the Electronic Frontier* (Cambridge, MA: MIT Press).

Rincé, J.-Y. (1994) *Le Minitel*, 2nd edn (Paris: Presses Universitaires de France).

STATS (2003): www.glreach.com/globstats

CHAPTER 7

Music

Chris Tinker

French popular music has never really achieved the kind of critical or commercial success in the English-speaking world that is enjoyed by, for example, the French film industry. For a long time the rather inward-looking French pop-music industry did little to promote French music abroad. However, producers, supported by public authorities and professional organizations representing authors and artists, created the Bureau Export de la Musique Française in 1993, and further export offices were set up in the UK, Germany, the USA, Brazil and Japan. French record sales abroad indeed rose from 1.5 million in 1992 to more than 39 million in 2000. Despite such progress, the hegemonic status of the English language has always represented a significant obstacle for French pop music. Subtitling may be a fairly effective and efficient means of translating film for a mass audience, but it does not lend itself well to pop music which is delivered to audiences through an ever-developing variety of electronic media.

In any case, when French pop has crossed the English Channel, it has generally been dismissed by cultural commentators as corny and outdated. For example, Charles Aznavour, the epitome of the French romantic singer figure, was parodied in 1975 by the UK comedy group, the Goodies, as 'Charles Aznovoice'. It is often assumed that French rock, in particular, can never achieve the quality and authenticity of the supposedly 'original' Anglo-American model. It is even claimed that 'French is a language that just does not rock' (Silverton, 2001). Nevertheless, British audiences and critics have occasionally succumbed to the exotic charm of French-language songs – hits such as Serge Gainsbourg's erotic 'Je t'aime moi non plus' ('I love you, me neither'), banned by the BBC for its raunchiness in 1969, Vanessa Paradis' 'Joe le taxi' (1986), and, more recently, Alizée's 'Moi… Lolita' (2002). These exceptions tend to confirm the general assumption of the Anglo-American pop industry that English-speaking audiences are unwilling to accept songs in the original French. In order for a French artist to sell in the English-speaking world, French lyrics are often absent, as can be seen in the recent successes of French electronic Dance/Techno artists such as Daft Punk, Air and Stardust. Otherwise, French pop music has had to be written with English lyrics, for example the 1970s disco classics of Cerrone ('Supernature', 1977) and Patrick Hernandez ('Born to be Alive', 1979). French song lyrics have also been translated into English, although these have often been altered drastically from the originals. Scott Walker and Marc Almond devoted entire albums to Jacques Brel songs translated into English, introducing his work to non-French-speaking audiences. Both had UK chart hits with 'Jacky', a translation of Brel's 'La Chanson de Jacky' (1966) – Walker in 1968 and Almond in 1991. In the United States, the 1968 musical and 1975 film *Jacques Brel is Alive and Well and Living in Paris* introduced Brel's songs to an American audience and still retains a cult following. The most successful and popular English-language cover version of Brel to date is 'Seasons in the Sun', whose original title was 'Le Moribond' ('The Dying Man', 1961). A huge chart hit on both sides of the Atlantic, in 1974 for the Canadian singer Terry Jacks and in 1999 for the Irish boy band Westlife (the Christmas number 1 in the UK pop charts), the somewhat sugary English lyrics and vocal delivery retain, however, little of the content or the spirit of Brel's original version.

In the light of what has often been a rather limited, if not clichéd, Anglo-American-centred view of French popular music, the aim of this chapter is to move towards a broader picture of contemporary music in France as a popular cultural activity. It will provide a survey of the industry, the main genres of music, as well as the iconic singer-songwriters who have marked the post-war era. We will then consider some of the key critical approaches towards popular music in a French context, before ending with a case study of a recent successful CD release by Zazie, an innovative singer-songwriter who inscribes herself within a specifically French tradition.

MARKETING AND MEDIATING POPULAR MUSIC

The French music industry possesses the fifth largest market in the world – the third largest in Europe. Although pirating, CD burning and illegal file sharing are currently of great concern to the music industry, not just in France but around the world, 168 million records were sold in 2001, producing a turnover of €2 billion. Music is France's second most successful cultural product, the first being books. Next comes the cinema (€1 billion), multimedia (€830 million) and video (€820 million). Around 130,000 people are employed in fields related to the record industry. Although centralized in Paris, the production of popular music in France is effectively dominated by the major multinational labels: BMG, EMI, Sony Music, Universal Music, Virgin Music France and Warner Music. Independent companies only represented around 3 per cent of the market in France during 2001. In fact, many so-called 'indie' products are actually distributed by major record companies. Most CD purchases are made in superstores such as Leclerc, Carrefour and Auchan, or in major music retailers such as Virgin Megastores and FNAC. These can advertise widely and offer discounts. As a result, independent chains and small shops are being increasingly squeezed out of the market, resulting in the reduction in the number of specialized shops. The record charts are not as popular in France as they are in various European countries, are broadcast less on TV and the radio, and have little influence on the sales of singles. SNEP (Syndicat National de l'Edition Phonographique), the leading association of the French phonographic industry, and IFOP (Institut Français d'Opinion Publique), the French institute for opinion polls, produce the top 100 singles, top 75 albums, and top 25 compilations charts.

The mass media is crucial to the successful promotion of artists. France has a strong network of radio stations, aimed particularly at the lucrative youth market such as NRJ, Skyrock, Europe 2, Fun, as well as over 300 independent radio stations outside Paris. The main terrestrial television channel offering music is M6. Thirty per cent of its broadcasting is devoted to music programmes and a strong emphasis is placed on Francophone music. Its objective is to present all musical styles through video clips and programmes as well as to showcase new talent. The advent of cable, satellite and digital broadcasting has led to the creation of several national and international music channels such as Fun TV, M6 Music, MCM and MTV. Recently, French television and record companies have been teaming up to produce fly-on-the-wall/talent shows, already popular in the USA and elsewhere in Europe. Shows such as *Popstars* (M6) and *Star Academy* (TF1), in which young hopefuls compete for the chance to secure a recording contract, have scored huge ratings, particularly with very young, pre-teen audiences. France has always had its fair share of manufactured pop artists, ever since the 1960s *yéyé* wave (see p. 93). The 1990s saw the development of the boy-band phenomenon (2B3, G Squad, Alliage), following the successes of Anglo-American groups such as New Kids on the Block, Take That and Boyzone.

PROLIFERATING GENRES: FROM *CHANSON* TO TECHNO

If you visit a record retailer in France, or browse its online catalogue, you will find an extensive and ever-changing range of generic categories covering home-grown, Anglo-American and world-music forms. The most popular form in France remains by far the mainstream French song (*variété française*). In 2001, 59 per cent of turnover came from the Francophone repertoire, while 36 per cent came from the international repertoire and 5 per cent from classical music. Furthermore, 90 per cent of the top 20 albums were recorded by French-speaking artists. France has a strong *chanson* tradition which emphasizes the importance of lyrics, and which may be traced as far back as the medieval troubadours. This tradition was epitomized by figures such as Maurice Chevalier, Charles Trenet and Edith Piaf whose careers began before the Second World War. The 1950s and 1960s saw the triumph of a new generation of singer-songwriters (*auteurs-compositeurs-interprètes*) such as Jacques Brel,

Georges Brassens and Léo Ferré who performed in the Paris cabarets before grad-uating to the music hall and television. All deal extensively with personal issues, par-ticularly the universal themes of love, friendship and death (the latter being less of a taboo in French popular music), as well as with social questions, adopting a stance which is anti-bourgeois (Brel's 'Les Bourgeois'), anti-clerical (Ferré's 'Monsieur Tout-Blanc' ('Mr Whiter-than-White')) and anti-nationalist (Brassens's 'Les Deux Oncles' ('The Two Uncles')). Singer-songwriters such as the anarchist Ferré and the communist sympathizer Jean Ferrat ('Camarade' ('Comrade'), 'En groupe en ligue en procession' (In a group, in league, in procession)), became embroiled in contemporary social and political debates, particularly during the Algerian War, and in the run-up to the unrest of May 1968.

During the 1970s, a new generation of politically aware artists emerged who inte-grated popular and rock forms into their *chansons*: Maxime Le Forestier, who wrote the anti-militarist 'Parachutiste' (1971); Bernard Lavilliers, who imported the Latin American influences he had discovered while on his travels; and Renaud, very much in the anarchist tradition of Brassens, who, along with Lavilliers, successfully culti-vated the image of the urban hooligan.

Although French *chanson* is a male-dominated world, there are some notable female singer-songwriters such as Barbara who represented the archetypal French *femme fatale,* and Anne Sylvestre, a writer of children's songs (*les fabulettes*) who also deals with social issues. While no artist has perhaps made such a lasting impact since Brassens and Brel, new generations of singer-songwriters who came to notice during the 1970s (Véronique Sanson, Alain Souchon, Laurent Voulzy) still enjoy a broad appeal. One notable development since the late 1990s is the resurgence in popularity of French stage musicals such as *Notre Dame de Paris* (based on Victor Hugo's novel *Roméo et Juliette*), *Les Dix Commandements* and *Cindy-Cendrillon 2002*. These shows have produced a new crop of popular singers and actors, among whom Garou is one of the most recent success stories.

Although the indigenous French *chanson* has always been the most popular style in France, this was to some extent undermined by Anglo-American pop music, which gained popularity in Europe from the late 1950s. *La chanson yéyé*, a French version of American rock 'n' roll, became popular in France during the early to mid-1960s, and was exemplified by teenage icons born in the 1940s such as Johnny Hallyday, Eddie Mitchell and Sylvie Vartan. However, by the time of the social and political unrest of 1968, youth audiences had turned away from old-fashioned *yéyé* singers towards more challenging artists from North America such as Bob Dylan and Jimi Hendrix.

Although the French popular music scene of the 1970s would remain heavily grounded in the French tradition with artists who had become famous during the 1960s, the 1980s marked another turning point. The 1981 victory of François Mitterrand, the first socialist president of the Republic, brought with it hopes for greater freedom of expression. France, influenced by British punk and new wave of the 1970s, produced a more distinctly French form of rock (Téléphone, Starshooter, Indochine), while a more non-conformist movement established what became known as 'alternative rock'. Although 'alternative' artists were originally signed to independent labels, many would eventually sign to majors such as Les Négresses Vertes, Mano Negra and Les Rita Mitsouko. While the latter are still going strong after more than 20 years with a new album in 2002 (*La Femme Trombone*), a more recent generation of successful 'alternative rock' artists emerged during the 1990s, reflecting two main tendencies: *rock métissé* which mixes Latin, North-African and Mediterranean influences (La Ruda Salska, Zebda); and retro rock music which mixes acoustic instruments, often features traditional *bal musette* (accordion music), and nostalgically draws on 1930s realism (Les Têtes Raides, Louise Attaque).

The 1980s also saw the arrival in France of hip-hop culture, not on the streets as in the USA, but via radio and television, which introduced the cultural practices of rapping, deejaying, breakdancing and graffiti art to youth audiences. Independent radio stations covering breakdancing and rap festivals began to emerge during the late 1980s. Although young rappers and dancers were mainly of immigrant origin, listeners and spectators came from a mixture of ethnic backgrounds. Hip-hop culture in France, by no means a pale imitation of its American forerunner, has often represented a site of collective resistance against racism, and a sense of marginalization experienced in France's suburbs. As Cannon observes, hip-hop culture deals with issues such as drugs, deliquency, discriminatory policing, anti-nationalism, and the integrationist model of race relations, as well as a colonialist/imperialist narrative of history. Over the years, rap music has become more and more mainstream in France, which now has the second largest market in the world. Although several French rap albums have gone gold (MC Solaar and IAM being key examples of this commercialization), there is nonetheless a diversity of styles, including hard-core artists such as Suprême NTM (Cannon in Hargreaves and McKinney, 1997: 150–64).

The appropriation of rap music is an indication that France is increasingly aware of its multicultural composition, and has become open to external influences. In recent years, France has become a key centre for the development of world music. One of the most successful forms of world music is currently *raï*, a style of music which originated in Oran, Algeria, during the 1920s, and which has been popularized in France by singers such as Cheb Khaled. At the same time, France has also seen a renewed interest in traditional regional music. One of the most significant figures is Alan Stivell, who, at the forefront of the Breton revival, produced a series of harp albums during the 1970s. However, describing himself as 'a citizen of the world before being a Breton' (see Latkovich, 2000), Stivell has fused traditional music with modern forms from hard rock to hip-hop, for example, in '1 douar (Une terre)' ('One Earth') (1998) where he collaborated with artists as diverse as Khaled, Youssou N'Dour, Jim Kerr and John Cale. Corsican music has also gained popularity in France.

I Muvrini, a leading group named after a wild sheep which lives in Corsica's mountain regions, feature traditional polyphonic sounds in their own compositions. They also recorded 'Terre d'oru' ('Fields of Gold') with Sting, in Corsican and in English, and Brel's 'Amsterdam' in their 'best of' album *A Strada – Best Of* (2000).

Although the French popular musical scene is subject to continuing globalization in its most homogenizing forms, France is nonetheless witnessing an increasing multiplication and cross-fertilization of musical genres and subgenres, which gives some cause for optimism.

POLITICAL AND CRITICAL DEBATES

Popular music in France makes a significant contribution to the continuing cultural and political debates, particularly around French national identities and prevailing notions of French exceptionalism. Language and culture have indeed become the site of a political and economic struggle in the face of the proliferation of Anglo-Saxon mass culture. Successive French governments have continued since the end of the Second World War to adopt a series of conservative, protectionist measures, designed to promote French culture and limit what is perceived as English-speaking cultural dominance and imperialism. Such alarm on the part of intellectuals or politicians, be it well-meaning or backward-looking, assumes the existence of a monolithic French cultural identity and heritage which are deemed worthy of preservation. Cultural protectionism was soon applied after the war, culminating in the 1949 Blum-Byrnes agreement, which sought to protect *bande dessinée* (cartoon strips) and cinema, and maintain French cultural specificity (Rigby, 1991: 171). Conservative intellectual figures such as Jacques Charpentreau, who dismissed *yéyé* as 'moronic trash', stoutly defended the virtues of 'intellectual' and 'literary' tradition in French song, and campaigned for forms of pop music that encouraged ethical awareness and civic responsibility (Rigby, 1991: 164).

In recent years, similar defences of French cultural identity against US and especially Anglophone rock-pop have been made by a new generation of intellectuals, the most notable of whom is Alain Finkielkraut. His famous pamphlet, *La Défaite de la pensée* (1987), advocated a return to the cultural and educational policies implemented during the early years of the Third Republic. Moreover, the French fear of Anglo-American cultural imperialism was highlighted by the mid-1990s GATT talks on film and television quotas, as well as the radio quotas for French songs. This involved setting quotas specifying a minimum amount of radio airtime for songs in the French language. The Pelchat amendment, which took effect from 1 January 1996, requires that at least 40 per cent of songs broadcast every month by French radio stations between 6.30 a.m. and 10.30 p.m. must be in the French language. Moreover, 20 per cent of the total number of songs broadcast must originate from new French talent.

While holding on to the idea of a distinctive French culture, French politicians and intellectuals continued for a long time to emphasize the preeminence of high culture over mass cultural forms such as pop music. In particular, André Malraux, the first French minister of culture under De Gaulle's presidency, pursued a *mission civilisatrice* (civilizing mission) during the 1960s to 'democratize' and promote 'high' culture through cinema, the Théâtre National Populaire (People's National Theatre), public libraries, *maisons de la culture* (community arts centres) and popular education. The maintenance of France's national cultural heritage and *grandeur* was of prime importance. However, by the 1980s, the socialist regime of François Mitterrand, represented by its flamboyant minister of culture, Jack Lang, began to attach greater importance to the cultural practices of young people. Popular music, especially rock, world music and rap, were to be viewed as an 'authentically national cultural phenomenon' (Looseley, 2003). On 21 June 1982, the minister created the first national music festival which is now well established in France (www.fetedelamusique.culture.fr). A programme of financial support at national and regional level was introduced, in order to make French music more competitive. Large concert halls for rock music which could hold thousands of people were constructed such as Le Zénith (1982), situated on the eastern edge of Paris and in the middle of the large La Villette park. Smaller concert halls in the provinces were built, and cities were encouraged to build rehearsal spaces for groups. The ministry provided support to annual popular music festivals such as Le Printemps de Bourges, Les Francofolies de la Rochelle and Les Transmusicales de Rennes. The legalization of pirate radio in 1981 allowed FM stations which would cater for specific genres of music. As mentioned earlier, M6 (formerly TV6) was created in 1987 with a strong youth audience remit. More recently, Catherine Trautmann, the socialist minister of culture, has attempted to push the popular music agenda further by recognizing techno as a national cultural form.

It is really only with the breaking-down of the hierarchical distinction in France between high and popular/mass culture, and the concomitant development of British-American cultural studies, that popular music has become a fully legitimate area of interest not just to politicians, but also to academics and intellectuals. Until recently, writing about French popular music, both in French and in English, tended to be limited to the more literary variety of French *chanson* which foregrounded lyrics, work of the 'great' *auteurs-compositeurs-interprètes* (singer-songwriters), canonical figures such as Brel, Brassens and Ferré. The writing on these tended to follow two general approaches, the first of which is biographically oriented. This assumed that the real author and the implied author (the various narrative voices within their songs) were one and the same. This type of intentionalist methodology which over-emphasizes the importance of the real author clearly has its limitations. A more constructivist approach allows one to dissociate the views of the real authors from those of their public personae. Within the collected works of a given singer-songwriter, there is a multiplicity of narrative voices or identities which generate meaning. It is impossible to regard such identities as a fixed, homogenous, stable entity, as they shift within a given song, from one song to another or from one version of a song to another.

The second approach to French song tended to limit itself to the literary analysis of song lyrics. While the work of certain artists certainly invites comparison with literary works, an approach which reduces a song to its lyrics as they appear on the written page ignores the other essential components of the song's text which make it a multichannelled form of communication. The processes of representation which operate within a given song should be considered not only in linguistic but also in musical, vocal and gestural terms. Although song lyrics are indeed crucial to the whole process of representation, musical expression also deserves consideration, especially when it informs our overall understanding of a given song. We also must not forget that a song is only fully concretized in the artist's voice, facial expressions, gestures and body movements in studio recordings, or performances in concert venues or on television. The extent to which we can build up a picture of artists ultimately depends on the existence and availability of recordings on audio/videotape/discs. An audiovisual approach necessitates reference to filmed or televized concert and documentary footage, drawn from commercial or off-air video recordings, as well as archive material. This mainly takes the form of one-to-one and panel interviews, as well as performances, filmed in concert venues, in the television studio or on location.

While representation – linguistic, musical, vocal and gestural – is crucial to our understanding of an artist's work, so are the other cultural 'processes and practices' which contribute as well to generating cultural meaning: production, consumption, regulation and identity (Du Gay, 1997: 10). While the artists are essential actors in the overall creative process, they are not solely responsible for the production and distribution of songs. They rely heavily on the personal, artistic, technical and commercial expertise of other individuals with whom they collaborate. The music industry, notably the record companies, as well as the mass media, also assume a regulative role which contributes enormously to overall public perceptions of artists. The way in which listeners buy and listen to songs may add to our overall understanding of the significance of an artist. Finally, popular music, in common with other French cultural forms, explores a multiplicity of personal and social identities. Music and song are indeed suitable vehicles for the exploration of such identities. As Simon Frith remarks, 'Music seems to be a key to identity because it offers, so intensely, a sense of both self and others, of the subjective in the collective' (Frith, 1996: 110).

It is with this broad, multifaceted methodological approach in mind – one which takes account of various cultural 'processes and practices' – that we shall now focus on Zazie's *La Zizanie*, a recent example of a successful record release in France.

CASE STUDY

ZAZIE'S *LA ZIZANIE*

Figure 7.1 *Zazie's La Zizanie album cover.*
Reproduced with permission of Jean-Baptiste Mondino

A former model, Zazie, whose real name is Isabelle de Truchis de Varennes (1964–), has, over the course of the last decade, become one of France's leading popular singer-song-writers (*auteur-compositeur-interprète*). Something of a tomboy as a child, she was nick-named Zazie by her parents, in reference to the main character in Raymond Queneau's novel *Zazie dans le métro* (1959), and Louis Malle's film adaptation of the same name (1960). In 1993 her first album earned her the best female newcomer award (*révélation féminine*) at the annual French music industry awards, Les Victoires de la Musique, the equivalent of the Grammy or Brit awards. She was subsequently voted best female per-former (*meilleur interprète féminine de l'année*) at the Victoires in 1997 and 2002. She has performed sell-out tours, including the Parisian concert halls, La Cigale (1996) and Le Zénith (1999). Zazie is signed to Universal/Mercury, and so benefits from the promo-tional might of a major label. *La Zizanie*, her fourth studio album, was released on 16 October 2001, following an extensive advertising campaign on radio and television, and in the press. On the release date, the record company even distributed a mock news-paper, *La Zizanie*, in French city centres. Zazie was also fortunate enough to collaborate with top image makers such as the fashion photographer and video maker, Jean Baptiste Mondino, who shot the rather provocative album cover. The use of an octagonal rather than a square CD case was designed to disorientate record buyers further.

Although, musically speaking, Zazie incorporates a variety of pop and rock idioms, and, in the case of this album, electronic dance music, she nonetheless inscribes herself broadly within the French *chanson* tradition. She has taken part in various television programmes celebrating the work of previous generations of singer-songwriters such as Georges Brassens (*Les Enfants de Brassens*, November 2001, France 2) and Serge Gainsbourg (*Nuit Gainsbourg*, March 2001, France 2). The love song, 'Sur toi', one of the tracks on the album, indeed makes explicit reference to Brel's 'Ne me quitte pas'. Like Gainsbourg, Zazie uses a good deal of wordplay in her songwriting, evident just from the titles of some of her songs; indeed her idiolect has been dubbed *le zazois* by fans. Although Zazie is appreciative of her fan base, as can be seen in her official and unofficial websites, her song, 'La Fan de sa vie' ('The fan of her life'), whose title is a homophonic play on the words *fin* and *fan*, argues that fan adulation is no substitute for more authentic relationships:

> *Tu es fan*
> *Tu es la fan de sa vie*
> *Puisque sa vie te rassure*
> *Et que la tienne est trop dure*
> *Tu es fan*
> *Tu le seras jusqu'au jour*
> *Où tu verras que l'amour*
> *N'est pas à vendre*
> *Mais à vivre*
> *A vivre*

> [You're a fan
> You're the fan of his life
> Because his life comforts you
> And yours is too difficult.
> You're a fan
> And will be until the day
> When you realize that love
> Isn't for sale
> But to be lived.]

Zazie composed all but one of the 13 tracks on an album which she views in rather autobiographical terms as a reflection of her current state of mind, as she has commented: 'Quand je fais un album, c'est d'abord pour moi-même, pour voir où j'en suis' ('When I make an album, I do it firstly for myself, so I can see where I am') (Spira, 1998). Her songs deal with personal and social issues, many of which are perennial themes within *la chanson française* such as friendship, previously fetishized by Brassens ('Les Copains d'abord'

('Friends First')) and by Brel ('Jojo'). However, Zazie attempts to present these themes from her own individual, original standpoint. 'Qui m'aime me fuit' ('Who loves me leaves me'), whose title is a reworking of the proverb 'Qui m'aime me suive!', recounts, for example, how the loyalty of Zazie's friends has been put to the test by her growing professional success and personal contentment. While love songs are a traditional staple of most songwriters' repertoires, Zazie resists this convention, as she explains in the autobiographical 'Sur toi' ('About You'), written for her partner:

> *On n'écrit pas sur ce qu'on aime*
> *sur ce qui ne pose pas*
> *problème*
> *voilà pourquoi*
> *je n'écris pas sur toi*
> *rassure-toi*

> [We don't write about what we love
> Or about what isn't a problem.
> That's why
> I don't write about you.
> Set your mind at rest]

Zazie's songs also tackle contemporary social issues. Indeed, the title track, 'La Zizanie', partly inspired by the Asterix *bande dessinée* of the same name (1970), identifies the singer-songwriter as a figure who sows 'un joyeux désordre, tout en gardant le sourire' ('merrily sows the seeds of a disorder, while retaining a smile') (interview in *Platine*, November 2001). Capitalist society is compared disparagingly to a Monopoly board in the first single release from the album, 'Rue de la Paix', the title of which refers to the most expensive street in the Paris version of the Monopoly game, famous for its very fashionable jewellers and clothing stores:

> *Je vends ma carte chance*
> *et je puise dans la caisse, on a bien mérité ...*
> *De toucher une avance*
> *si c'est pour rendre la caisse à la communauté*
> *Je passe à l'action quitte à monopoliser l'attention*
> *Et rester quelques tours en prison*

> [I'll sell my chance card
> And I'll dig into my coffers; we deserve ...
> An advance
> If it means giving the chest back to the community.
> I'll go into battle even if it means monopolizing attention
> And staying in prison while I miss a few turns.]

Zazie is highly aware that, in providing social comment, she could be accused of demagogy. Such was the case with the anti-racist song 'Tout le monde' ('Everybody'), taken from her previous album *Made in Love* (1998), a hit which took a swipe at Jean-Marie Le Pen, the leader of the extreme far-right *Front National*. Zazie has similarly been criticized by the press for 'Tais-toi et rap' ('Shut Up and Rap!'), which evokes the lack of opportunities for those living in France's troubled *banlieues* (suburbs). However, Zazie answers her critics by insisting that she is concerned specifically by *l'incommunicabilité* ('the difficulty in communication') (*Platine* interview, November 2001). 'Adam et Yves', a text written by Joëlle Kopf in defence of homosexuality, and which Zazie set to music, led to further charges of demagogy. Although the taboo of homosexuality has been broken in the past by singer-songwriters such as Charles Aznavour ('Comme ils disent', 1972), Zazie, aware that she has a significant gay following, felt that a more positive representation was still required, and one which did not rely on familiar gay stereotypes (Hermange, 2002). 'Adam et Yves' was indeed accompanied by a celebratory video clip, inspired by a scene in the recent film *Le Fabuleux Destin d'Amélie Poulain* (Jean-Pierre Jeunet, 2001) in which passport snaps, taken in a photo booth, come to life.

Zazie has, along with other popular artists, become involved in raising money for a variety of causes including the fight against poverty and hunger (Les Enfoirés) and AIDS (Solidarité enfants SIDA – Sol en si). The *chanson* form is a highly self-referential one, and Zazie is conscious of her role as a socially committed artist, as she showed by citing Brel, who saw himself in empathetic terms: 'J'écris quand j'ai mal aux autres' ('I write when I feel bad for other people'). Zazie also writes out of anger: 'Mon mode de fonctionnement et d'écriture est plutôt dans la chose qui ne me plaît pas et qui me met en colère' ('My work and my writing is inspired by things I don't like or which make me angry') (Labrio, 2002). Reflecting her acute awareness that she forms part of an industry which often values style over substance, the song 'Cheese' exposes the emptiness of fashion, consumerism and the beauty myth, as well as the high expectations which are placed on artists who are manufactured according to a rigid format. Zazie resists the pressures upon female artists to conform to traditional notions of femininity, insisting that she has a serious role: 'Ce qui me donne de la force, c'est d'avoir des choses à dire, et non d'être une jolie fille qui chante' ('What gives me strength, is having something to say, not being just a pretty girl who sings') (Spira, 1998). Although the song 'Aux armes Citoyennes' ('To Arms, Citizens') has been interpreted as a rousing *chanson féministe*, Zazie herself views it in broader terms as *une chanson féminine*, an inclusive call for both women and men to work together.

In sum, *La Zizanie* is illustrative of the kind of processes and practices involved today in the production of popular music in France. Although the industry, dominated by the multinational major labels, is subject to the demands of the global economy, a distinctive Francophone market nonetheless continues to thrive. Popular artists are commodified and highly mediatized. Nevertheless, Zazie, drawing on a rich tradition of French song with foregrounded and socially challenging lyrics, maintains her identity as an artist and as an intellectual, tackling issues of a personal, social, political and even philosophical nature.

SUGGESTIONS FOR FURTHER STUDY

The foregoing discussion has, I hope, identified several areas worthy of further investigation. Music raises many questions about national identities, especially, in relation to France, the notion of French cultural exceptionalism and the bearing this may have upon the development of various genres. Popular music in France may also be viewed from a broader, intercultural perspective, particularly in terms of the interchange which operates between France and the Anglophone world, and the question of the translatability/adaptability of songs from one language and culture to another (take, for example, Frank Sinatra's 'My Way', originally Claude François' 'Comme d'habitude', and Bing Crosby's 'Yesterday When I Was Young', originally Charles Aznavour's 'Hier encore').

Other areas worthy of further investigation include: the relationship between the music industry and the media in France (press, radio, television, internet), especially the development of programme formats (live performance, documentaries, reality, talent shows, etc.); the interplay between popular music and film; the issues of regulation and censorship (for example, the 1995 'affaire NTM'); the representation and the construction of gender and sexual identities (for example, gay icons such as Barbara, Dalida and Mylène Farmer, to name but a few).

FURTHER READING

Dauncey, H., and S. Cannon (eds) (2003) *French Popular Music: Modernizing Cultural Exceptionalism* (Aldershot: Ashgate). Provides an overview of the changes in French popular music, society, culture and politics from 1940 to the present.

Hargreaves, A. and M. Mckinney (1997) *Post-Colonial Cultures in France* (London: Routledge). Includes chapters on hip-hop culture by Steve Cannon and world music by Chris Warne.

Hawkins, P. (2000) *Chanson: The French Singer-songwriter from Bruant to the Present Day* (Aldershot: Ashgate). Situates the genre of *chanson* in theoretical terms, and provides a survey of individual singer-songwriters from the late nineteenth century onwards.

Looseley, D. (2003) *Popular Music in Contemporary France: Authenticity, Politics, Debate* (Oxford: Berg). Explores the segmentation of the French music scene since the late 1950s and 1960s, and the cultural debates this has generated.

The main trade journals in France are *Musique info hebdo* (www.musiqueinfo.com), *Lettre du disque*, *Ecran total* and *La Scène*. While the market for music magazines is ever-changing, *Les Inrockuptibles* (www1.lesinrocks.com) remains a key title, covering a variety of genres. See also the following:

- Pop and rock: *Rock'n'Folk* (www.musiqueinfo.com), *Magic, Rocksound*
- *Chanson*: *Chorus, les cahiers de la chanson* (www.chorus-chanson.fr), *Je chante!* (perso.wanadoo.fr/je.chante/), *Le Hall de la chanson* (www.lehall.com)
- Hip-hop: *Radikal* and *L'Affiche*
- Electronic music: *Coda* (www.codamagazine.com), *Remix, Trax* (www.traxxx.org)
- In English: *French Music Ezine* (www.frenchmusicezine.co.uk)

A useful starting point for studying the repertoire of established artists in France would be their 'greatest hits' albums, e.g. *L'Absolutely meilleur of Renaud* (Renaud, Virgin France, 2000) and *Histoires* (Lavilliers, Barclay, 2002). For essential information on individual artists, see A. Hughes and K. Reader (1998) *Encyclopedia of Contemporary French Culture* (London: Routledge). For fuller biographies, see rfimusique.com. Many artists have their own official sites, e.g. www.zazieonline.com, or fans have assembled their own unofficial sites (e.g. madeinweb.free.fr). Websites are also maintained by French music festivals (www.printemps-bourges.com; www.francofolies.fr), producers of French musicals (www.notredameonline.com) and charitable organizations (www.solensi.asso.fr.restosducoeur.org).

For up-to-date sales statistics on home and foreign markets as well as the SNEP/IFOP national sales charts, see disqueensfrance.com. The French Music Bureau also compiles up-to-date information, published on its website, along with information about its work and that of the other French music export offices (www.french-music.org).

BIBLIOGRAPHY

Du Gay, P. (1997) *Production of Cultures/Cultures of Production* (London: OU/Sage).

Frith, S. (1996) 'Music and Identity' in S. Hall and P. Du Gay (eds) *Questions of Cultural Identity* (London: Routledge).

Hargreaves, A. and M. McKinney (1997) *Post-Colonial Cultures in France* (London: Routledge).

Hermange, F. (2002) *L'Université* (magazine interview).

Labrio, P. (18 March 2002) *Ombre et lumière*, France 3 (television interview).

Latkovitch, P. (2000) *An interview with Alan Stivell*
    http://www.rootsworld.com/interview/stivell.html

Rigby, Brian (1991) *Popular Culture in Modern France: A Study of Cultural Discourse* (London and New York: Routledge).

Silverton, P. (29 April 2001) 'France Turns the Tables', *Observer*.

Spira, A. (July 1998) *Psychologies* (magazine interview).

CHAPTER 8

Fiction

Martine Guyot-Bender

The publication and the consumption of books are national issues in France. They are highlighted by the awarding of an infinite number of prizes; by such popular cultural events as the National Festival of Reading (La Fête du Livre) and the Paris Book Fair (Le Salon du Livre) which encourage the consumption of all types of books, and by innumerable government agencies which track the quantitative and qualitative evolution of French literary production in order to ensure that books (especially French books) and reading maintain their privileged position in the French cultural and leisure arenas. The results are that France still counts several hundred independent bookstores, including many specializing in popular fiction; the number of public libraries has tripled over the last 20 years; and French readers of all ages consider a visit to the Fnac, the main chain retailer of books in France, as an enlightening and exciting activity. Moreover, in a country where the educational system does not offer creative writing programmes, the book industry has maintained itself as a vast, prosperous activity (granted, with ups and downs). In spite of some pessimism and the constant fear that the French will stop reading, recent statistics are encouraging. They show increases between 1999–2000 and 2000–2001 of 13 per cent in the number of titles published (44,000), of 6.2 per cent in the number of books sold (353.6 million – almost six books per inhabitant), reading and of 4 per cent in revenue (€2 to 2.5 billion) (Centre National du Livre – CNL).

This is not say that everything is for the best in the realm of the book industry, but that public and national conversations as well as governmental financial support have allowed the market for books to stay rather healthy. Despite strong and sustained Anglo-American influence, for example, French popular fiction continues to develop along its own lines and reading has, over the last 50 years, become a popular activity which has extended beyond the scope of traditionally recognized popular subgenres.

In France, as elsewhere, the question of exactly what popular fiction is elicits such varied and contradictory responses that it sometimes seems as if almost anything that has been printed with a cover in the last 50 years could in one way or another fit the category. For most French readers 'popular fiction' equates to detective, science fiction or sentimental novels. Other readers immediately relate it to paperbacks – especially to the legendary pocket collection called, rather plainly, Le livre de poche,

'The Pocket Book'. Others consider any novel sold in super- or hypermarkets, news-stands and train stations to qualify as popular. Like beauty, what qualifies as popular in the world of fiction is primarily a matter of the eye of the beholder.

This chapter investigates the state of popular fiction in France according to two broad understandings of the phenomenon. It first examines characteristics of repre-sentative post-war popular icons, then it overviews some important editorial and retail events that transformed popular reading in France. Current practices and trends in the mass production of books will serve as a background for an examina-tion of the ways in which one contemporary author, Amélie Nothomb, increasingly notorious with readers of both popular and high literature, exemplifies the state of popular fiction in today's France.

POPULAR GENRES: DEFINITION AND ICONS

In her recent study of reading in France, Nicole Robine reminds us that readers of popular fiction choose their books according to their own desires rather than on the basis of duty or of social status, and that it is, before everything, a very personal endeavour (Robine, 2000: 12). French literary critics (and educators) do not all agree with Robine. In fact, many consider reading popular fiction a futile activity and their view is supported by the number of belittling designations of the genre such as: *para-littérature* ('pseudoliterature', as if it were illegitimate); *littérature alimentaire* ('sub-sistence literature', because authors of popular subgenres receive a fixed amount per book – a taboo obviously!); *roman à quatre sous* ('penny novels', wrongly sug-gesting that popular fiction is destined for the poor); *roman de gare* ('train station novels', because they are sold in ordinary public places rather than in specialized bookstores which attract book connoisseurs). Regardless, however, of how critics consider popular fiction, with a positive or condescending eye, popular genres are alive and well in France; they represent a wide production and readership from all backgrounds and all levels of education, and are integral parts of the general cultur-al landscape in France. And this is not a new phenomenon: readers once rushed to the most recent product of Rabelais' satirical pen at fairs or to the latest cheaply printed edition of Balzac at bookstalls. In many cases, indeed, yesterday's 'trash' becomes tomorrow's classics.

Apart from some notable recent exceptions – such as Michel Tournier's *Vendredi et les limbes du Pacifique* (Friday, 1980) or Alexandre Jardin's *L'Île des gauchers* (The Island of the Left-Handed, 2001) – the concept of adventure fiction, the first popular genre made famous by Jules Verne and Alexandre Dumas in the nineteenth century, has become the realm of detective, spy and science fiction, three subgenres that were so deeply influenced by mid-century Anglo-American naturalist production that, until the early 1960s, French authors often adopted English-sounding pen-names to ensure that their manuscripts would be accepted and their books sell. French readers' (and publishers') assumption was that the French just could not write detective fiction.

It is only gradually that publishers of detective fiction included French authors in catalogues otherwise mainly composed of translations from English – translations of Peter Cheney and Hadley Chase made the famous *série noire*'s reputation and they actually gave the French public its taste for detective fiction (this overwhelming influence of Anglo-American models is paradoxical considering that the word *roman noir* reflects an earlier French influence on the genre). Both post-war Anglo-American and French *polar* and spy novels used a similar and simple recipe based on, as Georges Duhamel's *série noire*'s founder described it, the subtle combination of touches of violence, existential blues, eroticism, sentimentality and mystery, without forgetting a touch of humour. Protagonists and situations are staged in expeditious, stereotypical ways that lead directly to the heart of the action; information – as little as possible – flows swiftly, in an unelaborated style, using street language and with few nuances and short descriptions. These characteristics apply especially to hybrid forms such as Gérard de Villiers' popular series *SAS* or *Brigade Mondaine* (Vice Squad), which add explicit eroticism to the basic mystery.

Increasing respect for locally produced detective fiction came with Auguste LeBreton, José Giovanni and Albert Simonin, who supplemented the traditional narrative models of detective fiction (good and evil dichotomies, closure and return to morality) with French sociopolitical references and concerns of the post-war era in Europe, often using the background of the French collaboration with the Nazis during the German occupation of France, or the growing shadow of the Cold War. Other great names in French detective fiction opted to confine their stories to resolutely provincial characters and environments. In contrast with any typical *polar*'s detectives (*polar* is a common abbreviation for 'police detection'), Georges Simenon's placid Maigret police deputy, for example, is an unflamboyant sleuth, caring of the most vulnerable individuals in small grey towns in Northern France and Belgium inhabited by people with little imagination or ambition. Maigret, a stern and down-to-earth grandfather figure, never runs into murky situations or tempting women, and he relies less on force than on an innate knowledge of human psychology to unravel his cases. Diametrically opposed to Maigret's middle-of-the-roadness, but nonetheless supposedly stereotypically French, stands the satirical Fleuve Noir series *San Antonio*, a legend in French popular fiction. Also inspired by, but not fully faithful to, the *roman noir* (Peter Cheney is one of his most obvious influences), San Antonio – both the author Frédéric Dard's penname and the name of the main protagonist of the series, 'the special service police deputy' – is a flirtatious bachelor in his late thirties whose politically incorrect language asserts the author's contempt for bourgeois standards and for moralistic literature:

Un médecin harassé sous le poids de l'alcool achève de soigner le nez de Godemiche qui patauge toujours dans des limbes comateux.
– Sûr que voulez pas porter plainte? bredouille le toubib d'une voix d'outre-biture.

[A doctor, exhausted by the weight of alcohol, finishes treating the nose of Dildy, who is still floating in a comatose cloud.
– Sure you don't want to sue? the doc mumbles in a beyond-the-bender voice.]

(*Céréal Killer*, Ch. 3)

In spite of the explicit vulgarity of his prose, devoted readers often defend San Antonio's unflattering descriptions of human behaviours, claiming that his work contains a true anthropological, sometimes even philosophical, flair (Boviatsis, 1979: 12). The chasm that exists between Maigret (whose readership is mostly female) and San Antonio (whose readership is mostly male) exemplifies the diversity of voices of the French *polar* since the 1960s, a clear reflection of the variety of expectations among *polar* fans.

Even though Jules Verne is acclaimed as a genuine ancestor of international sci fi and French author René Barjavel's 1920s novels were translated into many languages as soon as they were published, modern French science fiction also developed from Anglo-American imports. Indeed, not until 1978 did the volume of French science fiction sold in France equal that of Anglo-American translations. It is known that prime sci fi collections such as Fleuve Noir and the long-disappeared Rayon Fantastique first built their reputations on translations of Asimov, Bradbury, Van Goght and, later, of Philip K. Dick, who has stated that, if it were not for the French reading public, he would be starving (personal communication). It was indeed with great difficulty that French authors penetrated the realm of science fiction, and then mainly with narratives that reflect realistic contemporary social problems (pollution, overpopulation, poverty) rather than creative fantasies. In the early 1980s, *la SF* reached 9 per cent of French literary production and was finally recognized as a rightful element in French cultural life, a development largely due to the period's boom in *SF* festivals, specialized bookstores, magazines and collections. This popularity also owes something to the rise of new French authors including Jacques Sadoul, Serge Brussolo and especially Pierre Curval and Gérard Klein.

If it is true that detective and science fiction have become progressively legitimized forms of 'literature', it is as true that a veil of contempt continues to cast its shadow over sentimental fiction, a genre sometimes despised even by its own readers (millions of them!), notwithstanding its huge popularity and the fact that it fulfils social and psychological needs, as all popular literatures do, by providing imaginary outlets to disenfranchised women.

At the bottom of the ladder of romance stands the *roman-photo* (photo-romance), especially the bi-weekly Nous Deux ('Both of Us'), a mid-1950s Italian innovation embraced at once by French readers. Composed of photographs and minimum captions assembled into brief – very brief – plots, these short romances tell inconspicuously idealistic love stories intended for a public that is only minimally interested in reading, and not at all interested in the development of an intrigue. Nous Deux romances are bare-bone stories the sole goal of which is to reach the happy ending. Even at a time when popular fiction is 'going intellectual', each issue of Nous Deux still sells approximately 450,000 copies and has an estimated audience of about 2 million people – 25 per cent of whom are men.

Other, more literary, French romances offer far more complexity than romans-photos. Guy des Cars' lengthy romantic epics, for example, feature heroines who are not merely romantic idealists but are also daring, able to overcome obstacles in order to take control of their lives and/or the lives of others and to surmount hardship. Indeed, many of des Cars' titles – La Révoltée (The Revolted Woman), La Voleuse (The Woman Thief), La Tueuse (The Woman Killer), La Justicière (The Righter of Wrongs), L'Entremetteuse (The Matchmaker) – advocate female ambitions, self-determination and ability to take revenge on (or find fulfilment in) a supposedly male-ruled world dominated by racist, classist and sexist discrimination against which their heroines have to fight while they are searching for love. In some cases, love happens as they are fighting these causes. Consequently, Guy des Cars is often portrayed as one of women's best advocates among French romance writers, as is Cecil St. Laurent, whose humorous series Caroline Chérie (Dearest Caroline) also portrays a young, audacious, amusing and sexually driven heroine, a heroine who escapes the hardship of the French Revolution – a historical context traditionally reserved to male protagonists.

To the dismay of French publishers, the market for sentimental literature was forever transformed in 1978 when the Canadian trade publisher Harlequin penetrated and soon dominated the French market for sentimental fiction. Harlequin's success in France has been no different than in other places around the world. It sold 5 million books in its first 18 months, progressively bought out all its potential competitors and, within a couple of years, reached 80 per cent of the French market. Today, Harlequin is the second most successful publisher in France, with reported yearly sales reaching 30 million copies and an estimated 2 to 3 million readership – mostly, but not exclusively, women, usually also readers of the feminine press (CNRS, 1998).

Popular icons in France are no doubt more numerous than this brief overview can suggest. Indeed, one of the characteristics of popular genres is that they produce hybrids, which appear, disappear and metamorphose as trends require or at the whim of publishing houses. A popular genre that does not respond to consumer expectations would (and does) necessarily lose its popularity and be doomed to die. But some of the mid-twentieth century's most renowned French ones have been able to survive well thanks to some inner thematic transformation and to efficient marketing policies.

P O P U L A R I Z I N G   R E A D I N G

Popular reading does not mean reading popular genres for everyone. Indeed, many of today's best-sellers do not look anything like the scripted genres described above; playing the globalization card, publishers and retailers have succeeded in popularizing books that might very well have only had a restricted intellectual readership three or four decades ago.

The intense popularizing of reading can be traced to the launching of the first French pocket edition, Le Livre de Poche, by the Librairie Générale Française in January 1953. Henri Filipacchi, its founder, transformed the landscape of bookselling in France by applying popular fiction's modes of production to the republication of prominent French classics, for example replacing the dignified cover of classics with illustrated covers that suggested a plot and encouraged impulsive buying: in 1953, as in 2003, an image was worth a thousand words. Le Livre de Poche suddenly offered French readers of all socioeconomic backgrounds the illusion of democracy and equality, by making reading a pleasurable activity available to all, or, as purists of the time put it, by desacralizing literature.

The Livre de Poche did not maintain its monopoly for long. While it diversified its own collections, stiff competition soon appeared from detective novels and war studies published by *J'ai lu* and – a new revolution indeed – sold in low-priced supermarkets Prisunic and Monoprix, followed by other pocket editions, many of which are still available in 2003: Press Pocket, 10/18, Point, as well as crossbreeds *semi-poche* (Imaginaire-Gallimard). In 1993, the Italian-based Éditions Mille et Une Nuits revolutionized the French book industry yet another time with its Petite Collection of lightweight yet robust volumes ideal for the constraints of busy urban life, which sold for 10 fr. (€1.52, the equivalent of 9.97 fr., after January 2002) and included an integral text, a preface, biographical notes and a bibliography. Rock-bottom-priced publications now include Librio (Flammarion) with its popular fiction as well as its historical or current-affairs selections of articles from the national press; Maxi-Poche devoted to popular texts of the public domain; as well as Gallimard's recently unveiled €2 Folio collection. Unquestionably, the proliferation of bargain collections permits more reading to be squeezed into the cracks of hectic contemporary life; it has allowed literary classics and political/historical/economical books to become common reading for commuters, and often to replace traditional popular subgenres. There is no doubt that hard covers (often called *grands formats* – large formats – or *collections blanches* – white collections) have lost some of their readers to paperback's ever-wider choice of books. Regardless of how voluminous the number of paperbacks sold may seem, in 2000 it represented only 23 per cent of total French book production, 28 per cent of the number of sales and 12.4 per cent of the revenue in euros (CNL, 2002).

Retailers, too, have had their role in transforming the landscape of popular reading in France. Who knows if André Essel, a former Trotskyite and passionate amateur photographer, realized that he was going to turn the whole trade of book-selling upside down when he created, in 1954, the Fédération Nationale d'Achats (the National Purchasing Federation), a populist project aiming at selling cultural products more cheaply through mass buying. La Fnac, as it is known now, like the Livre de Poche, impacted reading and the popularizing of classic and avant-garde literature to an extent that is still difficult to evaluate. For one thing, the Fnac made the 'book' – a formerly sacred object – less intimidating by allowing its customers to wander around the store and read on the premises. Books became more visible and palpa-ble, thus more accessible and tempting to buy both to connoisseurs and to neo-phytes. The opening of a Fnac in a medium-sized town, is, even today, a major cultural and popular event. The success of the Fnac, which soon became the top book retailer in France, inspired temples of mass consumption of everyday products to sell books, such as Carrefour and Leclerc hypermarkets, which now rank respec-tively second and third among booksellers. (Some Leclerc stores include immense cultural centres, some of which sell over 10,000 books a month in a wide variety of genres, both popular and not popular.) But in 1969, even before hypermarkets start-ed to compete seriously with Fnac, book clubs began to offer an even less intimi-dating venue to buy books. Today, 4 million subscribers to France-Loisirs (the most renowned book club) can choose pre-selected books in the intimacy of their home, a practice that, even if all the books bought are not read – which is often the case – has helped disseminate reading among social groups who might not otherwise read.

There is one last – 'typically French' some will say – event that had a tremendous impact on popular reading in France. By requiring that retailers offer no more than a 5 per cent discount to buyers, La Loi Lang (Lang Law, 1981) transformed the politics of bookselling for ever. Almost overnight, competition between small bookstores and larger retailers became service-based rather than price-based, thus redirecting buyers towards specialized bookstores they had deserted for Fnacs. This drastic law, loathed by mass retailers, had an unforeseen long-term consequence: in response to the new competition from small stores, hypermarkets added more erudite books to their stocks, thus allowing buyers of such books the convenience of picking up one or two of them while grocery shopping rather than making a special trip to a small bookstore. While pro-tecting small bookstores, the Lang Law thus also spread the trade of high culture beyond the traditional boundaries of small selective bookstores and irremediably blurred the lines between popular and non-popular reading. On 15 January 2003, for example, the Relay newsstand in the Gare de l'Est in Paris offered travellers not only a wide choice of Harlequin, translations of Daniele Steele, Mary Higgins Clark and Patricia Cornwell (all in pocket editions), as well as French SASs, but also (this would have been very sur-prising three decades ago) erudite volumes by Stefan Sweig, Paulo Coelho, Amin Maalouf, Tolkien and the popular *La Vie sexuelle de Catherine M.* (2002) by Catherine Millet: an eclectic choice reflecting a wide range of popular readers with a wide range of tastes. Obviously, the train-station novel is no longer what it used to be.

In 2000, independent bookstores still account for 20.8 per cent of book sales; chain bookstores such as Fnac for 17.2 per cent; general supermarkets for 19.2 per cent; tobacco shops for 9.1 per cent; and 24 per cent of books were sold by reading clubs. The remaining 10 per cent were sold by various sources including newsstands (CNL, 2002). While the proportion of sales in small bookstores has certainly decreased over the last decades, there is no clear evidence that people buying books on impulse in supermarkets or ordering them from book clubs would ever push the door of a small exclusive (intimidating) bookstore if chain retailers did not exist. Common sense actually suggests that most of the supermarket buyers of books would be lost altogether were France to eliminate all forms of mass distribution (which, of course, is not going to happen).

ENSURING THE FUTURE OF POPULAR FICTION/READING

Regardless of how concerned observers are about reading practices in France, the French read much more, and more widely, than they did in the 1950s, and popular reading no longer means reading only traditional popular genres. The dawn of the twenty-first century may not be remembered as a new golden age for those popular genres, but they have incessantly been reinventing themselves to reflect new cultural and sociological trends. They have also sought ways to build up their readership by following some 'higher' literary movements' stylistic and thematic models. Very much like the new novel, many mass-produced fictions seem suspicious of linear storytelling and of narrative closure, and, very much like post-colonial theories, many also question archetypal race and gender categories.

The *neo-polar*, for example, has resolutely distanced itself from simple dichotomies between good and evil. After 1968, date of the gigantic student/worker May strikes, authors like Jean Patrick Manchette, Philippe Djan or Daniel Daenincks, representing a young generation unsupportive of the establishment, introduced cops who were no longer necessarily good guys or even motivated by their enquiries, and who could easily succumb to corruption in ambiguous novels that end without a traditional return to normality or morality, all this in highly charged political contexts. As some critics claim, contemporary *roman noir* – now dubbed *le poulpe*, after the English 'pulp' – has become really sombre, or as Fred Vargas, a rising (female) star of the genre, says, detective fiction style increasingly relies on narrative 'blanks' and ambiguities to mirror the uncertainties of life while boosting the reader's imagination. Along with Vargas, the last decade has seen the growing success of women authors – Yvonne Besson and Brigitte Aubert – in the traditionally male world of detective fiction. Their crafted, well-researched fictions have redefined the genre and attracted new readers, including readers sensitive to the literary quality of what they read, even in popular genres. Fostering readers' involvement in skilled, socially conscious stories is probably the main originality of French contemporary detective fiction, a genre which is steadily moving away from gendered or moral archetypes. In spite of the proliferation of small detective collections, the *série noire* continues to be the main reference for French detective fiction. As a result of globalization, the collection has opened its catalogue to translations of authors from Finland, Albania and Norway, thus diversifying even further the voices of detection in the Hexagon. The *série's* best-selling author in 2002 was local, however. It was Jean-Claude Izzo, who likes to situate the inspections conducted by his modern hero, inspector Fabio Montale, in his native southern town of Marseilles, arguably France's most racially diverse and politically charged unstable city.

French sci fi, too, has moved closer to realistic situations but it is struggling more than detective fiction to maintain its readership, which seems to be more and more restricted to connoisseurs. Although French sci fi is using contemporary issues such as cyberculture, spirituality and the environment as its background, its progress is timid; some fans like to claim that new trends could lead to a new golden age of the genre, especially if selective collections such as Gérard Klein's *Ailleurs et Demain* (Somewhere Else and Tomorrow) continue to provide high-quality texts. Steampunk has made a limited incursion into French SF domains. As in the USA, it draws upon a complex mixture of old-time stereotypes (i.e. aliens) and imaginary fantasy with technological, fictional and political resources of the nineteenth century. This is the path that Johan Heliot has taken in *Seule la lune le sait* (The Moon only Knows, 2002), a complex, well-crafted story that blends hyper and low technology thus fulfilling some French readers' combined taste for classic culture and modern development.

It is the transformations of everyday society that have affected sentimental fiction the most. Recent productions from Harlequin (which still accepts only Anglo-American authors), for example, mirror the diversification of family structures and the growing proportion of women holding top professional positions. Harlequin's new protagonists are often single-parent, marginal or professional women who seek respect in society. A recent release, *Le Combat d'une mère* (A Mother's Battle, 2002), opens with the heroine – the widow of a man who spent all the family's savings before dying – drinking beer from a bottle, alone in a smoky bar and pondering her lonely life as a private detective:

> *Elle était bel et bien dans son élément ici. Bien plus que dans une banlieue tranquille, à participer aux réunions des fédérations des parents d'élèves ou à vendre des gâteaux dans des kermesses scolaires.*

> [She was truly in her element there. Much more than in a quiet suburban neighbourhood meeting with the local PTAs or selling cookies at some school fundraiser.]

(Rawlins, 2002: 11)

So much for the traditional homemaker and the devoted mother! In the same vein, the growing recognition of bi- and homosexual cultures in France (another – welcome – Anglo-American influence) has encouraged the flourishing of gay popular fiction publishers such as the Éditions Gaies et Lesbiennes whose still modest 18 titles – which sell an average of 2,000 copies each – follow Harlequin's old codes but with non-traditional family structures, thus catering to readers' yearning to see various life choices reflected in what they read – but without the ideal happy ending, thus responding to an intellectually more sophisticated readership (personal communication with the author). Naturally, too, large publishing groups who are always on the lookout for novelty – but are rarely ready to take the risk of publishing novelty – are also trying to ride the wave of new trends, often discovered and first promoted by small publishers on shoestring budgets. In 2001, after the unexpected success of *Bridget Jones's Diary*, J'ai Lu launched the series Comédie Romantique intended for thirty-something professional women, a new genre sometimes designated as *littérature-trash*, that is borderline pornography, or, at the very least, sexually provocative. Authors of this new genre up to now are still mainly Anglo-American, except for Catherine Millet's successful *La vie sexuelle de Catherine M.* or *Confessions d'une radine* (Confessions of a Frugal Girl) by Catherine Cusset, both published in 2002.

Immigration and the diversification of France's former primarily European population has created a more diverse demand for and production of books. Most notably, the *roman beur*, novels written by authors of Maghrebi – mostly Algerian and Moroccan – origins, has become a genre of its own. *Beur* humour, for example, probably best represented by Driss Chraibi's best-seller *La Civilisation, ma mère!* (Mother Comes of Age, 1989), dedramatizes the shock between cultures associated with immigration and has given European French readers a glimpse of the life of immigrants (or children/grandchildren of immigrants) in France, in a lighter tone than most media representations.

> *L'appréhension devant l'inconnu. […] « Au nom du Tout-Puissant, Maître de l'Univers ! » Puis, elle a pressé sur le bouton de la poire – et la lumière fut dans la chambre, le soleil sur son visage.*
>
> [Apprehension in front of the unknown. […] « In the name of the Almighty! » Then, she [the mother] pushed the button of the pear-shaped light switch – and there was light in the room, sun on her face.] (32)

Humorous episodes such as this one in which an Algerian mother encounters electricity for the first time (later in the book, she will discover political activism in very much the same way) provide comic relief on the subject of immigration, typically treated in the media as problematic. The French *polar* also owes some of its most recent developments to *Beur* authors including Lakhdar Belaid and his celebrated *Sérail Killers* (an obvious homage to San Antonio's *Céréal Killer*). (The term *Beur* comes from the reverse pronunciation of the word *arabe* (arabic), inspired by street language called *verlan*, the reverse pronunciation of *à l'envers* – reverse – see Chapter 2.) As a tribute to the quality of *roman Beur*, the national origin of its authors is – as it should – progressively ceasing to be mentioned, a small indication that the world of French popular fiction/literature has adopted this new genre as its own.

Some new currents in popular fiction are harder to categorize than the ones described so far, and purists might even claim that they are not 'popular fiction'. While it is hard to determine a single format for this kaleidoscopic category, these books seem to owe more to 'high' literature (in terms of stylistic originality) and focus more on social problems – some more taboo than others – than archetypal popular genres do. If Marc Levy's *Et si c'était vrai?* (And If It Were True?, 2002) offers the fast read, simple recipe of love, mystery and happy ending that made traditional popular genres popular, it will take some time to determine if best-sellers such as Daniel Pennac's bittersweet fictions on youth culture and the inflexibility of the education system (*La Fée carabine* (The Fairy Gunmother), 1992, or *Messieurs les enfants* (Mister Kids), 1997), Christine Angot's tormented short novels (*L'inceste*, 2000) or Bernard Werber's fantastic epics about an imaginary ant realm that resembles turn-of-the-century struggling western societies will ever be considered as genuinely 'popular'. If the pigeonholed criteria that made the success of popular subgenres is absent from these fictions, the fact that they sell so well to a very diverse readership (up to 500,000 for Werber's *Les Fourmis* (The Empire of the Ants), 1995, when the average number of sales for a novel is 8,000) certainly suggests that they have met popularity. It might just be that the whole concept of popular fiction is currently being redefined by French popular readers' broader tastes when they read for pleasure.

The future of popular reading in France is tightly linked to the diversification of genres and to how closely authors and publishers respond to and anticipate public demand. It will also most likely depend on the relationship paper culture is able/willing to build with technology. Indeed, if the production of e-books is still far on the French horizon, the internet has, on the other hand, already shown a measurable, and somehow paradoxical, impact on the marketing of books/authors. There is little doubt, for example, that, while the internet does substitute for on-paper reading to a degree, it has also proved to be a great promoter of book purchasing (and maybe even reading) in much the same way as French televized literary programmes such as *Apostrophes* in the 1980s, at a time when pessimists claimed that television would ultimately kill books. Most publishers already advertise through elaborate websites that include catalogues, book summaries, links to authors they want to popularize, and other promotional material. Though only few French authors have created their own websites (SAS's Gérard de Villiers has), many of them benefit from an even better situation: fans' own websites featuring their books and often them, thus offering these writers and their publishers unsolicited, candid, enthusiastic and *free* advertising. As unpredictable as they might be, the ramifications of the internet in the

advancement of authors and books are indeed immense and can only grow as technology penetrates more and more French homes and schools.

THE ULTIMATE ZAPPER – AMÉLIE NOTHOMB'S (ANNOYING) POPULARITY

Among the plethora of new French/French-speaking authors, some, such as the very in-
your-face Amélie Nothomb, seem to have taken special advantage of all the recent developments in society, in readers' eagerness for novelty, and in marketing practices.

As is the case for Angot, Pennac or Werber, there are several reasons why Amélie
Nothomb, whose books sell like hot cakes, should *not* be in a chapter on French popular
fiction. For one, she saturates her novels with literary/philosophical references. Secondly,
her plots rely very little on the linearity or the closure that once characterized the popu-
lar novel. She also collects literary prizes, among them the Grand Prix de l'Académie
Française (not commonly bestowed on popular fiction!), which she received in 1999 for
Stupeur et tremblements (Fear and Trembling). One last reason, specific to Amélie
Nothomb and some other great names of 'French' popular culture, such as cartoonist
Hergé, singer Jacques Brel and of course author Georges Simenon, is that she is a
Belgian national. But Amélie Nothomb is widely read in France; her books sell in supermarkets, kiosks and independent bookstores, she is translated into a growing number of
languages and is a regular guest of literary television shows. Although it would be an exaggeration to say that Nothomb appeals to a typical popular audience, she is, for better or
for worse, a popular author, albeit an 'intellectual' one, who incarnates sort of a French
pop fiction's new wave.

Nothomb publishes one book a year (conveniently in September, right on time for the
autumn literary salons and prizes) and each of them contains between 140 and 160
pages (thus requesting a minimum reading-time investment). While her first novel,
L'hygiène de l'assassin (The Assassin's Hygiene, 1992) was inspired by detective fiction,
detection is not the path she pursued. Nor, for that matter, did she stick to any of the
paths she took in her subsequent novels. She is quintessentially a zapper of the imagination, constantly renewing herself – to the delight of her readers, who discover an entirely new world in each ensuing publication – although, paradoxically, nothing looks more like
one Amélie Nothomb novel than another Amélie Nothomb novel. Her writing style is pre-
cipitous, composed of short sentences, always written in an acidic tone. Her protagonists
are few, but she gives great importance to the internal dynamics of dialogues, turning
each of her novels into a kind of verbal combat, as if language were a protagonist in its
own right. In a very Kafkaesque way, her main characters meet and fight abjection, daily
horror, futile harassment, humiliation with a sense of *humour noir*, which makes up some
of the charm of her prose. Like many other writers of short fiction, she has perfected the
art of the first sentence, 'the grabber', immediately plunging the reader into the absurdity

of the subsequent plot. A collection of Amélie Nothomb's unsettling first sentences looks like this:

> *Cherchez à qui le crime profite. L'ensevelissement de Pompéi sous les cendres du Vésuve, en 79 avant Jésus Christ, a été le plus beau cadeau qui ait été offert aux archéologues. A votre avis qui a fait le coup?*
>
> [Look who benefits from crime. The burial of Pompeii under the ashes of Mount Vesuvius, in 79 BC, was the best present archaeologists could have dreamt of. Who do you think pulled that one?]
>
> (*Péplum*, 1996)

> *Pour habiter cette île, il faut avoir quelque chose à cacher.*
>
> [To live on this island, one must have something to hide.]
>
> (*Mercure*, 1998)

> *La première fois que je me vis dans un miroir, je ris. Je crus que ce n'était pas moi.*
>
> [The first time I saw myself in a mirror, I laughed. I thought it was not me.]
>
> (*Attentat*, 1997)

The tone is set from the start: her narrators are all watching for answers, for imaginary answers mind you, since Nothomb never attempts to pin down, and even less to solve, 'real' social issues. Her work is the result of a steaming imagination that transports readers into fast-moving, unrealistic worlds (even realism becomes unrealistic under her pen) in which demagogy has no place.

To say the least, Nothomb's writing and personality are buoyant and provocative. Together, they illustrate many of the more striking tendencies of contemporary popular fiction in France, including something of a show-business aura. Her appearance on a television programme is always an event. Viewers now expect she will display her eccentric personality in much the same way that they expect her novels to take them by surprise and propel them beyond the expected. Very much like the other new 'popular authors' mentioned before and many others, the intellectual nature of her writing satisfies a French literary tradition, while her plain style is accessible to a wide audience, making for a combination that, supported by the right publicity, can result in (as indeed it has) impressive book sales. Nothomb has shown that French (or at least French-language) literary/popular culture can develop successfully away from Anglo-American models and that books can combine reading for pleasure and reflection.

What better conclusion to give on the state of popular fiction and popular reading in today's France than one of Amélie Nothomb's protagonists' own words? The solemn declaration of *le professeur* in *Les Combustibles* (Flammable Material, 1994) to one of his students reveals the superficiality of the traditional dichotomy between popular and erudite reading/genres, while he is, symbolically, burning his gigantic library one book at a time to keep warm during a war:

Comment pouvez-vous accorder du crédit aux paroles d'un bonhomme qui démolit Blateck devant ses étudiants et qui s'en régale quand il est seul? [How can you trust the words of a guy who destroys Blateck [a imaginary popular author] in front of his students and relishes him when he is alone?] (62)

For the professor, an erudite man and mentor to his students, the very term 'popular fiction' must be taken with a grain of salt in an era when extremes often meet, or at least are no longer mutually exclusive.

Conclusion

While French traditional popular genres continue to develop with more success than failure, popular reading invites less formulaic works, intended to surprise readers rather than to cater to their expectations. The popularization of a certain type of intellectually motivated fiction has indeed forced critics to review the notion of reading for pleasure. French pessimists may worry about a decline in reading, but reading is more widespread now than after the war, and the fading of the dichotomy between low and high reading has allowed a broader, richer choice for French readers.

SUGGESTIONS FOR FURTHER READING

Few references in English, or in French, exist on present-day popular fiction. For current issues on French literature, including popular fiction, see: *Lire* (www.lire.fr) or www.mauvaisgenres.com, a complete website specializing in popular genres. The following volumes offer good historical or theoretical perspectives: Jean Ratford, *The Progress of Romance: The Politics of Popular Fiction* (London: Routledge, 1986) and Tony Bennett's *Popular Fiction: Technology, Ideology, Production, Reading* (London: Routledge, 1990).

To appreciate and think about French popular fiction, the first thing is probably to read it. Readers could start with the following selection of (mostly translated) works:
Dard, Frédéric (1968) *The Strangler* (London: G. Duckworth).
Klein, Gérard (1972) *The Day Before Tomorrow* (New York: Mass Market Paperback).
Nothomb, Amélie (1998) *The Stranger Next Door* (New York: Henry Holt & Company).
Simenon, Georges (1983) *Maigret and the Black Sheep* (Eugene, Oregon: Harvest/HBJ).
Vargas, Fred (2001) *Pars vite et reviens tard* (Paris: Vivian Hamy).
Werber, Bernard (1998) *Empire of the Ants* (New York: Bantam).

BIBLIOGRAPHY

Boviatsis, Renée (1979) *L'humanisme de San Antonio* (Paris: La Pensée Universelle).

Chraibi, Driss (1989) *La Civilisation, ma mère!* (Montreal: Éditions Aquila).

CNL (2002) *2000–2001 Sofres statistics* (Paris: Centre National du Livre and the Observatoire de l'Économie du Livre).

CNRS (1998) *L'édition française depuis 1945* (Paris: Éditions du Cercle de la Librairie).

Essel, André (2001) *Je voulais changer le monde, Mémoires* (Paris: Mémoire du Livre).

Miggozi, Jacques (1997) *Le roman populaire en question(s)* (Limoges: Presses Universitaires de Limoges).

Mollier, Jean-Yves (2002) *Où va le livre? Édition 2002–2003* (Paris: La Dispute/SNÉDIT).

Nothomb, Amélie (1992) *L'hygiène de l'assassin* (Paris: Albin Michel).

Nothomb, Amélie (1994) *Les Combustibles* (Paris: Albin Michel).

Nothomb, Amélie (1996) *Péplum* (Paris: Albin Michel).

Nothomb, Amélie (1997) *Attentat* (Paris: Albin Michel).

Nothomb, Amélie (1998) *Mercure* (Paris: Albin Michel).

Nothomb, Amélie (1999) *Stupeur et tremblements* (Paris: Albin Michel).

Raabe, Juliette (1999) *Fleuve noir. 50 ans d'édition populaire* (Paris: Bibliothèque des Littératures Policières).

Rawlins, Debbi (2002) *Le Combat d'une mère* (Paris: Harlequin).

Robine, Nicole (2000) *Lire des livres en France* (Paris: Editions du Cercle de la Librairie).

Sairigné, Guillemette de (1983) *L'aventure du Livre de Poche. L'enfant de Gutenberg et du XXème siècle* (Paris: Librairie Générale Française).

CHAPTER 9

Cinema

Phil Powrie

French cinema is, politically at least, a cinema with attitude. It is difficult to imagine Tony Blair inviting government ministers to a showing of *Trainspotting* (Boyle, 1996) so as to highlight and explain the drugs problem; difficult too to imagine President Clinton doing the same with *Kids* (Clark, 1995) to understand the disaffections of US youth. But *La Haine* (Kassovitz, 1995) and *Diên Biên Phu* (Schoendoerffer, 1992) had presidential endorsement: President Chirac had his ministers watch the former, and the latter was shown in Vietnam in the presence of President Mitterrand, who also attended the premiere of *Germinal* (Berri, 1993) in northern France, where the film was set, with a host of politicians and dignitaries. More importantly, the French government fought hard, and won what has become know as *l'exception culturelle*, meaning the exclusion and therefore protection of French cinema in the 1993 GATT trade agreements with the USA, just the latest chapter in the longstanding competition between the French and American national cinemas.

For the French, then, cinema matters, and matters in a very public way. Moreover, French cinema is the biggest European producer since the 1980s with an average of 140 films per annum (to the UK's 60 and Italy's 115). And it is the most glitzy of the European cinemas. Italy may have the Venice Film Festival, and the UK the London Film Festival; but France has Cannes, and it is Cannes that matters most after the Oscars.

Because cinema matters to the French, the state has been more supportive than most European countries, introducing subsidies based on tax breaks for private funders founded in the mid-1980s (the SOFICAs, or Société pour le Financement du Cinéma et de l'Audiovisuel). These have on the whole supported what is called the *cinéma d'art et d'essai* sector (the elite-culture cinema rather than the big-budget commercial sector). However, the state has also encouraged TV co-productions, which have benefited both elite and commercial cinema. TV channels have since the early 1970s invested increasingly large amounts in the making of films. Of the 145 films produced in 2000, for example, the subscription channel Canal Plus contributed to 115, and of those 100 were also supported by other channels. Of these, 20 belonged to TF1, which contributed altogether some 235 million fr., averaging almost 12 million fr. per film, considerably more than the 4–5 million per film for

France 2, France 3 and M6. A 'TF1 film' is most likely to be a big-budget popular comedy with well-known stars. The dependence of French cinema on TV funding marks a slow reversal which began in the post-war period.

In the sections which follow, I will explore first how the cinema industry tried to cope with diminishing audiences, many of them lost to TV. I will then outline the main stars and directors of the popular genres, before considering those genres – the police thriller, the literary adaptation and the comedy – and finishing with a case-study on the third most popular French film of all time, *Les Visiteurs*. As we shall see, there are three key dates for French cinema: unsurprisingly, 1968 marks a watershed for the three popular genres which we shall explore in this chapter; 1986 was the year in which French audiences went to see more American than French films, marking a low point; and 2000 saw a return of those same audiences as a spate of extremely successful French comedies persuaded them that French films weren't that bad after all (although I should point out that US films constituted 59 per cent of the national market in 2002, despite those popular French comedies).

INSTITUTIONS: CHANGING FORTUNES

Cinema became the prime leisure activity of the French in the immediate post-war period. There were some 6,000 35mm cinemas and a further 3,500 16mm projectors in use, and in the period 1945–60 there were an average of 340 million spectators per year. Cine-clubs, fostering public discussion and interest in film, spread throughout the country, reaching a peak in the 1960s.

The post-war consumer boom worked against this film culture. Television ownership was slow in France compared with the UK, but rose steadily from 2 million at the end of the 1950s, contributing to a decline in cinema audiences. The French bought more cars and travelled out to the country rather than staying in town to watch films. Spectator numbers fell dramatically during the 1960s, bottoming out at 170–200 million per annum during the 1970s and early 1980s, and some 3,500 cinemas closed in the period 1940–70. Cinema-going changed from a quasi-universal leisure activity to one concentrated in cities and large towns.

The industry tried to revive appetites by building multiscreens in urban centres from the early 1970s. New technologies were also invented to make films ever more spectacular, leading from the mid-1950s onwards to a concentration on 'blockbuster' films. Cinemascope was introduced in the early 1950s, quickly followed by other often short-lived wide-screen formats (Cinerama, Vistavision, Franscope, Kinopanorama). In the 1980s there was Dolby sound; in the 1990s THX and digital sound, and multiplexes with multiple leisure activities as well as multiscreens – the Kinépolis in Lille had as many as 23 screens – and, finally, the use of digital technology in many popular successes, including our case study *Les Visiteurs* (Poiré, 1993).

During the mid-1980s to mid-1990s, despite all of these inducements, there was a further sudden plunge in audiences, to an average of 130 million per annum (a staggering 40 per cent drop since 1945). Not only that, but in 1986–7 French audiences, for the very first time, went to see more American films than French films, a feature of film-going which did not change until a spate of highly successful French comedies in 2000–1. This shift back to French-made films proves the dictum that the popular genre par excellence is the comedy, as we shall see below.

STARS: MOSTLY MEN, SOME WOMEN, AND THE DIRECTOR AS STAR

Popular cinema in France as in other national cinemas is heavily dependent on a combination of specific genres and well-known stars. Of the 50 top films 1945–99, about half are comedies and a quarter are literary adaptations, the latter including costume dramas and swashbucklers as well as what has become known since the 1980s as the heritage film. The police thriller, or *polar*, may have less impressive audience figures, but it has consistently been a key popular genre.

The top box-office stars are generally associated with specific genres. Gérard Philipe (active mid-1940s–mid-1950s) is associated with historical dramas. Jean Marais, known to Anglophone art-house audiences for his films with Cocteau in the 1940s, is better known in France for his historical epics in the 1960s. Comedy has a number of major stars: Fernandel and Jacques Tati (1950s), Louis de Funès and Bourvil (1960s–1970s; indeed, these two stars appear in eight and six respectively of the top 50 French films since 1945), Pierre Richard (1960s–1980s), Jean Rochefort and Jean-Pierre Marielle (1970s), Coluche (mid-1979s–mid-1980s), Josiane Balasko, Christian Clavier and Thierry Lhermitte (1980s–1990s). The second most popular genre in France, the police thriller or *polar*, similarly has a number of major stars, all male. Jean Gabin, after his 'poetic realist' films with Marcel Carné in the 1930s, and for which Anglophone audiences are likely to know him best, is better known in France for his second career in the police thriller during the 1960s and early 1970s. There are also, in the same period, Alain Delon and Lino Ventura, the three stars famously appearing in one of the great popular thrillers of the 1960s, Verneuil's *Le Clan des Siciliens* (1969).

But there are superstars who cross over the genres, such as Jean-Paul Belmondo, who, after his early career in the new wave, went on to become one of the longest-lasting French stars, associated mainly but not exclusively with the thriller, dominating the box office from the early 1960s through to the late 1980s. Female stars have tended not to dominate the box office in quite the same way. Yet Catherine Deneuve is very much a superstar, busts modelled on her being until recently the image of the French state ('Marianne', the statuette in all French town halls); and Isabelle Adjani was one of the first stars to work in Hollywood, followed in the 1990s by Emmanuelle Béart and Sophie Marceau, well before Gérard Depardieu. Nevertheless, it is perhaps for many, both French and Anglophone, Depardieu who is the quintessential French superstar, at home in art-house films, in comedy, in heritage films and in thrillers, and who has dominated the box office since the mid-1970s, starring in four of the 50 top films.

Despite the female stars just mentioned, stardom in French cinema is more a matter for men than women, reflecting what might be considered a more misogynistic popular culture than in some European nations. It is not that there are no women stars: apart from those previously mentioned, there are Annie Girardot, Jeanne Moreau, Romy Schneider and Simone Signoret from the pre-1980s period, and Anémone, Fanny Ardant, Nathalie Baye, Isabelle Huppert and Miou-Miou in the last 20 years. However, the difference between the sexes lies in pulling power. Depardieu has had some 25 million spectators in the Paris region for some 60 films, whereas Catherine Deneuve and Miou-Miou tie with 9–10 million for their 30-odd films each. Similarly, the average number of spectators per film for the top 15 male stars is about 495,000, whereas it is only 218,000 for the top 15 female stars. The reason for this is that popular film par excellence is the comedy, and that few comic roles are offered to women, with the exception of two who have made their name in the genre, Anémone and Josiane Balasko.

The apparently solid star system has changed in the last decade. Stars, although clearly useful in attracting spectators, have not always been a guarantee of success for a film; this has been the case particularly with the ageing stars, such as Belmondo and Delon during the 1990s. On the other hand, successful films have frequently been directed by a small group of directors, suggesting that there has been a drift back to the *auteurism* associated more with the art cinema. The same directors appear on several occasions in the list of the top 50 French films. For one director representing the heritage film, Claude Berri (whose total number of spectators over ten films was almost 6 million, and his average per film over half a million), there are considerably more directors of comedies. Claude Zidi tops the list of total number of spectators for his 17 films at almost 11 million, and has two comedies in the top 50, as does Francis Veber (almost 4 million total for four films, an average of almost a million for each). The other directors in this hit parade are Gérard Oury, director of three de Funès/Bourvil comedies in the top 50, including the best-seller of all time, and Jean-Marie Poiré, whose *Les Visiteurs* is the second best-selling French film of all time. If many of the remainder in the top 15 are best known for their comedies (Bertrand Blier, Etienne Chatiliez, Georges Lautner, Claude Pinoteau, Coline Serreau – the only woman, but whose *Trois hommes et un couffin* of 1985 was the surprise best-seller of the 1980s with over 10 million spectators), there are nevertheless others: Claude Lelouch, a perennial popular director of sentimental dramas; Bertrand Tavernier, something of an all-rounder with a penchant for realist drama; and the directors associated with the stylish *cinéma du look* of the 1980s, Jean-Jacques Annaud and Luc Besson.

I will now turn to a brief outline of the major genres in which the stars appeared. As will have become clear, the definition of the popular used here is based on audience figures. In the sections on particular genres which follow, the statistics given – relying on Simsi (2000), which uses figures from the Centre National de la Cinématographie – are of total number of spectators in millions for a given film in the period 1945–2000 (so not just the number of spectators in the year the film was released); the ranking, when given, is the film's position in the top 20 French films (so excluding what are usually American films in the top 20).

THE *POLAR* AND THE *CINÉMA DU LOOK*: DISENGAGING FROM THE USA

The post-war thriller, or *polar*, was influenced by two things: the *série noire*, a new book list which focused on crime thrillers, many of them translations of US titles, and, second, US *film noir*. Consequently, many *polars* are dark in tone and located in cities rather than the provinces. Arguably, then, this genre, more than any other, betrays the French love-hate affair with American popular culture, although, as we shall see, the *cinéma du look* turns the tables on American influences.

During the 1950s and 1960s, the top 20 films usually included three or four *polars*, many of them adaptations of popular crime novels, such as those by Simenon, or novels in the *série noire*. Most popular *polars* attracted 3–4 million spectators, generally representing a minimum of 3–5 per cent of the audience numbers for the top 20 films in each year, but often as much as 10–11 per cent. If we take the years 1958 and 1963 as examples, we see the persistence of certain types of *polar* from one decade to the next. In 1958 three *polars* represented 10 per cent of the audience figures for the top 20 films (including non-French films). These were *En cas de malheur* (Autant-Lara, 3.2m, eighth) with Gabin and Brigitte Bardot, followed by a Simenon adaptation, again with Gabin, *Maigret tend un piège* (Delannoy, 3m, ninth) and *Le Gorille vous salue bien* (Borderie, 2.8m, 13th), with another stalwart of the genre, Lino Ventura. Five years later, we find much the same pattern of films, with the same actors, the same world-weary gangster played by Gabin, the same Maigret adaptation, representing 11.7 per cent of the total audience figures for the top 20 films that year: *Melodie en sous-sol* (Verneuil, 3.5m, second), with Gabin and Delon; *Les Tontons flingueurs* (Lautner, 3.5m, third), with Ventura; and *Maigret voit rouge* (Grangier, 2m, tenth), again with Gabin. The pattern of the genre did not change until after the events of May 1968, as we shall see below.

In this period there were several types of *polar*. Perhaps reflecting French guilt for collaboration during the Second World War, there was a strand dealing with criminality in very ordinary people, such as the evocatively titled *Nous sommes tous des assassins* (Cayatte, 1952, 3m, 14th), or *Le Fruit défendu* (Verneuil, 1952, 4m, fifth). However, many more focused on the underworld and the figure of the gangster, epitomized by Jean Gabin, as for example in *Touchez pas au grisbi* (1954, Becker, 4.7m, third).

But there was also the extremely popular comedy thriller with the character Lemmy Caution played by American Eddie Constantine. He starred as this and other characters in a long run of some 15 films, beginning in 1953 with *La Môme vert-de-gris* (Borderie, 3.8m, seventh), through to the early 1960s. These films, after the first few, regularly had 1–2 million spectators.

From the late 1960s to the 1980s, the *polar* was dominated by Belmondo and Delon in the more stylized gangster thriller, exemplified by the films of Jean-Pierre Melville. Belmondo starred in *Le Doulos* (1963, 1.5m), joined by Delon in *Le Deuxième Souffle* (1966, 2m), *Le Samouraï* (1967, 2m, 14th), *Le Cercle rouge* (1970, 4.3m, fifth). But the old guard of Gabin and Ventura were still crowd-pullers in the late 1960s. Indeed, successes in 1969 show the mixture of the old and new *polar* in a variety of ways. *Le Clan des Siciliens* (Verneuil, 4.8m, second) starred Gabin and Ventura, but also Delon, now an established if younger *polar* star. In first place, there was a comedy thriller starring Belmondo, *Le Cerveau* (Oury, 5.5m). But in third place, there was a new type of *polar*, the left-leaning political thriller, reflecting disenchantment with the state and its apparatus, now seen as oppressive: *Z* (Costas-Gavras, 4m), which the same director followed in 1970 by *L'Aveu* (2.1m, 13th). This type of *polar* was an important feature of post-'68 film culture. Yves Boisset was the director of a number of such films. *Un Condé* (1970, 1.3m) was banned because of scenes of police brutality. It was followed by *L'Attentat* (1972, 1.4m) and the very popular *Le Juge Fayard dit le 'Shériff'* (1976, 1.7 m), focusing on racism, and which reached the top 20.

In the 1980s, the traditional *polar* with its traditional stars still managed to pull large audiences. However, *La Balance*, directed by an American, was a new style of Americanized thriller (Swaim, 1982, 4.2m, fourth) with a new emphasis on the indistinguishability of police and criminals. This type of thriller suggests not just the increasing Americanization of French society as French cinema audiences began to be attracted more to American films, but also a more general amorality prevalent throughout the western world during the materialistic 1980s. Typically, it was women characters who carried the burden for a changing society which no longer quite knew what its identity was in a postmodern and increasingly Americanized environment. For example, the top-selling film of 1983, *L'Été meurtrier* (Becker, 5.1m, first) starred Isabelle Adjani as a disturbed *femme fatale*.

But, as had been the case in the politicized 1970s with the political thriller, in the

1980s the *polar* again took a new turn, this time apolitical and flashy, as the directors of the *cinéma du look* became popular among the ever larger youth audience. In 1981 the sleeper success *Diva* (Beineix, 1981, 2.3m, ninth), heralding the *cinéma du look*, was sandwiched between more traditional *polar* genres, one being a film directed by and starring Delon, *Pour la peau d'un flic* (2.4m, eighth), and the others being Tavernier's adaptation of a Jim Thompson novel, *Coup de torchon* (2.2m, tenth) and Miller's adaptation of a John Wainwright novel, *Garde à vue* (2.1m, 11th). A few years later, however, the *cinéma du look*'s *Subway* (Besson, 1985, 2.9m, third) was well ahead of a Delon vehicle, *Parole de flic* (Pinheiro, 2.5m, sixth).

The *polars* which subsequently did well were either comedies, such as the sequel *Ripoux contre Ripoux* (Zidi, 1990, 2.9m, fifth; this still only being half the number of spectators for the first film, *Les Ripoux*, 1984, 5.9m, second), or thrillers by Besson, such as *Nikita* (1990, 3.8m, fourth), and the New York-set, English-language *Léon* (1994, 3.6m, second). Although Besson's films in particular suggest that at least one French director was able to play the Americans at their own game by making spectacular action thrillers with a distinctly Gallic flavour, the genre in general was no longer so popular. In 1986, the year of the heritage film's success, for the first time, there were no *polars* in the top 20, and in the 1990s most *polars* stayed below the 500,000 spectator mark. The reason is partly that the genre had become an established feature of television with popular series such as *Navarro* and *Commissaire Moulin*, partly because another genre had taken its place in the top 20: heritage films, developing from the 1950s costume epic and 'quality cinema' frequently based on literary adaptations.

LITERATURE AND HERITAGE CINEMA

Literary or historical films featured regularly in the top 20 until they were displaced during the 1970s. They made a comeback as heritage films in the 1980s, partly because of state support, both political, as mentioned on p. 119, and, more importantly, financial as the newly elected socialist government undertook, under the minister of culture, Jack Lang, to promote what might hitherto have seemed a paradox: a quality popular French cinema. As we shall see, however, the focus in the 1980s and beyond was different.

The bulk of the films in this broad genre were swashbuckling literary adaptations of the nineteenth-century novel, especially those of Alexandre Dumas and Victor Hugo, focusing on either the Louis XIV period or the Revolution. Even films which were top-selling costume epics rather than literary adaptations were set in these two periods, for example Sacha Guitry's two mid-1950s films, *Si Versailles m'était conté* (1954, 7m, first) and *Napoléon* (1955, 5.4, second), or Gance's Napoleonic epic *Austerlitz* (1960, 3.5m, seventh), or a decade later *Les Mariés de l'An II* (Rappeneau,

1971, 2.8m, fifth). The appendix of popular literary adaptations (see pp. 133–4) shows not only the prevalence of nineteenth-century authors, but also a systematic use of the same stories, the same directors and the same actors.

Where stories are concerned, Hugo's *Les Misérables* occurs twice, as do several Dumas narratives: *Le Comte de Monte Cristo, Les Trois Mousquetaires* and *Le Bossu*. These narratives had been much adapted before 1945 as well: *Les Misérables* had been filmed in 1911, 1925 and 1934, and *Le Bossu* in 1923, 1925 and 1944. And, although *La Reine Margot* occurs only once in our list of best-sellers, it too had already been used in a Franco-Italian co-production starring Jeanne Moreau (Dréville, 1954, 2.6m). The pre-'68 directors who recur – Autant-Lara, Christian-Jaque, Delannoy, Hunebelle – were taken to task by Truffaut in a famous 1954 article in which they were characterized as representatives of a stultifying old men's cinema relying excessively on literary adaptations. After the 1970s lull in the genre, the post-'81 directors show more variety, but are dominated by Claude Berri. The stars, as we mentioned above in the section on genres and stars, are principally Jean Marais and Gérard Philipe in the first period, and, much as Berri dominates the directors, so does Depardieu dominate the stars who represent this genre in the post-'81 period.

There are differences, though. In the 1950s and 1960s, the prevalence of the high literary adaptation led to adaptations of novel series by best-selling contemporary authors set in the two favoured historical periods. There was the 1950s Caroline series set in the Revolution, based on novels by Cécil Saint-Laurent, and (for the first two) starring Martine Carol: *Caroline chérie* (Pottier, 1951, 3.6m, fifth); *Un caprice de Caroline chérie* (Devaivre, 1953, 2.8m); *Le Fils de Caroline chérie* (Devaivre, 1955, 1.7m). Then in the 1960s there was the Angélique series, starring Michèle Mercier and directed by Bernard Borderie, based on novels by Anne and Serge Golon, set in the other favoured period, the court of Louis XIV: *Angélique marquise des anges* (1964, 3m, eighth); *Merveilleuse Angélique* (1965, 2.5m, ninth); *Angélique et le roy* (1966, 2.2m, sixth); *Indomptable Angélique* (1967, 1.9m, 15th); *Angélique et le sultan* (1968, 1.8m). These cod-historical films are not a feature of the 1980s.

In the 1990s, many more non-literary heritage films attracted audiences than in the earlier period. Moreover, the focus of the films changed, and was more transparently concerned with political and social issues. Firstly, they addressed French decolonization, although not so much of Algeria as of French Indochina, with two popular successes in 1992, one a non-literary adaptation starring Catherine Deneuve, *Indochine* (Wargnier, 3.2m, first), the other a literary adaptation of a Marguerite Duras novel, *L'Amant* (Annaud, 3.2m, second). Secondly, as these two Indochina films suggest, several of the most popular heritage-style films focused on famous women, such as the Isabelle Adjani vehicle *Camille Claudel* (Nuttyen, 1988, 2.7m, fifth) and *Jeanne d'Arc* (Besson, 1999, 3m, second). We might think that this was a result of consciousness-raising French feminism, until we remember that in one film the heroine goes mad and is locked up, and in the other she is burnt at the stake, suggesting that stereotypical French misogyny dies hard. Thirdly, whereas in the 1945–70 period the genre tended to focus mostly on the seventeenth century and the Revolutionary or post-Revolutionary periods, in 1996 there were *Ridicule* (Leconte, 2.1, sixth) and *Beaumarchais l'insolent* (Molinaro, 1.9m, 17th), both set in the immediate pre-Revolutionary period, and both dealing with characters who reject a corrupt society, a feature of another heritage film set in the more usual seventeenth century, *Tous les matins du monde* (Corneau, 1991, 2.2m, first). Finally, the 1990s heritage film was dark in tone, with its piles of corpses in *Le Colonel Chabert* and *La Reine Margot*, and cholera-wracked vomiting victims in *Le Hussard sur le toit*. These last two features of the literary adaptation, it has been suggested, are connected to disenchantment with the French political system and what was seen as the gradual corruption of Mitterrandism and the great hopes attached to it in the early 1980s.

The watershed for the literary and non-literary historical films as a whole, however, was 1968. Prior to this, the genre conveyed a mixture of nostalgia and certainty, as solid as the nineteenth-century realist novel form itself, with the same periods, the same stars, the same 'saucy' series. Such repetition confirmed the immutability of France's greatness as a nation and its global domination in the period beginning with the golden age of Louis XIV, the Sun King, and ending with the Revolution and its aftermath (1640–1815). After 1968, however, the view of the historical past was more critical, more dystopian, and women played an increasingly important part as the focus of the narrative. It is hardly surprising, then, that with such dystopian narratives, it was the comedy, popular genre par excellence, which from 2000 reversed the mid-1980s trend where French spectators went to see more American than French films.

C O M E D Y

1968 also changed the nature of comedy. Prior to 1968, comedies demonstrated a conservative escapist impulse and fear of change in what had become a very rapidly changing society. Typical of the carnivalesque function of comedy, and typical indeed of the events of May 1968, order was momentarily subverted only to be reasserted. Although many popular comedies were broad sex farces, the most successful comedies were inextricably linked to individual performers in this period. After 1968, however, no doubt reflecting the mood of the nation after a moment of brief euphoria, popular comedies became more anarchic and corrosive, the humour frequently black, much in the same way as the heritage film went gloomy in the 1990s; and they tended to work around groups of comic performers which included an increasing number of women.

The pre-1968 period was dominated by Fernandel and Jacques Tati. Tati's 1950s films were successful partly because they chronicled naïve amazement at post-war change: *Jour de fête* (1949, 6.7m, first), *Les Vacances de Monsieur Hulot* (1953, 5m, fourth), *Mon Oncle* (1958, 4.6m, third); his later films, in 1967 and 1971, were less successful, partly because comic styles were changing. Similarly, Fernandel, who was already a star in the 1930s, waned by the early 1960s. Renowned for his toothy grin and thick Marseilles accent, he made anything from two to six films a year in the 1950s, most of them with 2–4 million spectators, and some with spectacular results, such as the Don Camillo series where he plays a priest at loggerheads with the communist mayor in an Italian village. The first in the series, *Le Petit monde de Don Camillo* (Duvivier, 12.8m) was released in 1951. It was the top-selling French film that year; remarkably, all of Fernandel's remaining films in 1952 were in the top 20 with 3–4 million spectators each (in fifth, sixth and 12th place). The following year, *Le Retour de Don Camillo* (Duvivier, 7.4m) was again the top French film. During the 1960s Fernandel's films generally fell below the million mark, but as late as 1963 he had a major success with *La Cuisine au beurre* (Grangier, 6.4, first).

Fernandel's place as the French public's favourite comedian was taken by Louis de Funès the following year when the first in a series of films in which he plays a policeman, *Le Gendarme de Saint-Tropez* (Girault, 7.8m), was the top-selling film of the year. From then until 1979, there was no year in which the top 20 did not include a de Funès film, and often there were as many as three. In 1965 he starred in the top three French films: *Le Corniaud* (Oury, 11.7m), the second in the Gendarme series, *Le Gendarme à New York* (Girault, 5.5m), and *Fantômas se déchaîne* (Hunebelle, 4.2m). In 1966 he starred in the best-selling French film of all time, *La Grande Vadrouille*, a Resistance comedy (Oury, 17.2m, first). In 1967, de Funès's three films were the top three French films, with almost 17 million spectators between them, and in subsequent years his films were usually the best-selling French films: *Les Aventures de Rabbi Jacob* (Oury, 1973, 7.3m); *L'Aile ou la cuisse* (Zidi, 1976, 5.8m); *Le Gendarme et les extraterrestres* (Girault, 1979, 6.3m). Whereas Fernandel's persona was that of the happy-go-lucky wily peasant, in some senses a pre-war throwback given the massive rural exodus in the post-war period (thus suggesting a romantic hankering for a lost rural paradise as France modernized), de Funès, more in tune with the silent majority's fear of rapid change post-war, tended to play the bigoted and angry lower-middle- or middle-class man on the street. Fernandel's grin was replaced by a face contorted by a pouting mouth and pop-eyed frustration.

As de Funès's career was ending, a new generation of comedians with a new form of libertarian comedy in tune with the post-1968 period was emerging from stand-up comic routines in the Paris *café-théâtres*. Depardieu was one of these; he starred, with Pierre Richard, in three films directed by Francis Veber, *La Chèvre* (1981, 7.1m, first), *Les Compères* (1983, 4.9m, third) and *Les Fugitifs* (1986, 4.5m, fourth).

Veber's films continued to be popular into the 1990s; *Le Dîner de cons* was the best-selling French film of 1998 (9.2m), and heralded the return of French spectators to French films rather than American films.

Another *café-théâtre* comedian was Coluche, associated with the Café de la Gare. He starred with Depardieu in *L'Inspecteur la bavure* (Zidi, 1980, 3.7m, third), and his films were frequently in the top 10 during the early 1980s. In 1983, for example, he had two in fifth and sixth positions, while in fourth was *Papy fait de la résistance* (Poiré, 4.1m) from the team of another group of *café-théâtre* performers, Le Splendid, who had started making films at the end of the 1970s. One of their first films, *Les Bronzés* (Leconte, 1978, 2.3m, sixth), was a series of sketches about the Club Med, and it had snapped at the heels of de Funès, whose *La Zizanie* (Zidi, 1978, 2.7m) was in third place that year.

The ideals of 1968 soon went sour during the mid-1970s, and comedy turned corrosive, just as the *polar* had become the paranoid political thriller. This new type of comedy took two very different forms, both articulated around male crisis as the feminist movement developed in the 1970s, the first directed by men, the second by women. In *La Grande Bouffe* (Ferreri, 1973, 2.8m, sixth), for example, a group of male friends commit suicide by over-eating, suggesting that the role of men post-'68 had been called into question. The films of Bertrand Blier were more in the mould of Luis Buñuel, and more voluntarily misogynistic than most comedies, generally a misogynistic genre. His most successful films starred Depardieu, either as a sexually liberated man in *Les Valseuses* (1974, 5.7m, second) or a bisexual in *Tenue de soirée* (1986, 3.1m, sixth), or, finally, caught between two women in *Trop belle pour toi* (2m, first), married to Carole Bouquet, the Chanel model, but attracted to his 'dumpy' secretary, played by Josiane Balasko. The second type of comedy to tackle male crisis was directed by women. Although not necessarily any less misogynistic, their films focused much more squarely on the discomfiture of men than films by their male counterparts. *Trois hommes et un couffin* (Serreau, 10.3m), eventually remade in Hollywood as *Three Men and a Baby* (Nimoy, 1987), was the surprise best-selling film of 1985, about a group of homosocial males learning how to become 'mothers'. Serreau's later *La Crise* focused on a middle-aged man's mid-life crisis (1992, 2.4m, fifth), although it did not do as well as *Gazon maudit*, a film about a threesome in which the director, Josiane Balasko, originally a member of Le Splendid, plays a lesbian who sets up house with a heterosexual couple (1995, 4m, fourth).

Ultimately, though, the greatest success for the Le Splendid team was the consistently good performance of the films directed by Jean-Marie Poiré during the 1980s and 1990s. His films with them, starting with *Les Hommes préfèrent les grosses* (1981, 1.9m, 14th), starring Josiane Balasko, generally had 1.5 million spectators; although nothing could have predicted the success of *Les Visiteurs* in 1993, whose 13.7 million spectators make it the second-best seller in the post-war period. *Les Visiteurs* took almost 10 per cent of the total number of spectators in France, whereas the top-seller, *La Grande vadrouille*, with its 17 million, only represented 7 per cent. For that reason I have chosen it as my case study (for further work on the film see Danan, 1999, and Jäckel, 2001), even if 2003 saw its audience figures beaten by *Astérix et Obélix: Mission Cléopâtre* (Chabat, 2002, 14.5m, first).

CASE STUDY

LES VISITEURS

The film recounts the time-travel adventures of a twelfth-century knight and his valet projected into the present of his descendants. The knight is desperate to return, appalled by what he discovers of the future (the Revolution, democracy, etc.), while the valet revels in the same developments and remains, engineering the return to the twelfth century of his descendant, a nouveau riche who has turned the knight's castle into a hotel.

Despite the low-key marketing for the film, over half a million spectators went to see it in its first week (released 27 January 1993), and it had had an unheard-of 4 million spectators by its fifth week. The film stayed in first place for ten weeks, by which time some 6 million spectators had been to see it. It returned to first place for the first month of the school holidays in mid-July, now at a total of 10 million spectators; and there was a final surge as it approached its 40th week, with well over half a million spectators across France in October, and still a position in the top 10 films. Some 1.5 million videocassettes were sold in the run-up to Christmas. By this time it had become a cult film, and the final surge of interest represented a second- or even third-time viewing for many spectators. Catchphrases from the film were in circulation: 'Mais qu-est-ce que c'est ce bin's' ('What's going on'), 'C'est dingue' ('It's crazy'; a normal colloquialism, but spoken in the film with an upper-class accent), the valet's 'OK', with the stress heavily on the second syllable, the cod-medieval French 'mangeaillons' (something like 'let us eateth'), and the term of abuse for modern French people who are 'fols dingos' (calqued on *fous/dingues*, or raving mad).

The film depends on various types of familiarity. The pairing of knight and valet (Jean Reno/Christian Clavier), apart from recalling the success of *Opération Corned Beef* (Poiré, 1991, 1.5m, fourth), would also have recalled previous comic pairs, such as Depardieu and Richard in Veber's 1980s comedies, or de Funès and Bourvil. The team particularly had the pairing of Jean Marais and Bourvil in *Le Capitan* in mind (Hunebelle, 1960, 5.2m, third), one of their stated aims being to reestablish traditional French popular film. Moreover, Chazel uses the broad accent of Arletty in *Hôtel du Nord* (Carné, 1938), recalling the classic cinema of the 1930s.

The setting in the middle ages is important too, recalling the great literary classics of the Chanson de Roland and the works of Rabelais. There is a particular flavour to this heritage reference, however, in that it is not to the golden age of Louis XIV, with its stilted etiquette, but to the era of farce, of boisterous carnival, when authors like Rabelais could revel in the scatological. When Godefroy and Jacquouille wash themselves in the toilet, then, there is a potent double return: to France's infancy as a nation-state, and to the spectator's early childhood. *Les Visiteurs* thus cleverly combines different types of nostalgia, whether cinematic, historical or psychological.

Gestured at obscurely through both these types of nostalgia is a paradox. The present may be egalitarian, and mod cons may make life easier, but it is at the price of one's soul, since money is king, the place is full of autocratic managers and upwardly mobile types out for a quick buck; in contrast, the past may have been unjust, but at least people knew their place, and values were stable. The film is a derisive satire on contemporary life consonant with post-'68 corrosive comedy, but underneath is a utopian longing for permanence, whether through the fantasy of immortality on one level, or the return to basic values on another.

Moreover, the film came at the right moment politically as well. There was public dismay with the political process; France was in recession, and Mitterrand was about to lose the election. The film allowed all political parties to claim that it represented their values. Ecologists saw it as a condemnation of modern pollution; the right saw it as a defence of French identity; the left saw it as a defence of egalitarianism. The film thus managed to suggest that things used to be better and at the same time it brought people and politicians together, generating serious debates about its historical and political significance. And, finally, it was released in the year of the GATT negotiations which catapulted France's cinema industry into the forefront of cultural politics, as mentioned on p. 119.

We said earlier that comedy is often seen as the least exportable genre. One of the feats of the genre since the mid-1980s has been its exportability. Apart from the remake of *Trois hommes et un couffin*, mentioned above, it is worth pointing out that *Les Visiteurs* was sold worldwide, and that it initiated a resurgence of French comedy not only in France, but abroad as well, as can be seen in *Le Fabuleux Destin d'Amélie Poulain*. Unlike the heritage film, then, French popular cinema does not need presidents to support it. Evidently, there is something compelling for both the French and the rest of the world in the spectacle of the French not taking themselves too seriously.

FURTHER THINKING AND READING

Underlying this chapter, there are two 'special relationships' which could be investigated further: cinema/TV and France/USA. You might also like to consider the question of why there was a loss of interest in the *polar* during the 1970s. Part of the answer lies in the reasons why very specific new genres took its place, the heritage film and the *cinéma du look*, both genres with high production values, even if the first might appeal more to a middle-class and middle-aged audience nourished on the French 'classic', and the latter more to the increasingly important youth audience. Another question: why do certain types become stars and not others? For example, why is Jean Reno's taciturnity preferred in the 1990s to the apoplectic anger that made de Funès popular in the 1970s? Again, many French films have been remade, but why is it that the majority of those remade in the 1980s were popular comedies, a genre which exports with difficulty, since it is heavily based on verbal humour? Finally, what do the successful comedies of 2000–1 tell us about the French? *Le Fabuleux Destin d'Amélie Poulain* (Jeunet, 2001) harks back to the *cinéma de quartier* of the 1930s, while the two Astérix films, quite apart from being based on one of the most successful series of cartoons in France, more particularly always revolve around a tight-knit French community faced with a globalizing imperial power – which perhaps returns us to one of those 'special relationships' mentioned above, France/USA.

To help get more of a feel for French cinema and the issues discussed here, the following reading would be particularly useful.

a) G. Austin, *Contemporary French Cinema: An Introduction* (Manchester: Manchester University Press, 1996). A good basic introduction on the post-'68 period covering art-films rather more than popular films; pp.138–40 on *Les Visiteurs*. Thematic sections on war, sexuality, women film-makers, thriller, *cinéma du look*, and heritage.

b) P. Powrie and K. Reader, *French Cinema: A Student's Guide* (London: Arnold, 2002). A more canonical view of French cinema history. Sections on the history of French film theory, writing about film; extensive statistical and historical information in appendices.

c) G. Vincendeau, *Stars and Stardom in French Cinema* (London: Continuum, 2000). Essential reading; the history and theory of French stardom; chapters on Gabin, Bardot, Moreau, de Funès, Belmondo, Delon, Deneuve, Depardieu and Binoche.

BIBLIOGRAPHY

Danan, M. (1999) 'Revisiting the myth of the French Nation: *Les Visiteurs* (Poiré, 1993)', in P. Powrie (ed.), *French Cinema in the 1990s: Continuity and Difference* (Oxford: Oxford University Press), pp. 92–103.

Jäckel, A. (2001) '*Les Visiteurs*: a feelgood movie for uncertain times', in L. Mazdon (ed.), *France on Film: Reflections on Popular French Cinema* (London: Wallflower), pp. 41–50.

Simsi, S. (2000) *Ciné-Passions: 7ᵉ art et industrie de 1945 à 2000* (Paris: Éditions Dixit).

APPENDIX: LITERARY ADAPTATIONS 1945–2000

Year	Title	Director	Author	Period set	Stars	Spectators	Position in top 10
1945	Carmen	Christian-Jaque	Mérimée	Late 19c	Romance, Marais	4.3m	3
1945	Boule de suif	Christian-Jaque	Maupassant	Late 19c	Presle	3m	10
1948	La Chartreuse de Parme	Christian-Jaque	Stendhal	Early 19c	Philipe	6.2m	1
1953	Les Trois Mousquetaires	Hunebelle	Dumas	17c	Marchal	5.4m	3
1954	Le Rouge et le noir	Autant-Lara	Stendhal	Early 19c	Philipe	4.3m	4
1955	Le Comte de Monte Cristo	Vernay	Dumas	Early 19c	Richard-Willm	7.8m	1
1956	Notre-Dame de Paris	Delannoy	Hugo	15c	Quinn	5.7m	2
1956	Gervaise	Clément	Zola	Late 19c	Schell	4.1m	6
1958	Les Misérables	Le Chanois	Hugo	Early 19c	Gabin	10m	1
1959	Les Liaisons dangereuses	Vadim	Laclos	18c	Moreau, Philipe	4.3m	4
1960	Le Bossu	Hunebelle	Féval	18c	Marais	5.9m	1
1961	Les Trois Mousquetaires	Borderie	Dumas	17c	Barray	4.5m	2
1961	Le Comte de Monte Cristo	Autant-Lara	Dumas	Early 19c	Richard-Willm	4.5m	3
1961	La Princess de Cleves	Delannoy	Lafayette	17c	Marais	3.4m	8
1961	Le Capitaine Fracasse	Gaspard-Huit	Gautier	17c	Marais	3.2m	9

cont. overleaf

Year	Title	Director	Author	Period set	Stars	Spectators	Position in top 10
1962	Les Mystères de Paris	Hunebelle	Sue	19c	Marais	2.7m	6
1962	Le Masque de fer	Decoin	Dumas	17c	Marais	2.4m	7
1964	La Tulipe noire	Christian-Jaque	Dumas	Revol	Delon	3.1m	6
1982	Les Misérables	Hossein	Hugo	Early 19c	Ventura	3.8m	6
1986	Jean de Florette	Berri	Pagnol	Early 20c	Depardieu, Montand	7.2m	1
1986	Manon des sources	Berri	Pagnol	Early 20c	Montand	6.7m	2
1990	La Gloire de mon père	Robert	Pagnol	Early 20c	Roussel	6.3m	1
1990	Cyrano de Bergerac	Rappeneau	Rostand	16c	Depardieu	4.7m	2
1990	Le Château de ma mère	Robert	Pagnol	Early 20c	Roussel	4.7m	3
1990	Uranus	Berri	Aymé	Second World War	Depardieu	2.6m	6
1993	Germinal	Berri	Zola	Late 19c	Depardieu	6.1m	2
1994	La Reine Margot	Chéreau	Dumas	16c	Adjani	2m	6
1994	Le Colonel Chabert	Angelo	Balzac	Early 19c	Depardieu	1.7m	7
1995	Le Hussard sur le toit	Rappeneau	Giono	Early 19c	Binoche	2.4m	6
1997	Le Bossu	De Broca	Féval	18c	Auteuil	2.3m	7

CHAPTER 10

Bande Dessinée

Ann Miller

If you live in an English-speaking country and are interested in *bande dessinée* you will be accustomed to the difficulty of trying to explain this cultural phenomenon to your friends. The first problem is the term itself: there is no satisfactory translation for *bande dessinée* in English. 'Comic strip' is misleading: although there is a long tradition of satirical and humorous BD, there are many BD genres such as the thriller or, more recently, autobiography, which do not fit into the category of 'comic'. Conversely, the faintly pretentious 'graphic novel' tends to be used in an Anglo-American context to refer to albums with minority appeal to intellectuals. The French term, literally 'drawn strip', has a much wider application: like cinema, BD ranges from escapist pulp to complex and artistically challenging work. The second problem is likely to be your friends' assumption that what you are studying is a branch of children's literature, since they may be familiar only with *Tintin* or *Astérix*, even if they are aware that the sophisticated wordplay and cultural references of the latter give it some appeal to older readers. You will have to explain that, in the 1960s, a politically and socially subversive current in BD gave it a cult status among adults, particularly students, which it has never lost. There is still a market for children's BD, but the typical BD reader, according to a 1994 survey carried out by the Institut Français d'Opinion Publique, is 15–34, and male. A further IFOP survey carried out in 2000 established that a third of French adults under the age of 50 regularly read BD, and that 44 per cent of the readership are graduates.

You will also need to impress upon your friends the sheer weight of BD in the book publishing market in France. Some indication of this is offered by the size of the section devoted to BD in 'cultural supermarkets', such as the FNAC, and further evidence is provided by best-seller lists, such as those produced by the magazine *Livres hebdo*, in which during most weeks between two and five BD albums feature among the top 10 best-selling books. However, the fact that you have to have this conversation at all with your friends (who could probably recognize the names of a few French film directors, for example) points to a certain invisibility of BD in the kinds of arena where French culture is on display outside France, such as the arts pages of newspapers and, with a few exceptions, the syllabuses of French departments in universities. This is not entirely surprising, since, even in France, acknowledgement of the claim of BD to be a legitimate art form has been slow in coming, and the story of the medium is, in part, the story of its struggle for recognition.

BD AS THE 'NINTH ART' IN THE FRENCH CULTURAL HIERARCHY

The first discussions about BD in print, far from giving it recognition, took the form of moralizing discourses. When American series first started appearing in France in translation in the 1930s, there was an outcry from various educationalists (across a spectrum from Jesuit to communist) about the seductive effects on impressionable young minds of this mass cultural medium, which abandoned any improving purpose in favour of entertainment. American magazines were banned during the Occupation but started to reappear later in the 1940s, and threatened to eclipse their tamer and more sanitized French rivals. The anti-American agenda of the Communist party moved it to join forces with the Catholic church to draft a law which aimed to protect young people from material deemed violent or morally unsuitable, by allowing for its prohibition. The law, passed in 1949, is still on the statute book and continues to be invoked as moral panics about BD are periodically reactivated: most recently, in the 1990s, a number of *mangas* (Japanese BD) were banned.

It was not until the 1960s that a small group of high-profile intellectuals, including the film director Alain Resnais, suggested that BD might be considered to be an art form rather than a disreputable subculture. To this end, they coined the term 'ninth art' (by analogy with 'seventh art', referring to cinema, and 'eighth art', referring to TV) in 1962 at the first meeting of the Club des Bandes Dessinées (Guillaume and Bocquet, 1997: 133). Their journal *Giff-Wiff* aimed to give the medium legitimacy by emphasizing its history, with a focus on classic American comic strips, some of which had provoked such indignation on their first appearance.

In spite of sporadic interventions by the censor, the process of legitimation gained momentum. An exhibition called Bande dessinée et narration figurative (BD and Figurative Narration), including Franco-Belgian as well as American artists, was held at the Musée des Arts Décoratifs in 1967, and attracted 500,000 visitors over three months. In 1974 a Salon de la Bande Dessinée was held in Angoulême, and went on to become an annual event. The Grand Prix de la Ville d'Angoulême went in the first year to the Belgian artist Franquin, creator of the incorrigibly indolent Gaston Lagaffe. By the 30th anniversary of the Salon (now called the Festival) in 2003, it was able to attract 200,000 visitors in four days.

In the 1980s BD became part of culture minister Jack Lang's strategy for promoting economic growth through the 'cultural industries'. He chose the 1983 Angoulême salon to unveil his '15 mesures pour la bande dessinée', which included the founding in Angoulême of the Centre National de la Bande Dessinée et de l'Image, to be numbered among Mitterrand's prestigious *grands projets présidentiels*. The president himself visited the salon in 1985. It is not clear, though, whether Lang's 15 measures (which did not include the ending of censorship) should be viewed simply as recognition of the contribution that BD could make as part of a home-grown mass culture which would help to combat the cultural and economic onslaught of the American mass media, or whether Lang intended to consecrate its status as art. The latter interpretation would be supported by his speech, in which he deplored the fact that BD had previously been seen as a *sous-produit littéraire* (second-rate literature), and by the conception of the CNBDI, which opened in 1990, as gallery space rather than fun palace. Roland Castro's spectacular building includes a museum dedicated to preserving the patrimony through the collection of original *planches* (BD pages), thereby associating the medium with a notion of heritage.

In December 2000 an exhibition called Maitres de la bande dessinée européenne (Masters of European BD) was held at the Bibliothèque Nationale de France at its recently inaugurated François Mitterrand site. The preface to the catalogue, written by the director of the BNF, a member of the Académie Française, compared BD artists such as Tardi and Régis France to the novelists Céline and Proust respectively, thereby suggesting that, like literature, BD has a canon and so a rightful place in this bastion of official culture (Angrémy, 2000: 9).

The cultural visibility of an art form may also be measured by the volume of critical work which it generates. In 1997 Harry Morgan and Manuel Hirtz catalogued over 700 books and special editions of journals devoted to BD, almost all of which were produced from the 1960s onwards. However, the vast majority of these works treat BD not as an art, to be discussed in aesthetic terms, but as an object of mass consumption, to be investigated for the mythologies that it embodies. *Astérix*, for example, has been variously viewed as a symbol of Gaullism through its narrative of resistance to invaders, or, alternatively, as a satire of the fifth republic project of modernization and centralization.

Some early theoretical work did set out to legitimize BD as an art form. Some writers, such as Blanchard (1969), traced a historical lineage for it, going back to cave paintings and the Bayeux tapestry. Others, such as Lacassin (1971), sought to raise the status of the medium by arguing that it shared certain formal features with cinema. However, the claim that BD is an art form seems more convincing if it can be demonstrated that, rather than being a variant of some prevously existing art, it has specific features all of its own. Rodolphe Töpffer, whose *histoires en estampes* (stories in the form of engravings), produced in the 1830s and 1840s, have been taken as the first examples of BD, was convinced that he had invented a new art form, the uniqueness of which lay in the indissociability of images and words (Töpffer, 1994: 161).

In the 1970s BD was taken up by the fashionable academic discourse of semiology, and its formal features were investigated in their own right: analyses of the codes and signifying practices of the medium were produced in prestigious journals such as *Communications*, which in 1976 devoted a whole issue to BD. It was here that Fresnault-Deruelle expounded a view that was to become influential: that there was a tension on a BD *planche* between the linear representation of a narrative sequence, which works through discontinuity, and the surface seen as a tableau-like continuous whole, in which effects such as symmetry may arrest the flow of the narrative. Fresnault-Deruelle's insight has been further developed by Peeters (1998), who argues that artists who exploit the medium's formal resources to maximum effect will use a 'productive' layout, in which the narrative is actually engendered by the creative tension between linear and tabular dimensions.

A number of different aspects of the medium have been put forward by other analysts in the search for specificity. The role of the inter-frame blank is frequently evoked. Van Lier (1988), for example, asserts that its importance lies in its capacity for facilitating transformations from one frame to the next, so that where film is essentially sequential, BD is 'mutational'. Groensteen (1999a) proposes a further dimension through which BD images may relate to each other, beyond relationships created by articulations and transformations between adjacent frames or through the formal patterning of a *planche* as a whole. He contends that resemblances and correspondences between spatially distant *vignettes* (BD frames) throughout an album create what he calls *tressage* (interwoven) series, serving to add symbolic and thematic resonance. The mode of reading of a BD, which allows for the reader to return to previous *planches*, means that these visual echoes can work to powerful effect.

The existence of a body of academic literature devoted to the analysis of BD, along with the creation of the CNBDI, suggest a certain institutionalization of the medium. Moreover, the area of BD production which is recognizably 'artistic' has expanded since the growth of independent publishing houses, a notable development since the 1990s. However, the place of BD within the cultural hierarchy still does not seem entirely secure: its coverage in the mainstream press is irregular, and the public image of the BD artist was strikingly portrayed by Dupuy and Berberian in their 1994 *Journal d'un album* (Diary of the Making of an Album). Here, in response to Berberian's admission of his occupation, a taxi driver says, 'Ah oui, je vois ... vous faites des conneries, quoi ...' ('Oh I see ... you do that kind of crap ... ').

POST-WAR BD FOR CHILDREN AND ADOLESCENTS; THE RISE OF ADULT BD IN THE 1960S AND AFTER MAY 1968

Although the origins of BD may be traced to the satirical and political journals of the nineteenth century, for the first half of the twentieth century it was restricted almost exclusively to children's magazines. In the post-war period the market was dominated by magazines such as *Le Journal de Mickey*, containing American strips, and by two Belgian publications: *Tintin* and *Spirou*, both owned by Catholic publishing houses. *Tintin* featured the work of Hergé and his fellow École de Bruxelles artists, E. P. Jacobs and Jacques Martin, all of whom employed the drawing style known as the *ligne claire*: clear outlines, absence of shading and geometrical precision of décors. The more exuberant graphic line of the *Spirou* artists, particularly Franquin, has been called the *style Atome* in reference to its fascination with modernity and machines.

The return of an adult readership can be attributed to the evolution of the French magazine *Pilote*, founded in 1959 and edited by Goscinny, in which his and Uderzo's *Astérix* series appeared from the beginning. By the end of the 1960s, the adolescent readers of *Pilote* had become students, and stayed with the magazine, which featured anti-heroes such as the unshaven, hard-drinking and gambling cavalry officer Blueberry, from Charlier's and Giraud's western series (from 1963). The codes of the medium were disrupted by artists who used reflexivity as a comic device: Greg's self-important bourgeois Achille Talon (from 1963) would repair the side of a speech balloon where the text was slipping out, and Gotlib would create complicity by a direct address to the reader.

Meanwhile, the satirical magazine *Hara-Kiri*, in which BD co-existed with other types of material, set about attacking taboos of all kinds, and the battle lines drawn up in 1968 were prefigured as the government used heavy-handed tactics to try to stifle the politically and sexually provocative work of artists including Wolinski, Reiser and Cavanna. The magazine was banned in 1961 and 1966. In 1969 the *Hara-Kiri* team brought out *Charlie Mensuel*, dedicated to ambitious and experimental BD, such as that of the South American expressionists Breccia and Munõz.

Many more artists felt the need to push the boundaries of both formal resources and subject matter in the aftermath of 1968, and, ironically, Goscinny, whose editorship of *Pilote* was felt by some to be over-directive, fell victim to the desire of certain artists to 'kill the father' (Groensteen, 2000: 180). Mandryka, Claire Bretécher and Gotlib left to launch the magazine *L'écho des savanes* in 1972. Unlike *Pilote*, it had no aim of being *tous publics* (for children and adults) and had *réservé aux adultes* on the cover. Mandryka could now give free rein to the intellectualizing delirium of his justice-dispensing vegetable, the *Concombre masqué* (Masked Cucumber), while artists such as Masse and Vuillemin railed against corruption and social injustice through the chaotic rage of the *ligne crade* (filthy line), in a radical break from the narrative and graphic clarity that underpinned the ideological certitudes of Hergé's *ligne claire* (which would however be resurrected in the 1980s in the form of pastiche and nostalgia).

The *Pilote* exiles' collective was short-lived: Bretécher soon left *L'écho des savanes*, and it was in the news magazine *Le Nouvel Observateur* that *Les Frustrés*, her famous satire of the neuroses and obsessions of a Parisian left-wing milieu, appeared. Gotlib left in 1975, to found *Fluide glacial*. They had, though, provided the inspiration for many more artists who wished to break away from more mainstream publications and set up alternative structures. Another *Pilote* author, Giraud, in his other incarnation as Moebius, was the co-founder in 1975 of the publishing house

Les Humanoïdes Associés whose magazine, *Métal hurlant*, was dedicated to science fiction with the philosophico-mystical tonality favoured by 1970s counterculture.

Censorship continued to be used against BD. The 1970s had opened with the banning of *Hebdo Hara Kiri* (a weekly version of the monthly *Hara-Kiri*), after its celebrated headline 'Bal tragique à Colombey: un mort' on the death of de Gaulle ('Tragic dance at Colombey [de Gaulle's village]: one death'.) With flagrant hypocrisy, the ban was announced as being occasioned by 'pornography' in a previous issue. Even under the more liberal régime of Giscard d'Estaing, elected in 1974, a number of bans were imposed (on the feminist magazine, *Ah Nana!*, for example, in 1978, after an issue on homosexuality), and the decade ended with a conference on freedom of expression at the Angoulême salon in 1979.

BD AS AN INDUSTRY

Up until the 1970s, BD was press-based: most people would buy their BD in a newspaper kiosk rather than a bookshop. Series were prepublished in magazines, and followed by an album only if they were deemed to be successful. A restructuring of the market took place in the recession-hit climate of the 1980s, however, as small publishing houses were bought out by major publishers. As a result, the magazines lost their cutting edge, readers deserted them and they closed down. Of all those founded in the 1970s, only *Fluide glacial* has survived into the twenty-first century, still selling 90,000 per month, although it was bought out by Flammarion in 1990. (*L'Écho des savanes* still exists, but was bought out by Albin Michel in 1985 and turned into an erotic magazine.)

BD had gradually started during the 1970s to occupy a more important position in the book-publishing sector. Where 50 albums had been published in 1965, by 1982 almost 1,000 albums a year were being produced, and sales were 18.5 million. The bubble then burst: in 1983 sales dropped to 12.3 million and went on falling gradually. The crisis was compounded as magazines folded and publishers no longer had the opportunity to absorb production costs by prepublishing series; by the end of the decade major publishers needed to sell 15,000 copies of an album to gain a return on their investment, compared with 7,000 ten years previously. Various strategies were adopted: the merchandising of BD-related products began to assume increasing importance, and, in contrast to the experimental and often politically radical BD of the 1970s, there was a general retreat into escapist genres, heroes and series. This tendency is exemplified by the best-selling *XIII* created by Vance and Van Hamme, the story of an amnesiac seeking both to discover his identity and to prove his innocence of the assassination of the president of the United States. The series began in 1984 and by the end of the decade was selling 200,000 per episode.

By the 1990s four publishing giants, Dupuis, Dargaud, Glénat and Casterman, controlled 80 per cent of the market. In 1999 Casterman was itself bought out by Flammarion. At the beginning of the 1990 the market for albums appeared to be stagnating, with annual sales running at 10 or 11 million, but in 1996 the enormous success of *L'Affaire Francis Blake,* in which E. P. Jacobs's heroes Blake and Mortimer (MI5 agent and professor of nuclear physics respectively) were resurrected nine years after their creator's death by Ted Benoît and Jean Van Hamme, had an electrifying effect on sales. The album sold 700,000 copies and was the best-selling book (across all sectors) of the year. Since 1996, BD sales have continued to rise; in 2000, 28 million albums were sold. Conservatism still reigns in the commercial sector, though, however buoyant the market: Groensteen has asserted that 90 per cent of all current BD falls into the category of genre or series. He suggests that the stranglehold of series leads to an industrialization of the process of creation and an infantilization of the readership (Groensteen, 1999b).

In a climate in which mainstream BD seems to have lost its ambition, two key developments stand out. The first of these is the growth of the *manga* phenomenon, the impact of which began with Glénat's publication of Otomo's *Akira* in 1990. This incursion into France of Japanese youth culture occasioned a flurry of press articles condemning *mangas* as both simplistic and violent. This charge is certainly exaggerated, and *mangas* should be credited with enabling BD to regain a following among younger readers, who had turned away from the medium towards computer games.

The second development is the resurgence of small independent publishing houses, which have set up alternative distribution systems with the aim of reaching a public who would see BD not as consumer product but as art form. They include L'Association, founded in 1992, which publishes the review *Lapin* alongside albums; Ego comme X, set up by a group of art students from Angoulême in 1994; Cornélius; Éditions Amok and the Belgian Fréon. Their output represents only 10 per cent of the sales of specialist bookshops (and a negligible percentage of those of outlets such as FNAC) and they are in no position to offer financial security to the artists who contribute to them. Their artistic influence has, however, outweighed their economic marginality; they have been innovative not only in visual and narrative terms but also through their subject matter, which has extended BD into areas of emotional life and subjectivity, notably through a focus on autobiographical material. Moreover, the independent sector has had its own best-selling phenomenon: the first volume of Marjane Satrapi's autobiographical *Persepolis*, recounting her childhood during the Islamic revolution in Iran, published by L'Association in 2000 with a print run of 3,000, had reached its seventh edition two years later and sold 36,000 copies. The following two volumes, dealing with her exile in Europe where she is confronted with a disorientingly different set of cultural norms around the female body, have been equally successful.

GENRES OF BD AND KEY AUTHORS

The figure of the *aventurier* was central to the children's BD of the first part of the twentieth century. Hergé's hero Tintin tirelessly embarked on missions to right wrongs in a career which lasted from 1929 to 1976. E. P. Jacobs's Blake and Mortimer were repeatedly called upon to save the free world from the machinations of totalitarian states between 1946 and 1970. In the 1980s and 1990s the genre evolved into reportage, and a new type of post-colonial, post-Cold War *aventurier* emerged, typified by Daniel Ceppi's Stéphane Clément, whose travels lead him to deal with unpalatable sociopolitical realities, such as a cover-up over the involvement of the British army in an explosion in Belfast. He himself becomes morally compromised, however, as he colludes with those in power in order to rescue individuals.

One variant of the adventure genre, science fiction, has been strongly represented in BD. The magazine *Vaillant*, published by a Communist party publishing house, included Poïvet's and Lecureux's series *Les Pionniers de l'espérance* (The Pioneers of Hope) from 1945. This was based on the adventures of a multi-ethnic group of space travellers who set out to spread a message of tolerance. In the 1960s science fiction became a vehicle for eroticism: Jean-Claude Forest's *Barbarella*, the first of a number of semi-clad heroines, appeared in 1962. In the 1970s, Druillet's work in *Métal hurlant* brought baroque full-page compositions and a grandiose cosmic vision to science fiction. In the same magazine Moebius further challenged narrative and graphic conventions: in the 1976 dialogue-free *Arzach*, for example, the hero's appearance changes from one frame to the next. *Métal hurlant* also included Chantal Montellier's more politicized science-fiction work, in which post-apocalyptic scenarios offer a critique of totalitarian regimes. This non-escapist tendency within the genre was continued in the work of Enki Bilal in the 1980s. His *Nikopol* trilogy has an atmosphere of dilapidation and squalor, albeit sensually depicted through the use of direct colour. The thematic is based on petty power struggles, whether among eastern-bloc politicians or gods from Egyptian mythology.

Heroic fantasy overtook science fiction in popularity in the 1980s. Science gave way to magic and the future was replaced by an indeterminate historical setting, usually medieval, although in the most commercially successful example of the genre, Rosinski and Van Hamme's *Thorgal* (from 1977), the hero has been brought up by Vikings. Many heroic fantasy series rework the trope of the quest, but replace the idealized knight by a more cynical or materialist figure. Bragon, the middle-aged knight of Loisel and Le Tendre's 1983–7 *La Quête de l'oiseau du temps* (The Quest for the Bird of Time), may meet spellbooks and elves on his journey, but his quest ends in madness and death. Alongside heroic fantasy, a number of albums which might more properly be called *fantastique* appeared in the 1980s, most famously in the work of Schuiten and Peeters. In their albums fictional worlds which seem to be constucted on rigorous architectural principles are gradually invaded by disturbing elements, such as, in the 1985 *La Fièvre d'Urbicande* (The Fever of Urbicande), a metallic cube which begins, uncannily, to expand into a steel network which engulfs the city.

Historical BD underwent a revival in the 1980s, but its tone of moral ambiguity broke with the tradition established by Jacques Martin's *Alix* series, which appeared in *Tintin* magazine from 1948. Martin's narratives of restoration of order and justice were renowned for the painstaking authenticity of their decors, often used by teachers to illustrate Roman architecture. In the 1980s, fidelity to history was taken to mean that sex and violence should be given their due place. Bourgeon's *Les Passagers du vent* (Passengers borne on the Wind) (1979–84), which features the journey of two white women on a slave ship, has its quota of nudity, but also offers a complex narrative which allows for the expression of conflicting ideological standpoints on slavery. *Les 7 Vies de l'épervier* (The Seven Lives of the Hawk) by Cothias and Juillard (1983–91) interweaves the historical narrative around the death of Henri IV, who is demystified by a naturalistic portrayal of his sexual indulgences, with a fictional narrative involving a masked *justicier*. The 1990s saw a greater concern for twentieth-century history: Tardi's 1993 *C'était la guerre des tranchées* (Trench Warfare) contrasted the nationalistic rhetoric of memorialization with the senseless slaughter in the trenches, while Lax and Giroud set out to uncover stories that had been suppressed from official histories: in the 1998–9 *Azrayen* they tackle the bloody reality of the 'peacekeeping' operation in Algeria.

The genre which marked the coming to adulthood of BD in the 1960s was above all social satire, and this vein has continued. Binet's working-class couple *Les Bidochon* have exemplified blinkered self-righteousness since 1977, while Margerin's more gentle satire of the suburban rockers Lucien and his friends, which first appeared in 1979, is nonetheless precise in its depiction of the cultural practices of Lucien's generation and that of his parents, signified through details of decor and possessions. Goossens has been ruthlessly demolishing the platitudinous discourse of television since the 1980s, most recently (since 1993) through the characters of *Georges et Louis*, media-age equivalents of Flaubert's earnest autodidacts Bouvard and Pécuchet. De Crécy and Chaumont are equally caustic in their representation of the Anglicism-filled discourse of management, in the 1995 *Léon la came* (Leon the Junkie). Baru, whose 1980s work had focused on male adolescent rituals in an Italian immigrant community in northern France, turned his attention in the 1990s to the crisis of masculinity in a post-industrial society in, for example, the 1995 road movie narrative of *L'autoroute du soleil* (Motorway to the Sun). Male anxiety also features in Dupuy's and Berberian's *Monsieur Jean* series, which began in 1991. The hero is a contemporary urban male, grappling with work, procrastination and the fear and attractions of commitment and fatherhood.

The thematic of contemporary society does not have to be treated on the mode of humour, however. In the 1990s, autobiography in BD became a major tendency, influenced by the highly introspective work of Edmond Baudoin, such as the 1983 *Passe le temps* (As Time Passes), in which he uses a raw, unfinished graphic line to give an intimate tonality to his depictions of (mostly) failed relationships. The permeability of inner and outer worlds in Baudoin's work is a feature of much subsequent autobiographical work. David B.'s five-volume *L'Ascension du haut mal* (1996–2000) recounts a childhood in which his family life was dominated by his older brother's epilepsy. As in Baudoin, subjectivity breaks through: here the inner turmoil of the narrator is expressed through battle scenes and the esoteric imagery of occult texts. David B.'s deceptively simple drawing style recalls wood engravings and is acknowledged by Marjane Satrapi as having influenced the stylized graphic line of *Persepolis*.

Dupuy's and Berberian's 1994 *Journal d'un album* is metanarrative in that it depicts not only the writing of one of their albums but the writing of the journal itself, which takes place during a period of marital crisis for one of the narrators, unsparingly recounted. Similarly, Lewis Trondheim's 1995 *Approximativement* (Approximately) and Jean-Christophe Menu's *Livret de phamille* (Family Record), published in the same year (*see* Figure 10.1), represent their personal lives and their immediate circle of collaborators in the micro-universe of BD with unstinting frankness. In all three of these albums, the everyday world is invaded by wish-fulfilment fantasies and by figurations of anxiety or guilt. The most complex and accomplished example of the BD autobiography genre is Fabrice Neaud's four-volume *Journal* (1996–2002). Neaud's realist graphic style offers, in places, an almost forensic rendition of life in an averagely homophobic small town, while elsewhere his experiences of marginality and of euphoria or rejection in a number of relationships are conveyed through metaphor or through blurred subjective images.

CASE STUDY

JEAN-CHRISTOPHE MENU

In 1987, in the magazine *Glob'off*, which was distributed to the Angoulême salon 'off' (fringe), Jean-Christophe Menu attacked the dominance of escapist and erotic BD, which was inhibiting the development of more ambitious work. After meeting Lewis Trondheim, an encounter which is chronicled in Menu's *Livret de phamille*, he was encouraged in his desire to launch a publication which would resist the formulaic agenda of commercial publishers, and reach all those who were prepared to leave behind both 'the middle ages and puberty' (Menu, 1990: 1). *L'Association*, set up in 1991 with five other artists (Trondheim, David B., Matt Konture, Stanislas and Killofer), is, literally, an association, financed in part from readers' subscriptions and in part by the Centre National du Livre. Its success in reaching a readership outside mainstream commercial circuits not only inspired other collectives to found their own independent publishing houses, but prompted major, non-BD, publishers such as Flammarion and Le Seuil to produce series which copied the format of the independent albums, and which were marketed as quality products for intellectuals.

As well as being instrumental in renewing both the landscape of BD publishing and its subject matter, Menu has also espoused the cause of formal experimentation. In 1993, he was involved in the creation of OUBAPO (Ouvroir de Bande Dessinée Potentielle) (Potential BD Sewing Circle), on the model of OULIPO, the Ouvroir de Littérature Potentielle, set up in 1960 by Raymond Queneau, among others, and later joined by Georges Perec. OUBAPO aimed to exploit the formal resources of the medium by building in constraints, a technique that had underlain Menu's and Trondheim's 1991 *Moins d'un quart de seconde pour vivre* (Less than a Quarter of a Second to Live), in which the visual element is restricted to permutations of the same eight images. The name chosen for this consciously avant-garde initiative alludes to the history of the medium through its homage to one of BD's greatest artists: the first two syllables of OUBAPO felicitously recall the cry of Franquin's Marsupilami, most legendary of all BD animals. In 1997, in the preface to a volume of theoretical texts and practical applications of OUBAPO principles, Menu pointed out that a large proportion of BD production was still entrenched in heroic fantasy and/or eroticism: 'les donjons-dragons et les nichons-ballons' (castles, dragons and tits) (Menu, 1997: 9). This is undeniable, but equally indisputable is the fact that the independent publishers have provided a space in which a more demanding version of the medium can continue to co-exist with its mass-market counterpart. Menu's own incarnation as a BD character in Trondheim's *Approximativement*, in which he disrupts the proceedings of an editorial meeting, recalls the many unruly brats who have inhabited the medium throughout its history. This brat must, however, be given much of the credit for ensuring that innovative BD has been able to survive and, modestly, flourish.

SUGGESTIONS FOR FURTHER READING AND FOLLOW-UP

You should now have some sense of the scope of BD, and the kinds of debates to which it gives rise in France. Many of the artists mentioned in this chapter have their own websites; that of Schuiten and Peeters, www.urbicande.be, is particularly impressive. If you go to www.bdparadisio.com you will find links to BD publishers in both the mainstream and the independent sectors, and you will get an impression of the visual style and the subject matter covered by both. Try to visit Angoulême during the festival at the end of January, where you will experience the buzz generated around the medium and you may meet some famous artists, as well as thousands of BD readers. Even if you can't get there in person, follow the awards ceremony in the press (both *Le Monde* and *Libération* cover it in detail, but it also gets mentioned in the English-speaking press), as the critics and columnists will not only tell you which artists and albums are most highly rated, but also give their views as to why. The CNBDI (www.cnbdi.fr) is, though, worth visiting all year round, as it has an extensive

Figure 10.1 Livret de phamille *by Jean-Christophe Menu*

library of albums and theoretical works as well as temporary and permanent exhibitions. The Centre Belge de la Bande Dessinée in Brussels (www.brusselsbd-tour.com/cbbd.htm), housed in a beautiful Horta building, also has a well-stocked library, and the second-hand BD shops in Brussels are a paradise for *bédéphiles*.

If you want to pursue the study of BD, it is useful to start by (re)acquainting yourself with Hergé, whose work laid down the codes of the medium in its most classic form but also prefigured, through the 1963 *Les Bijoux de la Castafiore*, the deconstruction of those codes. A considerable amount of the critical work that exists on BD concerns Hergé, and this album in particular, so it is as important for BD students to read it as it is for film studies students to watch *Citizen Kane*. There is less critical commentary to be found on the work of more recent artists, but Peeters (1998) and Groensteen (1999a), like Baetens and Lefèvre (1993), use multiple examples in their discussion of the formal resources of BD, and these may inspire you to follow up on the work of the artists cited. Have a look too at some of the work being done in the area of autobiography; if you don't read French you will find both David B.'s and Marjane Satrapi's work in English translation. Show them to your friends, and they will begin to understand the unique fascination of BD.

FURTHER READING

Baetens, J. and Lefèvre, P. (1993), *Pour une lecture moderne de la bande dessinée* (Brussels: CBBD). Through the discussion of seven key BD albums, the authors demonstrate a range of techniques of analysis.

BIBLIOGRAPHY

Angrémy, J. P. (2000) Preface to *Maîtres de la bande dessinée européenne*. (Paris: Bibliothèque Nationale de France/Seuil).

Blanchard, G. (1969) *La bande dessinée* (Verviers: Marabout Université).

Fresnault-Deruelle, P. (1976) 'Du linéaire au tabulaire', in *Communications*, 24, pp. 7–23.

Groensteen, T. (1999a) *Système de la bande dessinée* (Paris: Presses Universitaires de France).

Groensteen, T. (1999b) 'Genres et séries' in *9e Art*, 4, pp. 78–87.

Groensteen, T. (ed.) (2000) *Astérix, Barbarella & Cie: Histoire de la bande dessinée d'expression française* (Paris: Somogy Éditions d'art Angoulême: CNBDI).

Guillaume, M. A. and J. L. Bocquet (1997) *Goscinny* (Paris: Actes Sud).

Lacassin, F. (1971) *Pour un 9e art, la bande dessinée*. (Paris: Collection 10/18).

Menu, J. C. (1990) editorial in *Labo*, 1.

Menu, J. C. (1997) 'Ouvre-Boîte-Po', in *OUBAPO* (Paris: L'Association).

Morgan, H. and M. Hirtz (1997) *Le Petit Critique illustré* (Montrouge: PLG).

Peeters, B. (1998) *Case, planche récit: lire la bande dessinée* (Tournai: Casterman).

Töpffer, R. (1994) *L'invention de la bande dessinée*, ed. T. Groensteen and B. Peeters (Paris: Hermann).

Van Lier, H. (1988) 'La bande dessinée, une cosmogonie dure' in T. Groensteen (ed.), *Bande dessinée, récit et modernité* (Paris: Futuropolis, pp. 5–24).

CHAPTER 11

Leisure

Bert Gordon

Three years after the French government legislated a 35-hour work week (on 13 June 1998), an electrical worker in suburban Paris extolled the change, which, he said, enabled him to take three-day weekends, giving him time for both rest (*repos*) and leisure (*loisirs*). He no longer had to choose between the two (Rodrigues, 2002). Introduction of the 35-hour work week continued a trend in France, from the late nineteenth to the late twentieth century, which saw the average work time of a city laborer decline from 4,000 hours per year to 1,600. The increased leisure time allowed for the growth of a wide range of activities to supplement the time spent merely resting from physical labor. Post-Second World War French economic growth and productivity, especially during the *trente glorieuses* (the 30 glorious years) from the Liberation in 1944 through the oil crisis of 1973, underlay the expansion of leisure activities such as tourism, the cinema and television. In 1990, French sociologist Joffre Dumazedier suggested the coming of a leisure revolution, in which, for the first time in the history of technological societies, the average amount of free time in the week was more than that of work time (Dumazedier, 1990: xvii).

The state played an important role in the expansion of leisure time in France, starting with the Popular Front's introduction in 1936 of the eight-hour work day and two-week paid vacations (*congés payés*) the latter extended progressively, culminating with the legislation of a five-week paid vacation by the newly elected socialist government of François Mitterrand in 1981. An increase in average household purchasing power and a lowering of work hours for wage-earners (*salariés*) in France offered enhanced leisure opportunities to a new 'baby-boom' youth generation, women who entered the workforce in growing numbers and drew increased salaries, and an ageing population, healthier and wealthier than ever before. Young people in the 1960s watched Johnny Hallyday in theaters and on television at home, women increasingly enrolled in adult education programs, and an older population became consumers of a broad variety of leisure activities, including tourism and the purchase of secondary residences. Television, which grew exponentially as a leisure activity from the 1950s onward, brought urban mores increasingly to the rural and small-town population, now less isolated from Parisian styles and tastes.

By the beginning of the twenty-first century, some in France feared that the increase in leisure had devalued labor and the work ethic. Others saw in the increase in leisure a loss of traditional French values, sometimes called the *exception culturelle française*, and too much borrowing from America. The enhanced leisure world of France, especially the creation of Euro Disney and the popularizing of Halloween in the 1990s, was to these critics an Americanization or 'coca-colonization' of France. Greater market segmentation in leisure activities offered consumers more specialized magazines in place of general-interest publications, cinema multiplexes instead of single theaters, a variety of FM radio stations offering more diverse programming than before, and enhanced choices, notably among theme parks, in tourist destinations.

Life in France had changed dramatically since the Second World War and sociologists and historians struggled to understand it. Writing in the late 1990s, Alain Corbin, a French historian, suggested that not all the elements in the history of leisure had yet been understood (Corbin, 1998: 63). Paul Yonnet agreed, suggesting that the future history of leisure would be as complex and changing as those of labor, war and religion. The relationship of demographic and gender issues in the expansion of leisure in France is at issue in the study of leisure history but even more basic is the definition of leisure itself, as one person's leisure might be another person's work. Leisure and holidays are a large subject that include many of the activities addressed in other chapters in this book, especially in France in the second half of the twentieth century, for which so much documentation is available. Tourism, which grew dramatically after the Second World War, plays a major part in leisure, so it, too, will be addressed, as will vacations and free time.

SOME DEFINITIONS OF LEISURE AND RELATED TERMS

The French term *loisirs* is generally used in the plural, as by the suburban Parisian electrical worker mentioned above, to represent the many different forms of leisure pursuits and the fact that leisure is understood to mean activity rather than simply rest. Aristotle was the first to make leisure (*scholè*: meaning leisure and education together) the principal activity of the free man. The term 'leisure', according to the encyclopedic and etymological dictionary *Trésor de la langue française* (TLF), seems to have first appeared in French in the early twelfth century as 'the ability to do something'. As the term evolved in French, it acquired a double meaning, referring favorably to the honorable use of one's free time, in the spirit of the Roman *otium*, or, if unfavorably, to a wasteful idleness (*oisiveté*). Worse yet was the gendered 'woman of leisure' (*femme de loisir*), the courtesan, or woman of ill repute.

The post-Second World War growth of leisure was highlighted in 1962 when Joffre Dumazedier asked in the title of a book whether France was headed toward a leisured society (*Vers une civilisation du loisir?*). At a time when leisure was expanding in France, Dumazedier called attention to the need to give to the study of leisure the same attention that the subject of labor had already commanded. He noted that leisure included activities at the end of the work day, which had shrunk during the twentieth century, the weekend, and the progressively expanding annual *congés payés*. Underscoring the sheer size of the subject, Dumazedier addressed tourism, cinema, television, the book, education, shows, spectator sports and do-it-yourself household tasks (*bricolage*), which, he added, could be considered work by some but leisure activities by others. As if foreseeing the suburban Paris electrical worker's praise of the 35-hour work week, Dumazedier wrote that leisure satisfied the needs for rest (*délassement*), diversion or amusement (*divertissement*) and personal development or education (*développement*) (Dumazedier, 1962: 20 and 27). Reflecting Dumazedier's conceptualization, the TLF offers as synonyms for leisure: '*récréation, repos, vacances*'.

The French term *fête* for festivals and holidays is derived from the Latin *festa*, and is defined by the TLF as 'any event which delights especially in breaking with routine'. Terms related to 'holidays' include 'vacations' (*vacances*) and 'free time' (*temps libre*). 'Vacations' (*vacances*) is defined as a 'period during which one does not work'. 'Free time' (*temps libre*) referred in 1821 to time that one could dispose of as one wished, and, in 1967, to time devoted to non-professional activities or leisure, representing a 'traditional opposition' between labor and free time, between routine obligation and creative liberty. The word 'tourist' spread from the English and appeared in French in the early nineteenth century, although the phenomenon existed earlier.

THE POST-WAR LEISURE REVOLUTION

The post-war surge in leisure time had its origins in nineteenth-century industrialization. In the mid-nineteenth century, the effective work week in manufacturing approached 75 hours. Growing working-class organization and demands, however, combined with the increased productive ability of French society to offer more time away from work. In France, an unpaid week's holiday (*congé hebdomadaire*), legislated in 1906, and the *congés payés*, written into law in 1936, extended the leisure time available to industrial workers. Peasants in the early twentieth century also became more affluent and began to eat and dress better. They traveled to organized games and sports, such as football, with an attendant growth of stadiums, dance halls and beer halls.

The end of the Second World War marked the victory of leisure as a commodity and the intensification of what Alain Corbin called a 'fun morality' (Corbin, 1995: 10–11). In 1948 the Declaration of the Rights of Man, approved by the United Nations General Assembly, provided for the rights to rest and leisure, paid holidays, and for all to take part in the cultural life of the community, participate in the arts and benefit from scientific progress. Post-war expansion of leisure came largely in the areas of diversion and personal development, for example in movie attendance, television viewing, tourism and adult education programs, rather than in rest, to use Dumazedier's terms. The baby boom of the post-Liberation years and the 1950s set the stage for a shift toward development of family planning in 1960 and an enhanced youth culture of sexual freedom in the 1960s.

By 1962, when Dumazedier's book was published, baby-boomers had become teenagers, whose idols included singers Johnny Hallyday and Sylvie Vartan. *Salut les copains*, a radio show broadcasting popular music, began in 1959 and gained immediate success. A magazine with the same name was launched in July 1962 and three years later sold a million copies for the marriage of Johnny and Sylvie. One in three French persons, or 16 million, was under age 20 in 1962. Some 4 million, the oldest of this youth cohort, disposed of 50 billion fr., much of it spent on new styles of clothing. Again, in 1962, the Renault auto maker gave its workers a fourth week of paid holiday. It is hardly surprising that Dumazedier's *Vers une civilisation du loisir?* was published in the same year. The end of the Algerian War in 1962 ushered in an era of peace for France, which had been in almost continuous warfare, from the Second World War, 1939 through 1945; through the Indochina War, 1946 through 1954; and, finally, the Algerian War, which had begun in 1954.

The youth who came of age during the 1960s were better fed and arrived at puberty earlier than their predecessors, influencing youthful leisure expectations and activities, and sexual culture and gender roles, all highly impacted by the introduction of the birth-control pill in the early 1960s and its growing use after the May–June 1968 student revolt. Although the *gauchistes* (leftists) of 1968 often criticized the consumer society, they also looked toward sexual liberation and enhanced hedonism, claiming the right to leisure, which had been articulated in 1880 in Paul Lafargue's *Droit à la paresse*. Organized feminism in the early 1970s led to the Loi Veil, allowing for abortions, in 1975.

A 1967 INSEE (Institut National de la Statistique et des Études Économiques) survey of French leisure activities, which listed 24 of them, was repeated in 1987/88 to see what patterns had changed in France after 20 years of increased leisure. In the late 1980s, 48 per cent of those interviewed said that they went out at least one evening per month, for meals in the homes of parents and friends, in contrast to 30 per cent in 1967. Other leisure activities showing growth during the 20-year period included the playing of board games (*jeux de société*), the playing of music, and the assembling of various kinds of collections. There were also increases in visits to museums, historic monuments and exhibitions. Museum visiting grew more among the rural population, perhaps because of greater mobility with increased automobile use, which also favored tourism in general. From 1967 through 1987, automobile ownership in France increased from 50 per cent to nearly 75 per cent of all households.

The largest increase in French leisure-time activity over the 20-year period surveyed by INSEE came in watching television. *Télévision Programme Magazine*, established in 1955, recorded 60,000 French households with sets at the end of 1953 and over 220,000 in August 1955. Television viewing in France lagged behind the United States and Britain during the 1950s and 1960s but its impact was widely felt. On 18 April 1960 Johnny Hallyday, then an aspiring popular singer with only a small following, appeared on the television show *L'École des vedettes*, hosted by Aimée Mortimer. Sales of his records 'Laisse les filles' and 'T'aimer follement' jumped from 12,000 in a month to 100,000 in the days that followed. In 1967, according to INSEE, 7 per cent of French households owned a television set and 51 per cent of the population watched television, whether or not they owned a set. By 1987, 94 per cent of French households owned at least one set and 83 per cent of the population watched television every day. The time spent in front of the television by urban adults averaged two hours and ten minutes daily, an increase of 20 minutes between 1975 and 1986 (Dumontier and Valdelièvre, 1989: 3). This figure would increase to three hours and nine minutes in 1999, with adults 50 years and older watching an average of four hours and three minutes daily.

The only leisure activities that failed to do well were those in competition with television, specifically visits to cafés. Survey respondents visiting cafés at least once weekly declined between 1967 and 1987–8 from 24 per cent to 18 per cent and the reduction was especially noteworthy among men. As a site for masculine sociability, the café seemed to be in decline. In addition, with more receivers in homes, fewer people visited the cafés to watch television. Daily newspaper reading declined, while magazines gained readership. New leisure pastimes included computer use – the Minitel had gained popularity by the late 1980s – and video recording activities. Attendance in restaurants nearly tripled, from 8.4 per cent to 24.6 per cent in the 20-year period covered by the survey (Dumontier and Valdelièvre, 1989: 44–5).

Film attendance in theaters declined from 423 million in 1947 to 119 million in 1989, when only 47 per cent of the French over 15 years old reported having gone to the cinema more than once in the previous year. In 1986 there were 500 movie theaters in Paris, with a total of more than 5,000 theaters, holding some 1,100,000 seats, in all of France. These figures represented an increase in the number of theaters, from 4,200 in 1972, but a decrease in the number of seats, 1,900,000, during the 16-year period, indicating a shift to more but smaller theaters, with the creation of multiplexes for more specialized audiences. The number of films shown remained constant from 1976 through 1984, with a ratio of 35 per cent French in origin, an important issue for the government which continually promoted French films in preference to those of foreign, especially American, production. Comedy was the most popular form of film. Pornographic film attendance surged in the early 1970s, but after 1975 X-rated films stopped receiving state aid. By 1984, only 3 per cent of the surveyed public attended X-rated films, compared with 10–25 per cent in the early 1970s. In 1985, 950 feature-length films were shown on French television, with an estimated 4 billion viewers, or more than 20 times the number seeing films in the theaters (Université de Bourgogne, 1990: 9–12). The growth in television-viewing as opposed to theater-going also spoke of the increased comfort of French homes in the post-war period.

While reading the daily newspaper declined by 1990, magazine reading increased with the appearance of more specialized publications. In addition to the 95 per cent of French households that owned at least one television set in 1990, some 56 per cent of households owned a hi-fi radio receiver and a proliferation of FM radio stations allowed the broadcast of more music, especially to farmers and the retired. The most commonly listened to music types, in order, were: popular songs (*chansons*), instrumental music, rock, and jazz (Université de Bourgogne, 1990: 4–5). Among the most widely read books in France were how-to books, on subjects such as gardening, do-it-yourself home projects (*bricolage*), and diet for one's cat or dog. Laurence Pernoud's *J'attends un enfant* (I am Expecting a Baby) had sold more than 200,000 for each of the prior 30 years (Université de Bourgogne, 1990: 18).

In addition to a heightened youth culture, the second half of the twentieth century witnessed an ageing of France's population. Life expectancy at birth, 63 years for men and 68.7 for women in 1950, increased to 69 and 76.9, respectively, by 1974. Men aged 60 in 1974 could expect to live an additional 16.4 years, women an additional 21.3. As of 1978, more than 60 per cent of France's 7.3 million retirees over age 65 (*troisième age*, or 'third age') were women (Souyris and Delage, 1979: 34–5). By the year 2000, the life span in France for men was 75.2 years and for women 82.7. The effect of this feminization of the senior age groups meant that there was a preponderance of women seeking collective leisure activities such as university programs and group tours that offered them a replacement family network. With an older population and more adult children, family gatherings also became a leisure activity. In 1990, the state legislated the possibility of retiring at age 60 in France, enhancing the retiree community as a market for the many leisure activities available.

THE SECULARIZATION OF HOLIDAYS AND VACATIONS

During the middle ages the year was divided by a series of religious holidays, including Christmas, Carnival and Easter, with popular celebrations and feasting. In addition, local fairs (*fêtes foraines*), some with religious origins dating to medieval France, gave rise to traveling road shows and circuses with live animals. Jacques Tati's 1948 film, *Jour de fête*, offers a sense of the excitement generated by the annual visit of a traveling fair to a small French town. Changing social preferences and traffic problems led to a banning of live animal shows in the streets of Paris in 1954. France currently celebrates as legal holidays (*fêtes légales*): New Year's Day, Easter Monday, Labor Day (1 May), End of the Second World War Day (in Europe – 8 May), Ascension Day, Pentecost Monday, Bastille Day (14 July – *fête nationale*), Assumption Day, All Saints' Day (*Toussaint*), Armistice Day (11 November – end of the First World War) and Christmas. Celebrated each year with a fireworks show, the 2002 Paris *fête nationale* also commemorated the bicentennial of Victor Hugo's birth. If one of the holidays falls on a Tuesday or Thursday, the adjacent Monday or Friday is often treated informally, if not legally, as a holiday, to make a 'bridge' (*pont*) for an extended weekend.

Although many of the venerable religious holidays continue to be celebrated, the establishment of a school holiday in summer was a result of the Third Republic's policy of universal education in the late nineteenth century and was more a response to the need for help in the fields at harvest time than a desire to enhance leisure. For pedagogical reasons, some of the older religious holidays were privileged above others. New Year and Easter became legal holidays marking the end of trimesters of the school year. Currently the French school holidays are set several years in advance by the education ministry. They include a week off for Toussaint, two weeks for Christmas, a two-week winter vacation which varies in late February depending on where in three administrative zones in France a school is located, a two-week spring vacation, also varying by zone from early to late April, and a two-month summer break in July and August.

Christmas remains the favorite holiday in France, continuing a pattern dating back to the first survey on the subject in 1948. Although Christmas had long-standing religious roots, it was the Victorians who popularized it as a family holiday, expressing the bourgeois values of privacy and family joined together, in a refuge from the rapidly industrializing outside world. By the end of the nineteenth century, Santa Claus, or Père Noël in France, had developed as a giver to all children, regardless of their social status, and the image fit well with the expansion of large department stores and their advertising campaigns. The celebration of Halloween during the late 1990s was popularized with increases in Jack O'Lanterns, masks and related decorations, and so noted in 1996 by the *Washington Post*. Halloween's increased popularity led to renewed complaints about American influence in France but defenders of the new fashion argued that Halloween had developed in Ireland, and only later traveled to America, so that the holiday was not really American, after all. Others emphasized that Halloween was merely superimposed on the older religious Toussaint holiday and so did not represent an enlarged American influence. By 1999 three out of ten people in France celebrated Halloween, in contrast to eight out of ten celebrating Mother's Day and seven out of ten Easter. French bishops warned publicly that the *carnavalesque* Halloween atmosphere was subverting the respect to the dead previously associated with the festival.

The extension of school holidays and the introduction of the summer vacation meant that, whereas children of the bourgeoisie might have the chance to spend several weeks in the country, those of the urban poor, without rural relatives willing to accept them, were condemned to spend hot summer months in enforced idleness on city streets. To address this issue, vacation colonies (*colonies de vacances*) were created, the first one by Wilhelm Bion, a Zürich pastor, who sent 68 children into the nearby mountains in 1876. French *colonies*, serving both girls and boys, appeared during the early 1880s and were sponsored by the church religious charities, as well as secular teachers. The camps also began attracting middle-class children, sent to share the open-air experience, which came to be considered a vital part of their education. By 1902, the Paris *Colonie de Vacances* Committee alone sent 5,329 of a total 142,287 grade-school children to experience a rigorous hygienic rural outdoors regimen in camps with activities organized to instill a sense of rootedness in the French soil. During the inter-war years *colonies de vacances* continued to grow and the state played an increasingly important role. With the advent of the two-week *congés payés* in 1936, more than 5,000 colonies enrolled over 100,000 children in France. The government took over an ever-increasing role in the organization and administration of the *colonies* (Gordon, 2001b: 59).

Colonies de vacances continued to grow during the post-war years, serving a million children plus 200,000 adolescents in 1956. After 1958, however, the *colonies* became one of the few vacation activities that stagnated, as families, with greater resources, took more vacations together with their children. In the 1960s cultural attitudes shifted away from the more authoritarian and hierarchical practices of the *colonies*, as well as the Catholic Youth and the Young Communists. To survive, the *colonies* turned to more egalitarian programs that emphasized sports, often organized by theme, such as skiing, sailing, hiking or equestrianism.

THE PRIVATIZATION OF TOURISM

A major factor in the evolution of leisure in France during the second half of the twentieth century was the increase in tourism, facilitated for the French and others during the second half of the nineteenth and first half of the twentieth centuries by railway, steamship, automobile and airplane. Train service extended the possibilities for recreational bicycling and the first *Tour de France* bicycle race was staged in 1903. Railway construction was accompanied in France by an almost doubling in the extent of communal roads between 1871 and 1911. The first Michelin guidebook was published in 1900, and by the 1920s Michelin was reviewing restaurants. Improved hygiene eliminated many of the diseases common in the Mediterranean region, a necessary precursor to the tourist influx of the later twentieth century. In 1910 France established an Office National du Tourisme, to encourage tourism, under the minister of public works. Sun-tanning surged in popularity between the wars while the coming of the automobile made more regions accessible.

The post-Second World War increase in foreign tourism to France was symbolized in the American film *Rhapsody in Blue*, with music by George Gershwin, in 1945. Featuring the story of a romantic liaison of Gershwin's during a visit to Paris on his first trip abroad, the film includes Gershwin's music from *An American in Paris*, with scenes of Paris taxis, the Eiffel Tower, Montmartre, Notre Dame and its Portal, the Folies Bergères, and can-cans, the dance in which women lift their skirts, often associated with 1890s Montmartre. A reprise was produced as *An American in Paris* in 1951. In 1970 France ranked third, behind Italy and Canada, in the number of tourist visits measured by the World Tourism Organization (WTO). The French Revolution bicentennial celebrations helped move France into first place, where it has remained since 1988. During the 2002 summer tourist season France received some 76.5 million visitors. This figure is undoubtedly inflated because France counts arrivals in both directions, going to and from northern Europe to Spain, so tourists are frequently counted twice or more. In terms of tourist income, France drops to third place, behind the United States and Italy. From 1979 through 1989, the average stay in France was reduced from 9.4 to 7.3 days.

Domestic tourism within France was encouraged by the adoption of the *congés payés* in 1936, stimulating the developing youth hostel movement (*Auberges de jeunesse*) which emphasized touring in and becoming acquainted with the various regions of France, though few toured in comparison to the post-Second World War years. During the Second World War, thousands of German soldiers and civilian officials were given tours of occupied France by *Wehrmacht* authorities, and French hoteliers continued to ply their trade and plan for better times. A significant post-war revival in tourism began with the introduction of the inexpensive Renault 4CV and Citroën 2CV automobiles in France in 1947 – making automobile travel available to a growing number of workers – and the arrival of the first airborne package tour in Corsica in 1949. In 1951, 60 per cent of French vacationers used trains to go to their destinations compared with 24 per cent who used automobiles. By 1957 this ratio had shifted to 47 per cent on trains and 41 per cent in cars (Dumazedier, 1962: 131, note 2). The post-war economic recovery of the mid-1950s, together with the economic and political stability engendered by the Cold War and the coming of the Common Market, contributed to a large increase in tourism globally. French tourists traveling to foreign countries, however, remained relatively constant in number, in contrast to vacationers from Germany, Switzerland, Scandinavia and the Benelux countries who traveled abroad in greater numbers in the early 1990s.

Plans for 'social tourism' (*tourisme associatif*), where state and trade-union tourism organizations would make travel vacations available to all, in the image of the *colonies de vacances*, had accompanied the advent of *congés payés* in the 1930s but the social tourism model declined after the 1950s. The extension of the *congés payés* and the popularity of the small Renault and Citroën cars, together with Anglo-American styles of advertising appealing to a sense of individual well-being, reoriented the dreams of organizing the leisure of the worker away from *tourisme associatif* to a more individual and family-oriented model. Here again, the individualist American model seemed to triumph over a more socially oriented French structure. Club Med, conceived in 1950 as a non-profit organization to make seaside vacations available to the less affluent, evolved to a more market-oriented profit-making commercial model by the 1960s (see case study, pp. 161–2). In 1982 the National Agency for Vacation Checks (*Agence Nationale pour les Chèques-Vacances, or ANCV*), was established under the ministry of tourism to help make vacations accessible for those of modest means. Assistance in the form of *chèques-vacances* enabled more than 5 million people in France to take vacations away from home between 1982 and the 20th anniversary of the ANCV in March 2002. With the help of the *chèques-vacances* program, the per centage of French people staying home during their vacations was cut from one-half to one-third in the period between 1982 and 2002. Unlike the *colonies de vacances* participants, however, *chèques-vacances* beneficiaries generally traveled independently rather than in groups.

The growth in tourism by the end of the twentieth century transformed earlier economic sectors. In France, the Canal du Midi generated more income from tourism than from the shipment of industrial goods. Southern France drew more than half its income from the holiday trade. By the end of the twentieth century, the French continued to tour more extensively in their own country than did many of their European neighbors. Following the market segmentation pattern of other leisure activities (such as magazines, in which the general-interest publications gave way to the more specialized; cinema, in which general audience theaters gave way to multiplexes; and radio, in which the expansion of FM increased the specialization of the programming), the tourism market also diversified. Some travel agencies focused on 'cultural' or heritage tourism to museums, battlefields and other historic monuments; whereas others, under the rubric of 'urban tourism', specialized in touring within the cities, often Paris. Still other agencies sought clients for 'adventure tourism', meaning travel to distant and unusual places, mountain climbing or river-rafting. 'Eco-tourism' focused on natural parks and travel with as little disturbance as possible to the environment.

Theme parks, reflecting the segmentation of tourism in France, also gained popularity, with several competing sites opening in the late 1980s. In 1987, Futuroscope, a theme park oriented to high-tech video media, including 3-D film and virtual-reality rides, was opened 5 miles (8 km) north of Poitiers and attracted some 225,000 visitors. Futuroscope added big-screen films and Cinerama (wraparound film) and by 1994 attracted 2 million visitors. In 1989, Parc Astérix opened in a forest, 22 miles (35 km) north of Paris. Based on the popular cartoon figure, created by René Goscinny and Albert Uderzo and which first appeared in the French children's magazine *Pilote* in 1961, Astérix represented ancient Gallic resistance to Julius Caesar and the conquering Romans with an implicit resistance to American popular culture as well. Parc Astérix featured French history and attracted 1.35 million visitors, of whom 85 per cent were French, during its first year. At first, Parc Astérix attendance plateaued with the opening of Euro Disney in Marne-la-Vallée, just east of Paris, in 1992, but ultimately the two appear to have complemented one another and Astérix's attendance has risen steadily. The blockbuster French film, *Astérix et Obélix contre César*, produced in 1999 by Claude Berri and intended to break Hollywood's cinematic domination in France, also contributed to Parc Astérix's popularity.

Euro Disney lagged in popularity in the early 1990s partly because of poor infrastructure, such as insufficient space for buses, and partly because it had been patterned after the American model, and, as such, had been the subject of considerable controversy. Adjustments were made and, by the beginning of the twenty-first century, Euro Disney became the most popular tourist attraction in Europe, attracting 12.5 million visitors annually, more than twice the number of visitors to the Eiffel Tower. Euro Disney visitors were 40 per cent French, 57 per cent other European, with the remainder from the rest of the world. Walt Disney Studio Park opened in Paris on 16 March 2002 with a goal of extending the total visitor count to both Disney parks to 17 million per year. Its managers planned a 'Disneyland Resort', a mini-city comprising the 'magic kingdom' and its dependencies, the park cinema, Disney village, hotels and a 27-hole golf course, together with the commercial center of Val-d'Europe and an international business park. Euro Disney management anticipated an average stay of two or three days there, facilitated by the coming of the 35-hour work week. The company Pierre et Vacances planned to transform day trips to its Paris-Val-d'Europe leisure park into one- and two-week stays, and Marriott's Village Île-de-France park looked toward a clientele of golfers in 2003. A new theme-park competitor appeared in February 2002 when Vulcania, the project of former President Valéry Giscard d'Estaing, opened in Saint-Ours-les-Roches, near Clermont-Ferrand in the Auvergne. Conceived in 1992 by Giscard, then president of Auvergne's Conseil Régional, Vulcania was an underground volcanic park which drew more than 500,000 visitors during the 2002 tourist season.

The leisure parks sought to attract young families on school vacations and the growing population of retirees. A French government study in 1992, which addressed the growing population of younger retirees with longer life spans and increasing pensions, noted that they could anticipate more years of good health and had 'a curiosity for travel and discovery' (Ministère du Travail, 1992: 59). Retirement programs at earlier ages encouraged more travel and secondary residences, and contributed to the development of tourist centers such as the Côte d'Azur. Older tourists often provided vacation trips or secondary residences for grandchildren while the younger parents worked. Occasionally three generations, including children, parents and grandparents, took vacations and went on tour together. Retirees sometimes took up permanent residence in areas they had discovered during previous visits. However, an increased number of the French were taking vacations in their secondary residences, limiting their travel and thereby alarming the tourist industry at the beginning of the twenty-first century.

Perhaps the most significant change in French leisure patterns initiated by the coming of the 35-hour week in 1998 was the shift by many workers in the use of their leisure time – again using Dumazedier's categories – from the end of the work day to the end of the work week. Rather than reduce their work day by one hour, workers often accumulated their extra hours to take three-day weekends instead. The new Walt Disney Studio Park and the Pierre et Vacances trips to its Paris-Val-d'Europe leisure park were designed with the increased three-day weekends in mind, catering to a new clientele that included the suburban Parisian electrical worker who wanted *loisirs* along with his *repos*.

CASE STUDY

THE CLUB MED

The history of the Club Med encapsulates the demographic shift toward an older population and the change in emphasis from *tourisme associatif* to commercial and individualized tourism during the second half of the twentieth century. Created in 1950 to make seaside vacations available to all Europeans, Club Med evolved to become the seventh largest travel company in Europe and the largest in France in 2001.

On the Côte d'Azur in 1935, Russian refugee Dimitri Philipoff and some friends created the Club de l'Ours Blanc, a non-profit organization designed to make vacations affordable to people of modest means. The club emphasized sports and swimming in the Mediterranean and, more importantly, cavorting in skimpy swimsuits. Inspired by the Club de l'Ours Blanc, Gérard Blitz, a Belgian diamond cutter and champion swimmer, and his sister Didy, created Club Med in 1950 and established its first vacation villages in Mallorca. In preparation for the 1950 season, Blitz contacted Gilbert Trigano, a former French Second World War Resistance leader, who, in the fall of 1949, was in business selling American surplus tents. At first, guests slept in surplus army tents and cooked their own food. The early Club Med rejected both bourgeois hotels and popular-class hostels and emphasized the beauty of the body as a countercultural spectacle. Blitz and Trigano became partners in 1954. Those who joined the Club became 'gentle members' (*gentils membres*) or 'G.M.'s'; those who directed the villages became 'gentle organizers' (*gentils organisateurs*), 'G.O.'s'. In 1961 Club Med came under the financial control of Edmond de Rothschild, who kept the Blitz-Trigano team but steered the club in a more profit-oriented direction. During the economic expansion of the 1960s, Club Med villages were advertised as the escape from the commercial urban rat race. The introduction of the Boeing 747, which carried more passengers at less cost than previous airplanes, made Asia and the Americas more accessible to Club Med. By the 1970s, in what turned out to be a window between the coming of the birth-control pill in the 1960s and the AIDS epidemic of the 1980s, Club Med had become famous for its hedonistic youth culture of *bouffer, bronzer et baiser* (eat, tan and make love), which helped eroticize the images of the Mediterranean, Polynesia and the other tropical locations of the vacation villages (Gordon, 2001a: 59).

The ageing of the baby-boom generation and the fear of AIDS in the early 1980s, together with the development of sex tourism in Thailand and elsewhere, made it difficult for Club Med to maintain its market niche. To survive in the demographically older market of the late 1990s, Club Med sought to shed its hedonistic image, adopt a more family-oriented tone, and reposition itself by promoting a more 'cultural' tourism, focusing on visits by local music and dance troupes to the vacation villages and club visits to local historic sites. Attempts to diversify its offerings, with the creation of Oyyo, a cheaper style of vacation village, however, seemed to degrade Club Med's image. Impacted, as was much of the travel industry, by the 11 September 2001 attacks against the United States, Club Med posted financial losses in the first half of 2002 as bookings declined. In the six months up to 30 April 2002, the company lost €25 million in contrast to a €6 million profit a year earlier. As of June 2002, cumulative bookings were down by 14 per cent compared with the previous year, although evidence indicated a coming upturn with more people planning vacations for later in 2002. Club Med was struggling in a changing leisure and tourism market.

SUGGESTIONS FOR FURTHER THINKING AND STUDY

Alain Corbin's comment that not all the elements in the history of leisure have been fully understood is a call for greater conceptual clarity and further research. In addition to the work on leisure by Dumazedier, one may consult Roger Sue, *Le Loisir* (Paris: Presses Universitaires de France, 1993 [1980]) and Paul Yonnet, *Travail, loisir. Temps libre et lien social* (Paris: Gallimard, 1999), a sociological study of the development of leisure in France. Two books by André Rauch, a specialist in the history of vacations in France, are *Les Vacances* (Paris: Presses Universitaires de France, 1993) and *Vacances en France de 1830 à nos jours* (Paris: Hachette, 1996). The personal story of Gilbert Trigano, one of the principal figures in the Club Med, is told in Alain Faujas, *Trigano. L'aventure du Club Med; avec une postface de Gilbert Trigano* (Paris: Flammarion, 1994). Club Med's early history and its countercultural ethos are discussed by Alain Ehrenberg, 'Le Club Méditerranée 1935–1960', in *Autrement. Les Vacances. Un rêve, un produit, un miroir. Série Mutations*, 111 (January 1990).

In addition to historical and sociological studies, useful sources for further study include fictional literature, such as Jean-Jacques Sempé/René Goscinny, *Les vacances du petit Nicolas* (Paris: Denöel, 1994) and films, notably Roger Leenhardt's

Les Dernières Vacances (1947), the story of a boy regretting the last holiday in his family's sold country house; Jacques Tati's *Jour de fête* (1948), referenced above, and his *Les Vacances de M. Hulot* (1953), featuring the comic misadventures of Monsieur Hulot at a beach resort; and Bertrand Tavernier's *Une semaine de vacances* (1980) in which a young Lyon school teacher reflects on her career and personal life during a week's vacation.

Questions, however, remain for further consideration. Are the definitions of 'leisure' sufficiently precise to enable us to approach the subject systematically? Have the differences between 'leisure' and 'work' been clearly demarcated? Are Dumazedier's categories of rest, diversion and personal development valid or do they need to be refined? What does it mean to say that one person's leisure is another person's work? Can the expansion of leisure activities, and tourism in particular, be reconciled with the need to preserve ecological balances on earth? Much has been made of an *exception culturelle française* differentiating France from other countries. Is this concept valid for French leisure practices of the past half century? Is America really dominating French leisure practices?

Additional areas for study include the relationship of leisure, holidays and tourism to age cohorts in France. How was leisure impacted by the youth culture and student revolt of 1968? How did the emergence of an older population in the late twentieth century impact leisure pastimes? How are the leisure and tourism practices of these groups differentiated by gender, social class, religion and urban versus rural status? Has the trend toward more leisure and shorter work time, culminating in the 35-hour work week in France, devalued the work ethic, as some maintain?

Finally, a set of questions concerning sources for leisure and tourism in France. How may government and industry statistics be combined with written memoirs, travel accounts, works of fiction and films to broaden and deepen our understanding of French leisure? How may material objects be used, for example, in helping to analyze the development of *bricolage* in France? If a museum of French leisure were to be constructed, what kinds of objects should it display?

BIBLIOGRAPHY

Corbin, Alain (1995) 'L'avènement des loisirs', in Alain Corbin (ed.), *L'Avènement des loisirs 1850–1960* (Paris: Aubier).

Corbin, Alain (1998) 'La révolution des loisirs', in *L'Histoire*, 226 (November).

Dumazedier, Joffre (1962) *Vers une civilisation du loisir?* (Paris: Seuil).

Dumazedier, Joffre (1990) Preface, in F. Comte, J.-J. Luthi and G. Zananiri, *L'Univers des loisirs* (Paris: Letouzey and Ané).

Dumontier, Françoise and Hélène Valdelièvre (1989) *Les Pratiques de loisir vingt ans après 1967/1987–1988, Insee Résultats. Consommation – Modes de vie* (Paris: INSEE), no. 3.

Gordon, Bertram M. (2001a) 'Club Méditerranée', in Michael Kelly (ed.), *French Culture and*

Society: A Glossary (London: Arnold).

Gordon, Bertram M. (2001b) 'Colonies de vacances', in Michael Kelly (ed.), *French Culture and Society: A Glossary* (London: Arnold).

Ministère du Travail (1992) 'Direction des industries touristiques', *Le Tourisme social et familial* (Paris: La Documentation Française).

Rodrigues, Graziella (2002) 'Le vendredi, je ne travaille presque plus jamais', *Le Parisien*, 9 July, 3.

Souyris, Jean-Denis and Bernard Delage (1979) *Voyage et Troisième Age* (Talence: Maison des Sciences de l'Homme d'Aquitaine).

Université de Bourgogne (1990) *Étude de la France. Quelques aspects culturels, juillet 1990* (Paris: Centre International d'Études Françaises).

CHAPTER 12

Sport

Phil Dine

MAKING SENSE OF FRENCH SPORT

Sport is something that has become so familiar in developed industrial (or even post-industrial) societies like France that it is tempting to feel that it is already 'known' and 'understood'. However, deeper inspection will reveal that sport is a complex phenomenon that benefits from exploration using explanatory terms and techniques drawn from the major disciplines of the social sciences, including particularly history, geography, politics, sociology, economics and even philosophy. This is true in any society in which sport is played (which nowadays means the overwhelming majority of nations), but is particularly clearly the case in the French context. In the discussion that follows, attention will be drawn to some of the key issues raised by sport in contemporary France. As a popular cultural practice that touches the lives, at one level or another, of the overwhelming majority of French citizens, sport is certainly hard to ignore. Indeed, the simple fact that it matters so much even to those people who either consciously or unconsciously reject its system of values is evidence of its abiding social significance. So, whether it is the focus of passionate interest, verging sometimes on quasi-religious fanaticism, or rather an object of personal resentment or intellectual derision, sport has a symbolic resonance that cannot easily be disregarded. Sport in France is consequently a particularly rich site of tensions and conflicts, and may thus productively be considered by students of French society. For what is so often at stake in French sport is nothing less than a conception of France itself: *une certaine idée de la France (sportive)*, as it were. This explains why a variety of struggles have regularly occurred over such issues as the following: attitudes to the body, hygiene and fitness; the concept of the Republic and its achievement of *grandeur*, both at home and abroad; the conflict between intellectualism and 'sportiness', particularly in the education system; the preservation of bourgeois pleasures in the face of cultural democratization; and the defence of 'authentic' French activities and associated values, against first British and then American cultural domination. It is this pattern of individual and communal investment – and often over-investment – in sport, both in psychological and political terms, which underpins its importance as a major field of popular cultural activity in France.

THE HISTORICAL ORIGINS OF FRENCH SPORT

The historical origins of modern French sport are to be found in the later nineteenth century, and more specifically in the enthusiasm for all things British of a privileged section of the society of the day. Impressed by the military and industrial might of the British Empire, then in its heyday, an influential group of aristocrats and members of the emergent urban middle classes looked to the English (and to a lesser extent Scottish) public-school system for clues to the obvious successes at home and overseas of France's traditional rival. This search became all the more urgent in the wake of the country's disastrous defeat in her war with Germany in 1870, which, among other things, revealed the nation's youth to be significantly weaker and more inclined to illness – and thus less fit for military service – than that of her belligerent continental neighbour. What the French visitors to England discovered was an education system that placed at least as much emphasis on the physical and psychological training encouraged by regular involvement in sport as it did on its more obviously scholarly components. Impressed by what they found, these pioneers of French sport would seek to transform their own country's education system through the introduction of such familiar 'English' games as football – both in its association (soccer) and rugby forms – rowing and athletics.

While this influential group's impact was only limited as regards educational reforms, their initiatives would nevertheless lay the foundations for the modern French system of sports associations and federations. Indeed, such was their zeal as advocates of the new games that these sporting pioneers would have a lasting impact on the organization of modern sports well beyond the borders of France. So, for instance, football's world governing body is still the Fédération Internationale du Football Assocation (FIFA), while motor-sport, up to and including Formula 1, is similarly governed by the Fédération Internationale de l'Automobile (FIA). Similarly, Jules Rimet, the French president of FIFA and the founding father of the football World Cup competition, which was inaugurated in 1930, was commemorated with the famous trophy that bore his name – made of 1,800 grams of solid gold and designed by another French national, sculptor Abel Lafleur – and which was won outright by Brazil in 1970 and so replaced by the current trophy. However, it was Baron Pierre de Coubertin who was to have the most abiding French impact on the world organization of sport. As the founder of the modern Olympic Games, which first took place at Athens in 1896, Coubertin established the single most important sporting event in the world, and one which to this day has a global resonance that far surpasses even the most important manifestations in other cultural domains.

Although these pioneers and their successors were active in France from the later nineteenth century onwards, the new games only directly affected a small number of participants, almost exclusively male and drawn essentially from the privileged classes. In particular, this meant from the upper echelons of the education system – i.e. the most prestigious schools and colleges – and from certain high-status professions such as medicine. Of course, many more people followed sport as spectators than were directly involved in it as players, turning for information to the burgeoning popular press, before the radio and later television emerged to feed this new hunger for sporting information. This was particularly true of the first indigenous sport to emerge in France, cycle road-racing, which developed around the turn of the century as an off-shoot of the professional track competitions that had become popular in the purpose-built *vélodromes* that had sprung up in the main urban and industrial centres from the 1880s onwards. This new activity grew rapidly in importance to become the most important spectator sport in France, for reasons that have at least as much to do with geography (and demography) as they do with history.

GEOGRAPHY, DEMOGRAPHY AND THE TOUR DE FRANCE

As a large, relatively sparsely populated and predominantly agricultural country, the France of the late nineteenth and early twentieth centuries would see modern sports develop in ways that reflected its particular geographical and, especially, demographic characteristics. So, while Paris, as the national capital, was undoubtedly an important centre in the early days of French sport, other towns and cities subsequently overtook it as the various games were introduced and expanded. Rugby provides a particularly clear example in this regard, with its epicentre shifting first from Paris to Bordeaux, and then to Toulouse, even deeper in the south-west, which has long been regarded as the game's spiritual home (see pp. 174–5 for a more detailed case study). A similarly strong regional dimension is apparent in the case of football, where Paris, in spite of the periodic successes of the Paris Saint-Germain club, nowadays appears somewhat peripheral in comparison with other centres. These range from the former coal-mining and steel-working communities of the north and east (epitomized by Lens) to the Rhône valley at the other end of the country, with the great port of Marseille displaying an obsession with the local team's achievements (and failings) that has echoes of Naples and other Mediterranean football centres. Similar patterns of distinctly local sporting implantation and affiliation are visible in basketball (where small-town and suburban clubs such as Cholet, near Orléans, and Villeurbanne, on the edge of Lyon, play a disproportionately important role), handball and volleyball, as well as in authentically traditional sports such as *pelota* in the Basque country on France's border with Spain.

However, it was the sport of cycle road-racing that was to prove uniquely well adapted to the still characteristic French landscape of scattered villages and small towns. As epitomized since 1903 by the great annual event of the Tour de France,

professional cycle racing broke with the patterns of organization, and crucially investment, that would lead to the construction of ever larger stadiums for city-based and
ticket-paying sports spectators. It thus established a qualitatively new relationship
with the French spectator that has ensured its continued success for a century. Julian
Barnes has recently summed up its special character particularly well:

> [T]he Tour remains extremely popular in France. This is the more surprising given
> that the last French victory, by Bernard Hinault, came fifteen years ago. Since then
> the race has been won by two Americans, two Spaniards, an Irishman, a Dane, a
> German, and an Italian. In 1999, not a single stage was won by a Frenchman; in
> 2000, they managed just two out of twenty-one. Such robust zeal for the victories
> of others confirms the suspicion that the French sports fan tends to be as much a
> devotee of the sport itself as of the team or nation, to be more of a purist than his
> Anglo-Saxon equivalent.
>   [...] But cycling is also different in one key respect. In other sports, fans go to
> a stadium, where there are entrance fees, tacky souvenirs, overpriced food, a gen-
> eral marshalling and corralling, and a professional exploitation of the fan's emo-
> tions. With the Tour de France, the heroes come to you, to your village, your town,
> or arrange a rendezvous on the slopes of some spectacular mountain. The Tour is
> free, you choose where you watch it from, bring your own picnic, and the market-
> ing hard sell consists of little more than a van offering official Tour T-shirts at sixty
> francs a throw just before the race arrives. Then you get to see your heroes' gri-
> macing faces from merely a few feet away; every seat is a ringside seat. These
> aspects make the Tour unique, and still rightly cherished by the French.
>
> (Barnes, 2002: 90–2)

Moreover, this century-old appeal shows no sign of lessening, in spite not only of the
continuing lack of success of French competitors, but also of the periodic crises that
hit the event, such as the Festina drug scandal of 1998. Indeed, if there is a single
event that sums up modern French sport as a popular cultural *spectacle*, then that
event can only be the Tour de France.

MASS PARTICIPATION AND THE ROLE OF THE STATE

As regards contemporary French *participation* in sport, however, we need to look
elsewhere. Prior to the Second World War, actually taking part in any of the range of
sporting activities theoretically available still remained limited to a relatively small,
and often financially privileged, segment of the population. Indeed, it was only after
the catastrophic military defeat and occupation of France by the Germans in the
summer of 1940 that sport expanded from being the preoccupation of a social and

educational elite to become the passion of a significant minority, if not actually the majority, of the French population (including, for the first time, significant numbers of women). This paradoxical evolution may be understood in terms of the 'National Revolution' undertaken in the wake of the armistice by the collaborationist French administration based in the 'free' (i.e. unoccupied) southern zone of the defeated country. With its headquarters in the small spa-town of Vichy, the new regime set about a programme of moral and political improvement for the French population that also, for the first time, included a significant programme for physical education and sports. In fact, this area became one of the main priorities of the Vichy administration, and, in spite of the obvious practical difficulties that beset France, proved to be a major success.

Unprecedented levels of public investment were committed to sport at this time: at least 20 times the amount of money made available by even the most sport-friendly government in the pre-war period, the left-wing Popular Front of 1936–8. Under the leadership of Jean Borotra, a widely respected tennis star of the 1920s, Vichy's programme of state-sponsored sports development both established a precedent that has been followed by all subsequent French governments and laid the foundations for French sporting success in the post-war period. In particular, the funding by central government of both major sports infrastructure and a nationwide network of specialist sports personnel (administrators, coaches, teachers and the like) is a basic principle of the French sports system that has only been even slightly modified in very recent years, with a measure of decentralization towards the regions, but never seriously questioned. In short, the role of the state in French sport from 1945 to the present has been characterized by a willingness to provide significant levels of financial support in return for the right to establish the general organizational frameworks of both elite and mass sporting activities.

Central to this managerial approach is the state's legal assumption since 1945 of responsibility for the overall management of French sport and its formal recognition (since 1975) of the public-service mission of the national sports federations. This has meant that successive governments have continued to fund both mass and elite sport at levels significantly higher than would be the norm in neighbouring continental European countries, let alone in the Anglo-Saxon cultures of sporting private enterprise that prevail in Great Britain and, especially, the United States. This state support may take the form of direct grants, but also involves the maintenance of a large body of coaches and other technical advisers, who are made available to the sports federations at national, regional and departmental (i.e. county) levels, and who are all paid by central government, with the official status of *fonctionnaires* (civil servants).

In return, the ministry for youth and sport sets the broad parameters of sporting activity in France – for instance, by requiring the various sports federations to issue official *licences* for all players at all levels – and intervenes in the case of disputes or other perceived crises in particular federations. This leading role for the state has encouraged some commentators to see France's administrative regime as more akin to the former countries of the communist eastern bloc, and to speculate unfavourably on the relationship between the sporting decline of these nations since the fall of the Berlin Wall in 1989 and the remarkable achievements of France's state-managed system (most visibly at the Olympic Games) in the same period. Meanwhile, those more favourably disposed have pointed to the significant role played in this sustained competitive success by the Paris-based Institut National du Sport et de l'Éducation Physique (INSEP), which has, since its opening in 1975, been a cornerstone of government intervention in the sporting sphere, and particularly as regards the selection, preparation and support of the nation's elite athletes.

Over the five decades since the end of the Second World War, such state management has undoubtedly helped France to become an ever more obviously 'sporting' nation. This has been reflected not only in the high levels of success achieved by French competitors in international sporting competitions, but also in patterns of mass participation, and in the associated levels of spending by French households on sports-related items. So, for instance, according to figures published by the French ministry of foreign affairs in 1999, the number of sporting licenciés (officially registered members of the national federations responsible for individual sporting disciplines in France) had trebled over the period since 1970, to make up one in four of the total population (Ministère des Affaires Étrangères, 1999: 139). To this figure must be added the very many French men and women who regularly take part in some kind of sport-based leisure activity outside the national sports federations – anything from aerobics to skateboarding – which means that nowadays half of all French people state that they periodically participate in one sporting activity or another, as compared with around a third in the 1980s and just over a quarter in the 1960s (Cauhapé, 1997). The most popular competitive sports are football, tennis, judo, the quintessentially French form of bowls known as boule or pétanque, and basketball, in that order; while skiing remains the most important winter sport. Tennis and skiing, in particular, are important examples of the democratization of sports that were previously socially exclusive, and in which rapid advances in popularity were made – in part thanks to a variety of government-supported initiatives, such as the classes de neige for children – between the 1960s and the 1980s. The amount of money spent by French people on these and related activities (such as fees for fitness centres and leisure clubs, which, as elsewhere in Europe, have seen a very rapid expansion over the past decade) means that sports expenditure (including purchases of sports equipment) is now (at over 16 per cent) easily the biggest single item in the average French household's cultural and leisure budget (Cauhapé, 1997).

The specificity of the French approach to sport may further be perceived in the way in which the state has now brought physical education and sports fully into the national education system, thus conferring on such activities both academic authority and social legitimacy. This is essential if sport is to be taken seriously in a country that is still, to a very large extent, an educationally based meritocracy. The existence of competitive recruitment examinations (*concours administratifs*) for sports managers is one sign of the official recognition nowadays accorded to the sporting sphere, as is the inclusion of the assessment of performance in physical education and sports in the *baccalauréat* school-leaving examination. These sports elements thus contribute in a significant fashion (currently 16 per cent of the overall grade) to this all-important qualification, which gives students the right to enter university, where accredited modules (*unités de valeur*) in skiing and other sports are also now available. Moreover, such courses are increasingly taught by tutors with the highly prestigious *agrégation* teaching qualification, which has, since 1983, been opened up to those specializing in Sciences et Techniques des Activités Physiques et Sportives (STAPS).

FRENCH SUCCESS IN MAJOR INTERNATIONAL COMPETITIONS

Such institutional commitment to (and, indeed, popular investment in) mass sporting participation may, together with the state-sponsored structures of support described above, go some way to account for the remarkable success of elite French competitors, both as teams and as individuals, in recent years. From this point of view, the period 1996–2001 undoubtedly represents a high point in French sporting fortunes. The Atlanta Olympic Games of 1996 saw France emerge as the world's fifth most powerful sporting nation, after the giants of America, Russia, a unified Germany and China. In 1998 France significantly enhanced its reputation as a host nation for major international competitions when, following the 1968 (Grenoble) and the 1992 (Albertville) Winter Olympics, the country organized the 1998 football World Cup. This event was not only a great success both in administrative and financial terms, but a huge achievement for the hitherto not conspicuously successful national side. Against all expectations, *Les Bleus* emerged victorious, beating the mighty Brazil 3–0 in the purpose-built Stade de France in Paris in the final. This startling victory has been much discussed by journalists, politicians and other social commentators, both within France and elsewhere. The spectacular celebrations that followed the victory were themselves of interest to sociologists, with no fewer than a million French citizens, including many who would not previously have expressed any particular interest in sport, taking to the streets of the capital to celebrate, amid scenes that were to be repeated in towns and cities across the country.

However, of more abiding significance was the manner of the national side's victory, or rather the ethnic composition of the side that had managed to triumph over the world's finest teams. For the French team was made up of players drawn from a variety of immigrant backgrounds, including several whose parents or grandparents, if not actually they themselves, had originally come from the North African or sub-Saharan territories of the former French colonial empire. The team thus contained as many black and brown faces as it did white ones, with even those apparently 'indige-nous' players having Spanish, Armenian or other 'non-French' family names and ancestries in several cases. The victory of this multiracial side was widely hailed not only as a sporting success, but also as a triumph for a new, more inclusive, con-ception of France and French identity: one in which the *black, blanc, beur* (black, white and Arab) ethnicity of the national football team was at least as important as the *bleu, blanc, rouge* of the national colours that its members had worn with such distinction. When this same side went on to add the European Championship title to their World Cup in 2000, such optimism was significantly reinforced; as, indeed, it was by the (again multi-ethnic) French victory in the 2001 men's handball world cham-pionships. However, the longer-term social and political impacts of such on-field suc-cess remain to be seen. What cannot be doubted, however, is the importance of the France '98 triumph as a popular cultural phenomenon, with over 23.5 million French people (or just under half of the total population), tuning in to watch the final match on television on 12 July 1998 (*Antennes*, 2001).

THE MASS MEDIA AND THE CULT OF THE STAR

The obvious success of this and other high-profile sporting competitions as com-mercial spectacles has led, inevitably, to the media, and particularly television, play-ing an increasingly important role in the administration of sport in France. In the most recent of its major surveys of the nation's cultural practices, carried out in 1997, the French ministry of culture and communication found that 25 per cent of the popula-tion had personally attended at least one paying sporting spectacle in the previous 12 months (Donnat, 1998: 42). However, this huge market is itself only part of a much bigger one that includes particularly the very significant spending by television companies on the rights to transmit elite sports events, and above all professional football matches. The most obvious indicator of the importance of this market nowa-days is the dramatic increase in the value of the contracts dealing with these broad-casting rights. So, for instance, French television companies paid only 5 million fr. (£0.5 million) for the rights to televize football in 1984, but this had risen to 700 mil-lion fr. (£70 million) by 1996. As elsewhere in Europe, the previous state broadcast-ing monopoly gave way at this time to a privatized marketplace, with important new bidders emerging in the form of cable and satellite broadcasters. These companies have helped to maintain the buoyancy of sport as a televized commodity, with broad-casting rights for football alone continuing to rise dramatically: to 1,100 million fr. in

1999 (£110 million); 2, 200 in 2000 (£220 million); and 2,600 million in 2001 (£260 million) (Bourg, 2000: 131). An important popular cultural benchmark from this point of view was set on the weekend of 16–17 September 2000, when, for the first time ever, a French television channel – in the event, the subscription channel Canal Plus – broadcast no less than 44 hours of sport over a 48-hour period (Constant, 2000).

This modern fascination with sport is most obviously visible in France, as it is in so many countries, in the cult of the sports star. It is in football that French sportsmen are currently most readily apparent on the European and world stages, with Zinedine Zidane, born in Marseille of Algerian Kabyle parents, continuing to represent a very special case. Zidane was the principal playmaker and the most easily identifiable icon of the multiracial national team that triumphed in the France '98 World Cup and the 2000 European Nations Cup. His enormous contribution to these French successes was internationally recognized when he was named FIFA World Footballer of the Year in 1998 and again in 2000; he has also been a driving force for the Italian giants Juventus and now the great Real Madrid in Spain. Zidane's achievements have thus mirrored those of such earlier stars of immigrant origin as Michel Platini and before him Raymond Kopa. Although less exalted, many other players have made a significant impact outside France, as have a number of managers, particularly in the neighbouring English Premiership. This exporting of strength by what is a relatively weak domestic French football league may turn out to have unwelcome consequences for the future development of the game in that country. However, it seems set to continue for the foreseeable future, in spite of the disappointment of the 2002 World Cup, which saw a lacklustre French team knocked out in the first round, after failing to score in any of their three group matches, with coach Roger Lemerre losing his job in consequence.

With none of the current crop of French professional cyclists having achieved anything like the recognition both within and outside France of such famous rivals as Jacques Anquetil and Raymond Poulidor (in the 1950s and 1960s), and Laurent Fignon and Bernard Hinault (in the 1970s and 1980s), we must look elsewhere for contemporary French sporting icons. Prior to her dramatic return home before the 2000 (Sydney) Olympic Games had even started, Marie-José Pérec, the then reigning double Olympic champion at both 200 and 400 metres, was certainly the leading French female athlete and, as a very striking black woman, also an icon of the successful sporting integration of France's ethnic minority populations on a par with Zinedine Zidane. Few other French stars have successfully made the transition to the world sporting stage, although the tennis-player Amélie Mauresmo, both through her muscular approach to the game, and through her courageous refusal to fit in with prevailing gender stereotypes – and specifically her 'coming out' as a lesbian – has invited comparisons with the great Suzanne Lenglen, who as the dominant female force in world tennis in the 1920s was France's first ever 'superstar'.

RUGBY FOOTBALL

Rugby football was mentioned earlier in this discussion to illustrate the significant regional dimension in French sport. It may now usefully be considered further to demonstrate how some of the themes discussed elsewhere in this chapter apply to a specific sporting discipline, and particularly to emphasize how sport in France has historically served as a setting for the playing-out of a wide variety of societal tensions and ideological conflicts. Like association football (soccer), this 15-a-side handling game of 'football' had its origins in the English public-school system, and was introduced into France in the 1880s by British expatriates. However, it owed its initial popularity in its adoptive country to the enthusiasm with which it was taken up by the students at the most fashionable Parisian *lycées*. From this prestigious social base in the capital, the new sport rapidly expanded into the regions, thanks especially to university students and to schoolteachers trained either in Paris or in the major provincial centres. The game was taken up with particular enthusiasm in the south-west of the country, for reasons that include the exceptional zeal of local partisans of the new sport (such as Dr Philippe Tissié of Bordeaux), as well as the ready adaptability of the game to established patterns of sociability in the small towns and villages of the region, and even a deep-rooted tradition of hostility in this area to the church, which happened to favour soccer at this time, particularly in its national network of Catholic youth clubs or *patronages*.

In the period between the two world wars, rugby became not only a marker of regional identity in the south-west – as part of a broader anti-northern, and particularly anti-Parisian, tendency in these still essentially rural provinces – but also a focus for intense local rivalries, with serious incidents of violence up to and including deaths occurring both on and off the pitch. This violence almost certainly had its roots in age-old inter-communal animosities, which all too easily found their expression in a game of bruising physical contact. Moreover, the process of democratization that had accompanied the game's implantation and popularization in the south-west had also removed the constraints on violent play imposed by the codes of sportsmanship imported from Britain and wholeheartedly accepted by the Parisian pioneers of the game. However, the regularly vicious rugby culture of the region was also fuelled by hard cash, as the sport – officially amateur until 1995 – became precociously commercialized and, crucially, illicitly professional in France.

The French game's violence (including in international matches), together with its formally unacceptable payment of players, would see France banned from international competitions from 1931 to 1940, when the Second World War isolated the country even more completely. Yet, with the enthusiastic support of the collaborationist Vichy administration, rugby would, remarkably, grow significantly in popularity during the war years. Its principal rival, the 13-a-side, and officially professional, game of rugby league, was actually banned by government decree, while mass participation in sport in general was encouraged as part of a fascistic 'National Revolution' that sought to shape bodies as well as to control minds.

Such was the boost given to French rugby in this period of isolation that it emerged in 1945 as a major force in the world game, regularly beating the best teams that its British originators and their former colonial dominions had to offer. The characteristically adventurous French rugby of this period – *le rugby-champagne*, as it became known and widely appreciated both inside and outside the country – was effectively marketed to a new national audience by the state-controlled radio and television stations, and was systematically encouraged by General Charles de Gaulle and his supporters. The most pragmatic of politicians, and the leading figure in France's wartime survival and post-war renewal, de Gaulle adopted rugby as a symbol of French sporting success to compare with the rapid industrial and technological advances being made by the country's booming (and, characteristically, state-managed) economy. Gaullist politicians regularly organized receptions for successful French teams as part of this mutually beneficial process of identification, while de Gaulle's famous ban on government meetings whenever France was playing in an international match has become part of the folklore of sport and politics alike. The appointment of Jacques Chaban-Delmas, a former international player, to the post of prime minister, in 1969, significantly enhanced the institutional linkage between the Fifth Republic (inaugurated by General de Gaulle in 1958) and this particular sport.

In more recent years, French rugby has had to respond to a variety of new pressures, including especially the official advent of the professional game in 1995, and the resulting migration of leading players, both within France and to the other major rugby-playing countries. It has also had to adjust to the increasing globalization of the sport, with the rugby World Cup, which only began in 1987, now the undoubted focus of the professional game. Unlike association football, where the national team has achieved conspicuous success thanks in large part to the effective integration of the country's ethnic minorities, rugby has not, with a few notable exceptions, managed to extend its recruitment beyond its predominantly white heartlands in the south and west. Nor has the *XV de France*, for all its achievements in international competitions, ever achieved anything like the national acclaim and global recognition of the 1998 and 2000 football team. Whether the game is actually capable of developing beyond its current base of players and spectators must, in fact, remain in doubt, and its long-term future may, in consequence, even be open to question.

CONCLUSION: THE CULTURAL SIGNIFICANCE OF SPORT

While all of the personalities and activities described above may be of interest, and even of sociological importance, do they actually matter in cultural terms? Although a number of respected French writers have periodically followed pioneers like Jean Giraudoux and Pierre Mac Orlan in the 1920s in arguing for an artistic and intellectual appreciation of sport, the general tendency throughout the twentieth century has been for intellectuals in France to deride sport as the antithesis of 'high' or 'legitimate' culture, and above all the traditions that they value most highly and that they seek to defend, that is to say *la culture française*. Important critiques of the politics and economics of modern sport have thus been voiced by a variety of French cultural commentators, with leftist sociologists and social critics historically to the fore in the post-war period, from Roland Barthes in the 1950s (in a famous analysis of the Tour de France), via Jean-Marie Brohm and Pierre Bourdieu in the 1970s and 1980s, to Michel Caillat and the political philosopher Robert Redeker most recently.

However, as Robert Donnat has pointed out in his analysis of the French government's most recent nationwide survey of cultural practices, carried out in 1997, the intellectually perceived antagonism between sport (and, by implication, other aspects of 'popular' culture) and the 'high' arts no longer, in fact, exists for the mass of French men and women. For the modern French citizen, in fact, it is no longer a question – if, indeed, it ever was – of being *either* 'sporting' *or* 'cultural': one can perfectly well play football one day and go to the opera the next. This cultural convergence, at the level of everyday experience, may be explained as follows:

> Many activities, and notably those which take place outside the home, mainly involve the same categories of the population [...] because they require the fulfilment of the same conditions: a certain level of financial resources and a certain independence as regards available time, but also a representation of leisure that favours contact with others and activity outside the home. Thus, for instance, being involved in physical and sporting activities and making use of cultural facilities, far from being opposed, tend rather, at the level of the French population as a whole, to go hand in hand.
>
> (Donnat, 1998: 29–30)

With this characteristic mixture of sporting individualism and social conformism, societal continuity and personal change, we have, perhaps, arrived at a convenient parting image of the current position of sport in the popular cultural landscape of modern France.

SUGGESTIONS FOR FURTHER THINKING READING AND STUDY

If you want to take your study of French sport further, you might usefully begin by looking at media coverage of the various sports, particularly in the light of the issues raised in this chapter: newspapers, radio, television and internet websites are all useful sources of up-to-date information. Much has been written in English on French sport in recent years, but the best historical survey remains Richard Holt, *Sport and Society in Modern France* (London: Macmillan, 1981). On individual sports, the following all provide helpful overviews and ample bibliographical references: Hugh Dauncey and Geoff Hare (eds), *France and the 1998 World Cup: The National Impact* of a World Sporting Event (London: Frank Cass, 1999); Philip Dine, French Rugby Football: A Cultural History (Oxford: Berg, 2001); Geoff Hare, Football in France: A Cultural History (Oxford: Berg, 2003); Hugh Dauncey and Geoff Hare (eds), The Tour de France, 1903–2003: A Century of Sporting Structures, Meanings and Values (London: Frank Cass, 2003). A useful place to start thinking about French academic analyses of sport is Ronald Hubscher et al., L'Histoire en mouvements. Le Sport dans la société française (XIXe–XXe siècle) (Paris: Armand Colin, 1992). For sheer enjoyment, and a wealth of fascinating anecdotes and observations regarding France's premier sporting event, Tim Moore, French Revolutions: Cycling the Tour de France (London: Yellow Jersey Press, 2001) is also warmly recommended.

BIBLIOGRAPHY

Antennes (2001) 'Football. Droits des images, droit à l'image', Antennes, 151, December.

Barnes, Julian (2002) 'Tour de France 2000', in Something to Declare (London: Picador), pp. 79–97.

Bourg, Jean-François (2000) 'L'économie du sport', in Pierre Arnaud (ed.), Le Sport en France. Un approche politique, économique et sociale (Paris: La Documentation Française), pp. 115–37.

Cauhapé, Véronique (1997) 'Le Culte du corps', Le Monde, 11 November.

Constant, Alain (2000) 'Le Week-end le plus sport de Canal', Le Monde, 18 September.

Donnat, Olivier (1998) Les Pratiques culturelles des Français. Enquête 1997 (Paris: La Documentation Française).

Ministère des Affaires Étrangères (1999) France (Paris: La Documentation Française).

CHAPTER 13

Food

John Marks

In order to talk about the cultural and social significance of food in France it is necessary to distinguish between three distinct areas: *la cuisine, la gastronomie* and *l'alimentation*. Broadly speaking, *la cuisine* refers to the selection, preparation, cooking and presentation of food, but in more specific terms it is often synonymous with the 'high' cultural tradition of *la cuisine française*; *la gastronomie* refers to a tradition of writing about food in France, which might be thought of as a literary theorizing of food, and is again a 'high' cultural activity; and *l'alimentation* refers to the production and consumption of foodstuffs. Obviously, these three areas overlap: it is difficult to establish clear boundaries between *la cuisine* and *la gastronomie*, particularly when considering the development of a notion of French national cuisine. Similarly, if we take the example of the development of *la nouvelle cuisine* in the post-war era, it is inevitably accompanied by a discourse on food, and is influenced by changing patterns in food production. Although *la cuisine* and *la gastronomie* should be considered as broadly 'high' cultural forms, it is important to understand that it is often very difficult to distinguish between high or popular modes when considering food in France. There are, in general terms, two reasons for this. Firstly, food is a *practice*, a way of doing things which draws on any number of sources and influences. Secondly, there is an often implicit, rather idealistic attitude in discourses on food in France, which assumes – a lot more than would be the case in other cultural fields – that the 'high' and the 'popular' inform one another, and are in fact versions of one another. A straightforward expression of this assumption would be the respect that a French chef or *gastronome* would pay something as simple as a well-cooked omelette.

In general terms, issues around food in France might usefully be considered in terms of a series of ongoing oppositions or tensions: modernity and tradition; simplicity and elaboration; national and regional; national and global; popular and elite. In this way, it is possible to detect a series of recurring themes, which take the form of a recasting of these basic tensions. So, for example, successive shifts in the direction of French cuisine are prompted by a general call for greater simplicity in the preparation of meals. Also, the importance of regional or local foodstuffs and dishes is constantly reaffirmed against both the centralizing tendency of the national and the homogenizing tendency of the global. Bearing these oppositions in mind, this chapter will look at some of the ways in which *la cuisine* and *la gastronomie* have influenced food culture in France, as well as considering a wider spectrum of French cuisines and everyday food practices. The chapter then moves on to a consideration of *alimentation*, and takes as a case study some of the issues which have arisen around the now famous interventions of the leader of the Confédération paysanne, José Bové, who has coined the term *malbouffe*. Any discussion of food in France should ideally, of course, be accompanied by a discussion of wine. However, for reasons of space this has not been possible, and mention of writing on wine is limited to the suggestions for further reading.

LA CUISINE FRANÇAISE

La cuisine française is undoubtedly a 'high' cultural form, implicated in the national prestige of France. However, the fact that the Revolution played such an important role in its development means that this essentially elite form is also implicated in discourses of democratization and popularization. The celebrated French tradition of cooking, *haute cuisine* or *la grande cuisine française*, can be traced back to courtly circles in the *ancien régime*. The general move, in the late seventeenth and early eighteenth centuries, towards a greater diversity of dishes, but also a greater simplicity and delicacy in ingredients and preparation, inaugurates a recurring motif in French cuisine: the notion of a *nouvelle cuisine*. As Stephen Mennell points out, the history of cookery in France is marked by a series of developments that signal both 'an advance in complication' and a move towards greater elegance and simplification (Mennell, 1996: 147). The idea of a *nouvelle cuisine*, or *cuisine moderne*, a further stage in the break with medieval practices, began to be talked about explicitly in the late 1730s, and Mennell perceives a parallel between changes in *cuisine* and changing styles of architecture at this time, in that both are concerned with the elimination of excess and the cultivation of delicacy.

The Revolution had a direct impact on the next stage in the development of French *haute cuisine*. This was the age of the great French restaurants, associated with the development of a *grande cuisine*, which widened the gap even further between domestic and professional cookery (Mennell, 1996: 134). At the same time, as French society became increasingly centralized after the Revolution, so elite cuisine became associated with the French nation. This *grande cuisine* was developed and codified by Antonin Carême. In the course of the nineteenth century, France established an international culinary dominance, and it has been argued that France's 'culinary nationalism' was a reflection of the more general process of cultural nationalization, whereby the French republican sought to centralize and unify the nation.

One of the key figures in this 'nationalization' of French cuisine was Georges

Auguste Escoffier, and his codification of French *haute cuisine* was exported around the world. However, in response to this internationalization of the principles of French cuisine, a reaction began to develop in France. This reaction combined, once again, a demand for greater lightness of touch, along with a call for fresher, simpler ingredients. In short, another *nouvelle cuisine* was beginning to emerge. The term originated with Henri Gault and Christian Millau, referring to the work of chefs such as Paul Bocuse and the Troisgros brothers. In all, and this illustrates the self-consciously programmatic nature of their intervention, they outline *ten* principles of *la nouvelle cuisine*. The essential drive was towards a lighter style of cooking, moving away from heavy sauces and spurning the use of flour and other starches, with an emphasis on both inventiveness and dietary considerations. Ingredients were often rapidly cooked in a manner that was almost certainly influenced by Chinese methods. They admired and encouraged the new chefs' use of modern kitchen equipment, and put much emphasis on the use of fresh foodstuffs, reacting against the tendency to mask inferior ingredients with strong sauces. They conceived of this new cuisine as a *cuisine de marché*, whereby chefs would buy fresh ingredients daily at the market, and also favoured a return to regional dishes as opposed to Parisian *haute cuisine*. In this way, the *nouvelle cuisine* movement of the post-war era can be seen to bring together high and popular concerns. That is to say, it is concerned with the aesthetics of food as an 'art' form, but also more everyday, practical issues, such as diet and the purchasing of food.

In retrospect, it can be seen that this *nouvelle cuisine* was in many ways a symptom of the so-called *trente glorieuses*, the 30 years or so of relatively rapid economic development that France experienced after the Second World War. For example, whereas it had once regarded technological advances with suspicion, the culinary sphere now responded enthusiastically to the opportunities offered by innovations such as refrigeration and new devices in the kitchen (mixers, blenders, etc.) There was also a growing awareness of the 'dietetic' dimensions of cuisine, and medical issues such as the dangers of cholesterol were increasingly discussed. In general terms, the principal values of *la nouvelle cuisine* – simplicity, lightness, imagination and innovation – can be seen as expressions of the shift in values that French society was undergoing. *Nouvelle cuisine* was associated with the bright new world of the emerging France, which was attempting to divest itself of some of the rigidities of the past.

In the 1980s, as the influence of *la nouvelle cuisine* began to wane, there was a move towards more traditional, regional forms of cuisine, sometimes known as *cuisine de grand-mère*, and seen by some commentators as symptomatic of a wider turn towards nostalgia and 'heritage' culture which has characterized much of French cultural life in the 1980s and 1990s. Marion Demossier feels that this interest in local culinary traditions is part of a wider nostalgic search for collective landmarks – *lieux de mémoire* – in an increasingly fragmented France (Demossier, 2000: 150). As

Demossier points out, the notion of *produits de terroir* emerges, in part at least, from a long-standing awareness of French culinary diversity (Demossier, 2000: 143). After this, the development of mass tourism also added to the awareness of regional culinary diversity. However, the modernization of the post-war period, as we will see with the discussion of *alimentation*, tended to undermine the tradition of regional foods and dishes. In reaction to this perceived erosion of traditional practices and regional diversity the Centre National des Arts Culinaires (CNAC), an inter-ministerial institution, instigated a project to put together a compilation of the culinary heritage of France. This project has been particularly concerned with *produits de terroir*, defined as local and traditional food products with a unique and identifiable, frequently regional character. Demossier considers that the publication of an ongoing multi-volume project dedicated to these *produits de terroir* has contributed significantly to the reconstruction and repositioning of a French culinary heritage within a European framework (Demossier, 2000: 146).

FRENCH ANXIETIES

In recent years, a general anxiety has been expressed in France with regard to *la cuisine*. The promotion of *produits de terroir*, for example, has been widely viewed as a reaction to the pressures of globalization on notions of French identity. For many in France the standardization of food, along with the arrival of *le fast food*, has been an everyday reminder of the threat to 'French' identity posed by economic globalization. The consumption and appreciation of regional products has become synonymous with a desire for more 'stable', 'authentic' forms of identity in a time of economic change, increased social mobility and cultural fragmentation. Not surprisingly, the perceived threat to the great tradition of *la cuisine française* has led certain more conservative commentators to lament the effects of modernization. Luc Rosenzweig, for example, writing in *Le Monde* in 1998, looks back to 1968 as a turning point (Rosenzweig, 1998). He regrets the fact that subjects such as gardening and cookery disappeared from the school curriculum after 1968. He understands that such moves had the generally progressive aim of responding to changes in French society, and of no longer presupposing that women would remain within the domestic sphere. However, he feels that the effect has been to create a sort of gap in culinary know-how, which is now being felt acutely. *La grande cuisine francaise*, as he calls it, has not been able to draw on a more general, collective and popular understanding of culinary matters, which would ideally be passed from generation to generation. Urbanization and the mass movement of women into the world of work have, in his opinion, undermined the transmission of this essential *patrimoine collectif*. Rosenzweig subscribes to the view that the most refined and celebrated forms of cuisine can only exist in the context of an educated public of consumers.

Philippe Faure, the president of Gault-Millau, which publishes a series of guide-books relating to cuisine and tourism in France, has expressed worries relating to the effects of globalization on French cuisine, and in particular on restaurants (Faure, 1999). In coining the term 'McGault' he seeks to draw attention to the fact that the practices and principles that underpin the production of fast food have also had an influence on some of France's most celebrated restaurants. He identifies three poten-tially damaging effects of globalization on French restaurants. Firstly, he considers the very notion of a 'French' restaurant to be under threat. In a global economy French chefs are able to overcome the limitations imposed by seasons and geogra-phy, but Faure wonders whether the application of French techniques to imported ingredients merits the description 'French'. The second damaging effect of global-ization is identified with Alain Ducasse's restaurant Spoon. Here, diners are invited to indulge in a form of culinary 'zapping', creating meals by choosing, according to pref-erence, from a range of foodstuffs, condiments, cooking methods, national cuisines, etc. Faure's obvious distaste for this sort of 'fusion' cuisine is expressed in similar terms to the way in which some cultural commentators in France have dismissed what they perceive to be the shallow consumerism of 'postmodernism'. In short, Faure considers this to be symptomatic of a drive towards subjugating French cuisine to the fashion-led demands of marketing and the ultimately fickle demands of consumers. Finally, Faure is concerned by the possibility that more and more French chefs will be tempted to 'franchise' their talents in the form of an international chain of restaurants which are run in their name and under their general guidance. Whereas Faure defends, unsurprisingly, the model of a *cuisine de marché*, which was one of the key principles of *nouvelle cuisine*, Ducasse argues that French cuisine needs to adapt to the contemporary global context, and must respond to the shifting tastes of the consumer. For Ducasse, the model of the chef-proprietor should be replaced by that of the chef as an ambassador and facilitator, disseminating French know-how and learning from other food cultures (Ducasse, 1997).

LA GASTRONOMIE

The tradition of gastronomy – writing about food in a lyrical or quasi-philosophical mode – is closely associated with the tradition of French cuisine. The development of a culture of restaurants and *grande cuisine* around the time of the Revolution was accompanied by the development of a cultivated eating public. Culinary innovation and fine dining were in effect moved from the private sphere – of which the ultimate example would be the court – to a more public sphere. In this way, the restaurant constituted one of the spaces in which the emerging elite could establish its social credentials. Consequently, in the early nineteenth century there emerged the figure of the bourgeois *gastronome* who was an expert in the refined art of eating, and who would act as an arbiter of public taste in culinary matters. The *gastronome* is not a cook, but rather a critic.

The emergence of the term *gastronomie* can be located quite precisely at the beginning of the nineteenth century, and Alexandre Grimod de La Reynière's *Almanach des gourmands* (1803) as the first real work of gastronomy. If Grimod, as the first gastronomic journalist, established a code for the consumer of food, it was Antonin Carême who educated the professional practitioners. The third crucial figure in the establishment of the field of *la gastronomie* was Anthelme Brillat-Savarin. He is the author of *La Physiologie du goût* (1826), notable for its anecdotal, witty and playful style, which contains the aphorism 'Tell me what you eat: I will tell you what you are.' He was keen that gastronomy should draw on up-to-date knowledge in the natural sciences, as well as diverse fields such as commerce, political economy and medicine. His humanist approach is epitomized in his assertion that, whereas animals merely seek to consume food to satisfy hunger in the most basic way, it is only 'man' who truly knows how to eat.

In the twentieth century, Maurice Edmond Sailland, who worked under the pseudonym Curnonsky, established himself as the *prince élu des gastronomes*. One of his major innovations in the field of gastronomy was the close association that he established between food and tourism. The appearance, following the First World War, of the motorcar and a rediscovery of the pleasures of food after a period of scarcity, were key factors in Curnonsky's invention of the *gastronomad*. Curnonsky's *gastronomadisme* inevitably meant that he favoured a return to more 'authentic', regional peasant cuisine. (In fact, the 'traditional' cuisine that Curnonsky and his associates promoted was, to a certain extent, invented, since they sought out recipes that were prepared on special occasions.)

EVERYDAY FOOD PRACTICES

The notion of cuisine, however pluralistic, is inevitably somewhat artificial and prescriptive. As we have seen with the example of *cuisine paysanne*, everyday practices are sometimes overlooked or ignored. In order to consider food as a form of popular culture it is also necessary to look at it as an everyday cultural practice, which is embedded within, and which itself generates, a series of cultural signs. Before mentioning some recent sociological or 'semiotic' approaches to domestic food practices, we will consider the issue of eating out, and in particular the phenomenon of *le fast food*, and particularly fast-food-type restaurants in France. Restaurants such as McDonald's, but also French chains such as Hippopotamus and Bar B Q Grill, have become part of daily life in France in recent years. Their success might initially appear to be somewhat anomalous, given the fact that fast food in general, and 'McDo' in particular, are frequently criticized in France, but this is perhaps one area in which the idealized continuity between high and popular culture breaks down. As Jean-Michel Normand notes, it is not uncommon for even the most vehement critics of McDonald's to take their children there for a weekly treat (Normand, 1999: 29). This might well be seen simply as evidence of the determination of McDonald's to market fast food to children, but it might also indicate that McDonald's has been successful in creating a type of restaurant for young people and families who would previously have found restaurants intimidating. There is a fairly widespread view in France that restaurants and cafés have not done enough in recent years to cater for and to welcome families and young people. More expensive restaurants have, perhaps, been too elitist, inflexible and intimidating, and this may be one of the reasons that young people in France have turned to American-style fast food. Brasseries and cafés have suffered particularly from the growth of the fast-food industry in France, and by the end of the 1990s their number had declined from an estimated 200,000 to a little over 50,000.

In recent times sociologists such as Michel de Certeau and his colleagues and Pierre Bourdieu have given serious scholarly attention to domestic everyday food practices, while Roland Barthes, writing in the 1950s, famously looks at the symbolic significance that certain foodstuffs and dishes play in French life. Bourdieu, in his celebrated sociological work on taste, *Distinction*, offers a class reading of attitudes towards food in France. Drawing on sociological field research carried out in the 1960s, he notes that middle- and upper-class French people are concerned rather more with form than with the actual substance of the meal. There are, he finds, a series of pauses and restraints which constitute the 'form' of the typical domestic bourgeois meal. The meal is generally structured around a relatively strict sequence of dishes and it is important to wait for the last person to be served until starting to eat, just as it is important to take modest helpings of food. In this way, the bourgeois integrates fairly ordered rules into the activities of everyday life. In contrast, the working-class meal is characterized by a greater freedom, and the emphasis is on pleasure and abundance. (Although Bourdieu also notes that in this milieu abundance is frequently the privilege of men, while women are encouraged to 'do without'.) The strict rhythm of the bourgeois meal is replaced by a more relaxed attitude, whereby sometimes everything is put on the table at the same time, and children are free to take their plates and watch television.

In the 1970s in France, Michel de Certeau and his colleagues carried out a research project on what they called the 'practice of everyday life', which they distinguished from both 'high' and 'mass' culture (Certeau *et al.*, 1998). In the published version of this research, Luce Giard analyses cooking, or 'doing cooking' as she calls it, as an exemplary 'ordinary' practice from a feminine point of view. That is to say, in contrast to the codified and self-reflexive gastronomic tradition, which takes delight in recounting its own history and which prescribes certain practices, there exists practice of 'everyday' cooking that is all too frequently passed over in silence.

These practices are ignored partly because women often carry them out, and Giard's intention is to emphasize that these activities require just as much intelligence, imagination and skill as those traditionally held to be superior. She also emphasizes that these 'nourishing arts' often express themselves as a series of bodily gestures. In order to illustrate this, Giard draws on her own life. She recalls that, when for the first time in her life she was in a position to cook for herself, she initially felt that she had no experience to draw on. However, she was surprised to find that she did have a sort of 'woman's knowledge' which she had absorbed unconsciously. Whereas the discourse of *haute cuisine* and gastronomy does not really acknowledge material limitations, Giard draws attention to the fact that a major aspect of the 'tradition' that is inherited by us today is constraint and scarcity. In considering the food practices of peasants in France, she contests the very notion of a peasant 'cuisine'. The truly poor do not have a cuisine, but rather a few basic foodstuffs, and frequently little more than a single method of cooking, such as an all-purpose pot.

Giard provides a useful challenge to 'high' cultural food practices, but sometimes her analysis lapses into essentialism. She points out, for example, that the appropriation and integration of regional cooking into the celebrated tradition of French cuisine is in fact highly selective. However, her own notion of *terroir* seems to look back to a lost authenticity, as when she laments the fact that regional cuisine has lost its internal coherence. She also appears to disapprove of the fact that the post-war society of spectatorship and travel has led to a multiplication of borrowings, with the result that we happily sample the 'shreds' of local cultures that are losing their integrity in the contemporary world. More useful perhaps, in considering contemporary food practices, is her claim that part of 'doing cooking' in a modern society is inevitably about individuals absorbing a multiplicity of influences which often go beyond the realm of the immediate family. The presence of North African cuisine in France today is particularly relevant in this respect. A recent survey has shown that couscous – the North African dish which has as its base a form of steamed semolina – is now the third-favourite dish of the French population (after pasta and meat). It would be unrealistic to suppose that all of the French domestic cooks who prepare a couscous dish are involved in creating something which is faithful to an 'authentic' North African regional cuisine. In the same way, practically every amateur domestic cook in Britain will have a version of a curry dish in their repertoire, which they will prepare possibly in imitation of food they have eaten in a restaurant.

In *Mythologies* (1973) Roland Barthes deals with some of the cultural assumptions of France in the 1950s, and he shows how these assumptions are woven into the texture of everyday life and practices. In his essays 'Wine and Milk', 'Steak and Chips' and 'Ornamental Cookery' (on recipes from *Elle* and *L'Express*), Barthes deals with class issues, and frequently seeks to problematize the generalized assumption of an idealized continuity between elite and popular forms. Writing about wine, for example, he notes that this 'totem-drink' is seen as an essential accompaniment to a range of activities, from the snack to the feast, and from the informal conviviality of the local café to the formal dinner. Similarly, he considers steak to be a 'basic element' of the French cultural landscape, from the flat yellow-edged 'sole of a shoe' of cheap restaurants to the thick and juicy fillet served in specialist bistros, and from the bachelor's bohemian snack to the comfortable bourgeois meal. 'Ornamental Cookery', on the other hand, seeks, like much of the material in *Mythologies*, to remind the reader that behind the myth of a classless national cultural field lie acute class differences and prejudices. The 'ornamental' cookery of *Elle* – golden partridges studded with cherries, charlotte with glacé fruit designs, mould of crayfish, etc. – sells a mythical version of 'smartness' and glamour to what is essentially a working-class audience. These dishes are not meant to be made, but rather represent an aspirational image of something unattainable. The recipes in *L'Express*, however, are aimed at a more solidly middle-class readership, are really meant to be made. In recent times Philippe Delerm has had a certain amount of success in France with a collection of short pieces called *La Première Gorgée de bière*, which celebrates the 'minuscule' pleasures of everyday life, some of which relate to food and drink, including drinking beer in a bar, eating Turkish delight on the street, buying pastries on a Sunday morning, shelling peas, the slightly guilty pleasure of eating a banana-split, and reading the daily newspaper while eating a leisurely breakfast (Delerm, 1997). In contrast to Barthes, Delerm seeks to provide his readers with a reassuring and relatively unproblematic compendium of everyday French pleasures.

In contemporary society, one of the major influences on everyday food practices is the mass media. Television chefs and the phenomenon of high-profile books on cookery and food and wine might be viewed as a contemporary mass-media version of gastronomic discourse. They are an attempt to popularize culinary know-how, as are television programmes devoted to cooking. It is sometimes claimed that France's particular culinary heritage means that there is less demand for recipe books than there is in Britain, given the fact that, relatively speaking, culinary know-how is still passed on in the domestic sphere. There is undoubtedly some truth in this claim, but that does not mean that the phenomenon of the TV chef, for example, has not appeared in France. In fact, France's first TV chef, Raymond Oliver, dates back to the very beginnings of television in France. Oliver is widely credited with being one of the first chefs to have used the modern mass media in order to promote cookery. He established his reputation in Paris after the Second World War as the proprietor of the Grand Véfour restaurant. At that time, Parisian restaurants in particular tended to specialize in particular dishes, but Oliver, drawing on his background in the Gironde, introduced the notion of a more seasonal cuisine. In this way, Oliver was one of the main precursors of *nouvelle cuisine*, in that he encouraged chefs to respond on an almost daily basis to what they could buy (he frequented the market at Les Halles). This worked against the tendency of restaurants specializing in particular dishes to preprepare dishes, or parts of dishes. Oliver appeared on French television for the first time in 1953, and was to appear every week for the next 14 years. It was the first time that *la grande cuisine* found its way into French living-rooms, and Oliver used his profile to influence culinary tastes in France. He appeared on the scene at a time in France when recipe books were relatively rare, and books by chefs were even rarer. Oliver changed this, publishing a variety of books on culinary matters from the mid-1950s onwards.

Today, there are several popular television programmes devoted to food and cookery, including the daily *Bon appetit, bien sûr!* presented by Joël Robuchon, which adopts the format of inviting a chef to prepare a dish each day. The aim of this programme, together with the ongoing series of accompanying recipe books, is to give fairly precise instructions for the preparation of often classic dishes. Vincent Ferniot, France 2's resident *chroniqueur gastronomique* on the early-morning *Télématin*, has recently had a good deal of success with his book *Mon carnet de recettes*. Here, the approach is slightly less formal, with recipes, which are suggested by friends and family as well as well-known chefs, for dishes such as 'quick' Gazpacho pizza on toast. Finally, Jean-Pierre Coffe, known for his television programmes on *cuisine du terroir*, has recently presented a programme in which he attempts to feed a family of four for €15 a day.

ALIMENTATION

In recent times, issues of food production and consumption have been widely discussed in France. The issue, for example, of 'mad cow disease' (known as *la vache folle* in France) has, perhaps more so than in Britain, served as a clear illustration for many in France that the separation between producers and consumers of food has become too wide. Also, the issue of genetically modified foodstuffs has occasioned much public debate. In July 2000, for example, the French government announced the creation of 66 local forums as the basis for a 'national debate' on OGMs as they are called in French. For many in France, the debates in food production relate to a wider tension between distinctively French traditions of welfare and state intervention and global capitalism driven by American neo-liberalism. In general, it seems that now, more than ever, discussions on the subject of French cuisine will be likely to refer to questions relating to *alimentation*. For example, when considering the future status of the 'French restaurant', one of the possibilities that Philippe Faure puts forward is that of the restaurant as a locus of active resistance to genetically modified foodstuffs, dioxins and the prions found in beef products infected with BSE. Faure suggests that France, with its great culinary tradition, might take a lead in this form of resistance.

This growing awareness of what one might call the 'politics' of food production stems in part from French anxieties relating to globalization, but also from a reassessment of the important changes that took place in French agriculture in the post-war era. In France, one of the features of the *trente glorieuses* was a move towards a greater intensification and 'industrialization' of agriculture. At the end of the Second World War French agriculture was still, to a certain extent, stuck in the nineteenth century. Farms tended to be small, often without a proper water supply, and there was generally little mechanization. France at this time was far from being self-sufficient in food production, whereas today only the USA is a greater exporter of food. This modernized, industrial production of foodstuffs means that food is produced abundantly and cheaply, but there is a growing dissatisfaction with this system of production in France.

The modernization of agriculture in France is part of a wider 'European' success story of reconstruction and agricultural legislation in the post-war era. The drive towards food security for Europe in the post-war era was seen as a legitimate and necessary political goal. However, many feel that the objectives of achieving food autonomy in Europe, providing cheap food, and protecting certain European agricultural products – cereals, sugar, milk, meat and wine – have been attained at a high cost.

CASE STUDY

JOSÉ BOVÉ AND *LA MALBOUFFE*

On 12 August 1999 in Millau in south-west France, a group of local sheep farmers 'dismantled' a partially constructed McDonald's. Five farmers were subsequently imprisoned for their part in the demonstration. Their actions were a response to America's decision to tax their main source of income, Roquefort cheese. America had introduced this measure in retaliation for Europe's refusal to import hormone-fed American beef. McDonald's was chosen as a symbol of American cultural and economic imperialism. It was here that José Bové, a spokesperson for the farmers' union the Confédération Paysanne, is credited with having coined the neologism *malbouffe* – a term which has gained a certain general currency in France – to describe the standardized products of much of the food industry. The nearest translation in English is 'junk food', but the French has more general connotations of unhealthy or contaminated food. Bové and Dufour even claim that the sound of the word itself provokes a kind of nausea to the French ear (Bové and Dufour, 2001: 77–8). Bové became the figurehead for a generalized protest movement, which forged strong connections with what has become known as the anti-globalization movement. Bové has been instrumental in articulating a rejection of 'industrialized' forms of food production by articulating a strong resistance to what he sees as the damaging rationale of globalization, and drawing on 'traditional' notions of food within French culture. Bové feels that self-sufficiency could have been maintained without the excessive industrialization that exists today. He is critical of the negative effects of industrialized modernization, specialization, concentration of farm ownership, and the creation of complex chains of production. In general terms, he argues that the industrialization of agriculture and food production is a strategy of global capitalism, which has much more to do with profit than with the production of good food. Bové is particularly critical of the over-production of cereal in France, and of the way in which agriculture has adopted a highly specialized 'production-line' form of organization. For example, one farm might specialize in the production of one-day-old chicks, another in larger chicks, and another in laying hens (Bové and Dufour, 2001: 89–90). In this way, Bové's campaign against *la malbouffe* has inevitably become linked with the promotion of *produits de terroir*.

Bové is opposed to standardized industrial food products on cultural, economic and health grounds. Culturally, they work against diversity and undermine traditional regional modes of food production. Economically, they work against the interests of the majority of producers, and it is for this reason that the Confédération Paysanne expresses soli-darity with other anti-globalization movements around the world. Finally, Bové associates industrialized food production with the use of hormones, pesticides and GMOs. McDonald's provides the clearest example of such products – Bové calls them 'food from nowhere' – but he extends his critique to products such as battery-farmed chickens and the industrially produced pasteurized cheeses.

The anti-globalization discourse that José Bové and his colleagues have been so instru-mental in constructing draws on a range of distinctively French cultural notions, and artic-ulates them primarily – but not exclusively – around issues relating to food. He certainly draws on a well-established anti-Americanism in certain sectors of French society, and combines a defence and promotion of what he regards as distinctive and traditional 'French' ways of living with some of the anti-consumerist ideas of the 1960s and 1970s. Fast food is identified with any number of tendencies in contemporary society which are alienating and which work against collective conviviality. The fact that food goes through a whole series of processes between the point of production and that of consumption is just one aspect of today's 'junk living' (*le mal-vivre*). Bové regrets the fact that the family meal has declined in importance, and sees this loss of conviviality and pleasure as a symptom of the 'vacuity' of much modern life ('un certain vide spirituel'), although he does note that there are some positive signs of resistance to this relentless industrialization.

In this way, Bové appears to lament the loss of a distinctively French form of everyday popular culture. He fears that the art of cooking and eating together as a family will not be passed on to future generations, and that this will lead to a loss of family cohesion and of a positive link to the land or a particular locality. For Bové, the move away from these arts of the everyday can be equated with a similar inability to confront and embrace the processes of birth and death as everyday realities. As far as Bové is concerned, the stan-dardization of food and the fact that agriculture has become a producer of raw materials for a global 'food industry' is part of a wider drift towards alienation in contemporary soci-eties. The fact that the dominant experience of food is that of a finished, processed prod-uct means that we are denying ourselves one important connection with the authentic texture of everyday life. We eat, Bové says, but we do not 'nourish' ourselves (Bové and Dufour, 2001: 57). There is little place for *haute cuisine* or *gastronomie* in José Bové's conception of what should constitute French food. However, although he adopts an explicitly anti-elitist and popular position, he is undoubtedly idealistic in his approach to food. He is also keen to place the popular understanding of food that he promotes within a broader cultural context. He suggests that food production and consumption offers one way in which individuals might be able to regain some control over their lives in the face of the apparently inexorable march of the global economy. Bové has become a popular icon of Gallic resistance to American-led globalization, and in a recent *Arte* documentary, *Bové en campagne contre burger*, he was shown publicizing the cause of the Confédération Paysanne across the length and breadth of France. Here, the *steak frites* myth that Barthes analyses in *Mythologies* receives a contemporary twist when Bové is shown enjoying *de la bonne bouffe* at a meeting with fellow farmers. Seated at a trestle table, he and like-minded farmers are served a simple meal of locally produced steaks and green salad.

CONCLUSION

In the course of some general comments on recent trends relating to food in France, John Ardagh talks of a 'curious polarization of eating habits': everyday, routine meals have tended to become increasingly utilitarian, whereas dining out and 'good eating' have become less regular but more special. The traditional 'gastronomic zeal' of the French has, he feels, been channelled increasingly into an outing to a good restaurant, a carefully prepared Sunday lunch, or a dinner party at home. In this way, Ardagh claims, the French are becoming somewhat more like other nations in their approach and attitudes towards food (Ardagh, 2000: 641). The very fact that it is remarkable that the French are becoming more like other nations in this respect reveals something about the particular cultural position that food holds in France. Although this chapter has conceived of food practices in terms of 'high' culture and, broadly speaking, 'popular' and 'everyday' culture, there has often tended to be an unspoken assumption in France that even the most 'everyday' act of cooking and eating is informed by a superior food culture. We might consider this to be the republican ideal of food as a symbol of national cohesion. However, this chapter has attempted to show that, although this conception of the particularity of food culture in France is still undoubtedly potent, it is descriptively inadequate for two reasons. Firstly, a plurality of food practices and 'cuisines', some of which have been largely ignored, have always existed. Secondly, the pressures of modernization and globalization have challenged some of constructions of identity in which food played a large part.

SUGGESTIONS FOR FURTHER READING

In the area of cultural studies, Allen S. Weiss and Lawrence R. Schehr (eds), *French Food: On the Table, On the Page, and in French Culture* (London: Routledge, 2001) presents a series of essays on cultural aspects of food in France, including essays on the significance of food in film and literature, along with subjects such as the origins of French gastronomy. Pierre Boisard's *Camembert: A National Myth* (Berkeley: University of California Press, 2003) looks at the development of the production of this one particular cheese, which is so closely associated with 'Frenchness', in social and cultural terms. The most comprehensive overview of the historical development of food culture in France and Britain, which has been referred to in the main text, is Stephen Mennell's *All Manners of Food: Eating and Taste in England and France from the Middle Ages to the Present* (Urbana and Chicago: University of Illinois Press, 1996). There is now a good deal of material relating to the issues of *la malbouffe* and genetically modified foodstuffs. Good places to start would be with Arnaud Apoteker, *Du poisson dans les fraises* (Paris: La Découverte, 1999), and also Gilles-Éric Séralini, *OGM, le vrai débat* (Paris: Flammarion, 2000). A good deal of writing on wine in France is fairly technical in orientation, but one or two titles do touch upon a wider social, cultural and scientific significance. Harry W. Paul's *Science, Vine and Wine in Modern France* (Cambridge: Cambridge University Press, 2002) offers an extensive analysis of the historical role of science in modern wine-production techniques. Although James Wilson's *Terroir: The Role of Soil, Climate and Culture in the Making of French Wine* (London: Mitchell Beazley, 1998) is primarily geological in orientation, it also combines natural history with social history. There are several comprehensive works in the field of food studies that do not relate directly to France but nonetheless give a broad social, cultural and economic assessment of food production and consumption in global terms. In this area *Food in Society: Economy, Culture, Geography* (London: Arnold, 2001) by Peter Atkins and Ian Bowler is well worth consulting.

BIBLIOGRAPHY

Ardagh, John (2000) *France in the New Century: Portrait of a Changing Society* (Harmondsworth: Penguin).

Barthes, Roland (1973) *Mythologies* (London: Paladin).

Bourdieu, Pierre (1984) *Distinction: A Social Critique of the Judgement of Taste*, trans. Richard Nice (London: Routledge & Kegan Paul).

Bové, José and François Dufour, interviewed by Gilles Luneau (2001) *The World Is Not For Sale: Farmers Against Junk Food*, trans. Anna de Casparis (London: Verso).

Certeau, Michel de, Luce Giard and Pierre Mayol (1998) *The Practice of Everyday Life, volume 2: Living and Cooking*, ed. Luce Giard, trans. Timothy J. Tomasik (Minneapolis and London: University of Minnesota Press).

Delerm, Philippe (1997) *La Première Gorgée de bière: et autres plaisirs minuscules* (Paris: Gallimard).

Demossier, Marion (2000) 'Culinary Heritage and *Produits de Terroir* in France', in Sarah Blowen, Marion Demossier and Jeanne Picard (eds), *Recollections of France: Memories, Identities and Heritage in Contemporary France* (Oxford and New York: Berghahn), pp. 141–53.

Ducasse, Alain (1997) 'Demain, c'est tout un plat', *Le Monde,* 25 December, p. 1.

Faure, Philippe (1999) 'McGault', *Le Monde,* 23 November, p. 15.

Mennell, Stephen (1996) *All Manners of Food: Eating and Taste in England and France from the Middle Ages to the Present* (Urbana and Chicago: University of Illinois Press).

Normand, Jean-Michel (1999) 'McDonald's, critiqué mais toujours fréquenté', *Le Monde,* 24 September, p. 29.

Rosenzweig, Luc (1998) 'Rallumons les fourneaux pédagogiques!', *Le Monde,* 28 March, p. 15.

CHAPTER 14

Fashion

Caroline Weber

Throughout the twentieth century, French fashion has more or less consistently been held to be synonymous with the Parisian *couture*, an institution regulated by the government's Chambre Syndicale de la Couture Parisienne and comprised of a handful of leading fashion designers specializing in the custom creation of luxury garments for a small, select and extremely wealthy clientele. This inherent elitism aside, however, the Parisian couture has always been and remains to this day a bellwether of style both in France and abroad: its innovations are the ones showcased every year at the biannual fashion shows in Paris, New York and Milan, and depicted monthly on the cover of leading fashion magazines around the globe. In fact, as this mass dissemination of its inventions suggests, the history of the *couture* in France, particularly from 1950 onward, offers quite a wide-ranging glimpse of sartorial trends and practices among the non-*couture*-buying majority, as well as a close look at the rarefied sources of Parisian style properly speaking.

In the past five decades, French *couturiers* have been influential not just in outfitting the rich and famous, and thus in setting trends among society's best-heeled echelons; just as importantly, these designers, often prompted by contemporaneous social and historical changes, have played a crucial role in altering the very dynamics and demographics of the clothing industry as a whole. The pages that follow trace the interweaving of stylistic advances made in the *couture* proper with the shifts, both sartorial and commercial, that occurred as the luminaries of the Paris *couture* were moved to reconfigure the horizons of their operations. In both its exclusive and its more populist manifestations, 'French fashion' from 1950 to the present is thus to be understood as the product of a complex interplay between the genius of individual designers and the demands of the marketplace, unfolding in a societal landscape that encompasses and inflects both of these powerful forces.

DIOR, THE NEW LOOK AND THE 1950S

During the Second World War, the French *couture*'s long-established preeminence in the international fashion community was disrupted by the Vichy regime's restrictions on luxury, its campaign against Jewish involvement in the clothing industry, and its isolationist stance with respect to Allied nations. After the war ended, however, the *couture* returned with a vengeance, spearheaded by Christian Dior, whose 'New Look', first lauched in 1947 and so baptized in English by American fashion editor Carmel Snow, became arguably the dominant sartorial influence of the 1950s, both within and beyond French borders. Extravagant by wartime standards, according to which fabric was strictly rationed and clothes constructed along stark, quasi-military lines, the dresses of the 'New Look', created by Dior with the financial and material backing of the wealthy textile manufacturer Marcel Boussac, boasted skirts comprised of 15 to 50 meters of fabric each. The result was a curvaceous, highly structured, unmistakably feminine silhouette: 'soft rounded shoulders without padding; nipped in waists; wide, wide shirts about four inches below the knee … A tight bodice [kept] bust and waist as small as small; then a crinoline-like underskirt of tulle, stiffened, [kept] the skirt to the ballet skirt tutu effect that Mr. Dior want[ed] to set off the tiny waist' (Alsop, 1975: 93). Although reactions ran the gamut from indignation at the New Look's costliness to enthusiasm for its beauty, and although its longish hemline in particular inspired disgust in some and fervid loyalty in others, Dior's esthetic established him definitively as French fashion's savior and its guiding light. Indeed, in 1954 his annual sales of $15 million accounted for roughly two-thirds of the *couture*'s total exports abroad. Wealthy post-war America betrayed a particularly insatiable appetite for Dior's work; accordingly, and in a radical departure from the *couture*'s traditional restriction to a tiny audience, he set up luxury boutiques in New York and London and entered into licensing agreements with American stocking and tie manufacturers whose products thereby bore his name. Just as importantly, the designer's creations appealed to an extremely high-profile cadre of film stars, heiresses and aristocrats whose patronage led his variations on his signature style to be detailed in the fashion press (itself newly vigorous in France since the creation of *Elle* magazine in 1945) as dutifully and thoroughly 'as [any] war' (Robinson, 1953: 31). As a function of all these factors, the New Look spurred an unprecedented wave of relatively cheap, mass-produced copies. The resulting paradox was that a style originally targeted at a select demographic of just a few wealthy women became the signature look of middle-class housewives everywhere – a harbinger of the copy-cat trends that would beset French fashion designers for the remainder of the twentieth century and continue to do so to this day.

Despite the ubiquity of the New Look, however, Dior was by no means the only important player in the 1950s revival of the *couture*. During this period, Pierre Balmain and Hubert de Givenchy, whose Parisian fashion houses opened in 1945 and 1952, respectively, became famous for their own luxurious, ultra-feminine creations. In terms of their market, these dresses resembled Dior's in the enthusiasm they elicited from a highly visible and moneyed international elite (Marlene Dietrich for Balmain; Audrey Hepburn for Givenchy). At the level of style, moreover, Balmain's and Givenchy's confections also recalled Dior's insofar as they too were composed with stiff fabrics and rigid boning: as *Vogue* noted in 1955, these garments had 'so strong a shape that they look[ed] as if they could walk across the room alone' (Howell, 1975: 239). Contemporaneous with these developments, feminine style received quite a different articulation from Gabrielle 'Coco' Chanel and Cristobal Balenciaga, both of whom favored clothes that took their silhouette more directly from that of the wearer herself. In 1954, Chanel returned to Paris from her wartime exile abroad and reopened business with softly draped variations of the trim, sporty styles and elegantly simple suits for which she had been renowned since the end of the First World War. Also a well-established *couturier* since before the war, Balenciaga too eschewed the restrictive architectural lines of the New Look and produced, from 1955 to 1959, a series of masterfully cut, superlatively flattering dresses that included the tunic, the chemise, the kimono and the *sac*. In 1957, the last year of his life, Christian Dior scandalized partisans of his signature style by issuing his own version of the *sac* dress, which with the Balenciaga prototype established the precedent for the loose-fitting, knee-skimming 'trapeze' shapes of the decade to come. Yves Saint Laurent, the young designer who took over artistic directorship at the House of Dior upon the master's death, made this triangular silhouette a staple of his early creations, as in his celebrated 'Mondrian' dress of 1965.

'*COUTURE* IS FOR GRANNIES': THE 1960S FASHION REVOLUTION

With the 'Mondrian' dress, in fact, the young Saint Laurent turned out to be Dior's heir in more ways than one. Like the New Look in its day, this smart, boldly colored crepe shift was pirated the world over almost immediately after its appearance on the cover of *Vogue* magazine, costing Saint Laurent inestimable sums in unrealized revenues, and prompting him to launch his own *prêt-à-porter* (ready-to-wear) line in 1966. For Saint Laurent, this move represented a chance not simply to recapture the economic benefits being reaped by his mass-market copiers, but to challenge many of the long-standing restrictions of the *couture* itself. In a pointed symbolic move, the young designer located his new company, co-founded with business partner Pierre Bergé, not on Paris's Right Bank, the traditional home of *couture*, but on its Left Bank, which at the time was held to be the epicenter of alternative French culture. Aptly named Saint Laurent Rive Gauche, the company served as a new paradigm in the fashion world by breaking with the *couture*'s injunctions against manufacturing (the Chambre Syndicale de la Couture Parisienne forbade member houses even to use sewing machines), and establishing direct collaborative relationships with textile producers and factory workers. The result was a formidable and unprecedented challenge from which the *couture* would never entirely recover: high-quality, mass-produced clothing at relatively affordable prices, which led even international trend-setters like Brigitte Bardot to scoff, 'the couture is for grannies' (Madsen, 1979: 266), and sent eager customers hurrying in droves to the Rive Gauche boutique. This formula proved so successful that Saint Laurent and Bergé soon replicated it in boutiques around the world, and, with the notable exception of the lofty, elegant Balenciaga, the rest of the Parisian houses followed suit, either opening retail shops of their own or selling exclusive rights to their designs in select department stores. As in Dior's day but on a significantly larger scale, French fashion was becoming big business.

The economic revolution that the *prêt-à-porter* instigated in fashion in the 1960s went hand in glove with radical changes at the level of sartorial style. Notable along these lines were the *yéyés*, a disparate group of young female designers who drew their inspiration from London's burgeoning youth culture – of which France at the time had no equivalent – and their name from a French pronunciation of the Beatles' lyric, 'yeah, yeah, yeah'. Probably the most influential of this group was Emmanuelle Khanh, a former Balenciaga model whose fanciful culottes and floppy, exaggerated lapels borrowed from the exuberant styles of Carnaby Street and the King's Road and appealed to a young, sartorially irreverent audience with little or no interest in stuffy Parisian fashion. Echoing Bardot's pronouncement about the death of the *couture*, Khanh asserted her desire 'to design for the street … a socialist kind of fashion for the grand mass' (Steele, 1998: 286), and was echoed in this by fellow *yéyés* like Michèle Rosier, whose deployment of cheap industrial fabrics like vinyl and plastic led to a veritable revolution in the world of textiles and clothing manufacture. Saint Laurent, a self-proclaimed fan of the *yéyés*, also offered variations on the stylistic idioms of contemporary 'street' culture, deploying bold, pop-art palettes; materials as humble as oilskin and as splashy as sequins; and, perhaps most ground-breaking of all, miniskirts and trousers. The latter development, which Saint Laurent pioneered out of allegiance to the gender revolutions occurring both in the sexual sphere and in the workplace, created a sensation in 1966 when his sleek feminine version of a man's *smoking* (tuxedo) was spotted on popular singer Françoise Hardy, and made women's trouser suits the new standard for stylish ease. Just as important in the introduction of pants to the fashion mainstream was Saint Laurent's contemporary André Courrèges, who during the 1950s had worked as the head tailor at Balenciaga, and whose own design house, founded in 1961, made waves in the international fashion press in 1965 with the launch of his all-white collection. Featuring monochromatic, minimalist miniskirts and skinny trousers paired with white vinyl go-go boots and astronaut-style 'space helmets', this collection was hailed – and is still described in the annals of fashion history – as perhaps the most influential since the New Look.

Certainly, Courrèges' designs ushered in a trend toward slick futurism which would dominate dress for the next several years, and of which Paco Rabanne and Pierre Cardin also became key proponents. Like the *yéyés*, Paco Rabanne relied in his clothing design on inexpensive industrial materials; he became best known for minidresses made entirely of small plastic discs held together by metal links and brass rivets. The assembly of these garments called for pliers and metal-cutters – a dramatic departure from the *prêt-à-porter*'s sewing machine, not to mention the *couture*'s requisite needle and thread. The effect, however, was a form of costume jewelry for the body, and inspired the widespread motto, 'Le plastique, c'est chic!'

Although, unlike Rabanne, Pierre Cardin had serious training in the conventional methods of *couture*, the latter too pushed the boundaries of fashion by devising a 'space-age' esthetic based on modern materials and unexpected shapes. From the 'satellite' miniskirt to the 'porthole' pinafore, and from the 'computer' coat to the 'rollerskate' pantsuit, Cardin's creations participated in and popularized the space-age sensibility in French fashion. In sharp contrast to Courrèges, for whom expensive, high-quality fabrics and *couture* craftsmanship were prerequisites of clothing design, Cardin willingly experimented with synthetic fabrics, often under contract from manufacturers wishing to enhance their products' profile. Moreover, unlike the majority of his fellow designers, Cardin extended his stylistic innovations to the realm of men's fashion by replacing menswear's traditional shapes and proportions with oddly attenuated, radically androgynous silhouettes. In fact, the men's collections that he produced in the late 1960s and early 1970s suggested possibilities for male style that would perhaps not be fully exploited until Jean-Paul Gaultier, Cardin's one-time assistant, came into his own over a decade later. For the time being, though, the only other *couturier* committed to exploring new directions in men's clothing was Ted Lapidus, probably the first designer to open a deluxe, ready-to-wear boutique for men. Although his designs were aimed at a relatively upscale clientele, Lapidus shared his peers' passion for unconventional materials, and in 1968 became infamous for his introduction of denim into the *couture*. The closing of Balenciaga's house in that same year seemed only to confirm the sea change that the *couture* had undergone in the near-decade since Dior's passing: more and more, the interest and the money were in the *prêt-à-porter*, with *couture* serving principally to whet the public's appetite for styles adapted to a mass market.

BACKLASH: ANTI-STYLE AFTER 1968

But 1968, as it so happened, became a turning point in French fashion for reasons that went far beyond the designers' bold iconoclasm and the *couture*'s concomitant decline. In May of that year, student protesters rioted en masse in the streets of Paris, and their brutal repression by the authorities resulted in an increased cynicism and anti-authoritarianism that would come to define 1970s youth culture as a whole. At the level of dress, this disenchanted, disenfranchised spirit declared itself a force to be reckoned with through a style known as *baba cool*. A French updating of the

Woodstock generation's scruffy 'hippie' look, the *babas* declared their social and sartorial independence by sporting battered parkas, knit scarves, baggy sweaters and military surplus gear. With the oil crisis of 1973, luxurious clothing came to appear more sociopolitically suspect than ever, and French youth remained true to the *babas*' anti-fashion stance by cultivating an interest in earthy, non-western garb. Although these developments posed problems for the *couture* and the *prêt-à-porter* alike, the savviest of the Parisian designers adapted their output to the new sensibility. Most notably, Yves Saint Laurent retained his cachet and his relevance through an eclectic range of offerings such as the safari jacket, the leopard-print caftan and the all-in-one jumpsuit. With his 'Gypsy' line he drew on the mass popularity of patchwork and crochet (also adopted by Guy Laroche), while his sumptuous 'Russian' and 'Chinese' collections of 1976–7 and 1977–8, respectively, brought the widespread 'ethnic' look to the *couture*, and in all cases he benefited greatly from the star power of Catherine Deneuve, Saint Laurent's acknowledged muse and a loyal wearer of his fashions. During the same period, Pierre Cardin too caught pace with the times by moving away from edgy space-age materials and silhouettes; he now used soft, draped jersey to create flowing capes, clingy knit tops and extra-long 'maxiskirts' that sounded the death knell for the miniskirt of the previous decade. Sonia Rykiel, who opened her ready-to-wear boutique in 1968 and who came to be known as the 'Coco Chanel of the 1970s' (Coco herself having died in 1971), also made extensive use of jersey and knits to set the tone for the era's new, anti-fashion esthetic. Rendered in a restricted palette at times enlivened by horizontal stripes, her clothing was versatile, easy to wear and exceedingly popular with the women of France. The comfortable yet elegant Rykiel look was so sought after that her shop was regularly mobbed and her confections widely imitated.

The craze for Rykiel's knitwear in fact attested to a growing appetite for sporty, relaxed clothing which Italy's Giorgio Armani and America's Calvin Klein were pioneering with considerable success, in France as well as in their native countries. But, despite these not insignificant threats to its position as world fashion leader, France rose to the occasion by producing several distinguished figures in the sportswear vogue. The Lacoste company, for instance, became internationally known in the late 1960s for its hallmark 'crocodile' shirt: a short-sleeved cotton polo shirt with a small crocodile emblazoned on the chest. The shirt had in fact been invented in 1933 by tennis player René Lacoste, for obscure reasons nicknamed 'the Crocodile', for his own personal use, but only became a staple of the casual male and female wardrobe some 25 years later. Invariably paired with twill trousers, shorts, and/or traditionally cut blazers, the Lacoste shirt's appropriation by the American 'preppies' and British 'Sloane Rangers' gave birth to a style that in France became known as *BCBG*, or *Bon chic bon genre* (Good style, good sort). While inflected with an altogether different socioeconomic valence than that of the *babas*, this crisp, clean, 'natural' look presented another form of anti-fashion, insofar as it privileged timeless classics and simple lines over the constant variation and eye-catching extravagance proper to the *couture*. In keeping with this esthetic, Agnès Troublé became France's answer to the preppy American standard-bearer Ralph Lauren by producing casual, traditionalist 'basics' for both sexes, sold under the label Agnès B. One-time *yéyé* Emmanuelle Khanh followed suit with her own line of sporty clothes for everyday wear.

Forcefully propagated by this talented cadre, *BCBG* held sway in France until the mid- to late 1970s, when British punk began to exert a countervailing influence on fashions across the Channel and restrained moderation ceased to be a watchword among the stylish. To some extent the German Karl Lagerfeld, artistic director of the house of Chloé since 1964, had anticipated this shift earlier on in the decade by pro-claiming the creative value of kitsch and betraying a marked sense of humor in his boldly designed, brightly colored collections. Another foreign designer living and working in Paris, the Japanese-born Kenzo Takada, drew his inspiration from both eastern and western folk garments. His unusual prints and energetic lines brought an unprecedented vivacity to the ready-to-wear market, in which he was principally inter-ested, and established him as one of the Paris fashion world's genuine stars. In 1976 he opened up a big flagship store on the Place des Victoires, to which young cus-tomers flocked as avidly as to Rykiel's boutique. As for French-born innovators dur-ing this period, two of the most significant were Thierry Mugler and Claude Montana, young designers committed to cultivating a look that Mugler dubbed 'extreme style': an exaggeratedly vampish, quasi-futuristic silhouette produced more often than not in clingy materials like Lycra and leather. Both men exploited the sculptural possibil-ities of shoulders and hips to create aggressive, figure-hugging designs that evoked the brash confidence of the Women's Lib generation. Accordingly, Montana and Mugler also became famous for their fashion shows, produced on a grand scale with music, lighting and elaborate choreography that combined to produce startling effects.

The excitement and controversy generated by these happenings injected the French fashion industry with a new vitality – not to mention a new mandate to shock. After the launch of his first collection (a series of woven straw 'tablemat' dresses) in 1976, Jean-Paul Gaultier rapidly came to exceed even Mugler's and Montana's repu-tations for outlandishness with clothes that irreverently mixed the lavishness of the couture with the grittiness of the street. Gaultier shared Lagerfeld's passion for kitsch and expressed this taste by creating unexpected combinations that hovered uneasily on the border between the beautiful and the ugly. As a result, he earned a reputation as French fashion's *enfant terrible*, a reputation in which he delighted and which only increased as the 1970s gave way to the 1980s. Indeed, the excesses that Gaultier and his fellow Young Turks perpetrated in the name of style paved the way for the period which rightly became known as the 'decade of fashion', and in which French designs again assumed predominance on an international scale.

GLITZ AND GLAMOUR IN THE 1980S

As in the 1970s, fashion in the 1980s was in many ways a product of vast changes taking place in the social, political and economic spheres. Just as futuristic modishness had yielded at the end of the previous decade to the deliberate shabbiness of *baba cool*, the rebellious attitude of the punk era now dissolved into unabashed conservatism and consumerism, a rehabilitation of the rich presided over by leaders like Margaret Thatcher, Ronald Reagan and François Mitterrand. Ironically enough, the designers who at the outset best captured the spirit of the new age were precisely those whose original orientation had been subversive and countercultural in nature. Thierry Mugler, for example, began to fabricate unapologetically glamorous yet conservatively ladylike dresses whose retro pronounced busts and nipped waists recalled the femininity of Dior and Givenchy. Similarly Karl Lagerfeld, appointed to head the house of Chanel in 1983, reconfigured his playful kitsch sensibility to endow his clothing with a markedly luxurious brand identity that targeted the wealthy. The 'Homage to Coco Chanel' dress from his début collection, for instance, featured elaborate *trompe l'oeil* beadwork meant to evoke the jewel-bedecked esthetic of the house's founder. This piece foreshadowed a continued emphasis on rich, abundant accessories whose provenance and prestige Lagerfeld emphasized by having them all stamped with gold, interlocking CC's. Like the Lacoste shirt's crocodile, the Chanel logo immediately became a favored status symbol not just among the privileged classes (old money socialites, *nouveaux riches* trophy wives), but also among those who aspired to join their ranks (Parisian teenagers, New York rappers). The latter demographic's appetite for CC-emblazoned items gave rise to a massive pirating industry which Lagerfeld combatted by continually reconfiguring his company's 'must have' accessories: handbags, belts, shoes and costume jewels that differed sufficiently from season to season to demand immediate adoption by the intiated. Equally sought-after were the designs of the Tunisian-born Azzedine Alaïa, who came to the forefront of the Parisian couture in 1981 with beautifully cut, seductively body-conscious women's garments affordable only to the very few. In fashion circles Alaïa was revered as a genius who, like Pierre Cardin, combined a true *couturier*'s tailoring abilities with a receptivity to relatively unconventional materials like Lycra and viscose; with these he effected the form-fitting silhouette that became not only his personal hallmark but one of the defining looks of the decade.

Along with Lagerfeld and Alaïa, though, it was Gaultier who perhaps most powerfully established the 1980s as the age of sartorial excess. The stylization and subversion of conventional gender categories became one of his foremost preoccupations during this period. In 1984 he also made a splash by introducing a line of exaggerated conical bras and corsets which, though designed as women's outwear, he showed on male models further to enhance their scandalous novelty. The following year, in a collection called 'And God Created Man' (a punning reference to the

Brigitte Bardot vehicle *And God Created Woman*), he released a series of apron-fronted men's trousers whose resemblance to skirts entranced the fashion world, even as it alienated the 'average' male consumer. If, however, Gaultier's gender-bending variations on sexpot style failed to catch hold among male clothing buyers, to fashionable women they exerted considerable appeal, receiving perhaps the ultimate validation when quintessential style-maker Madonna adopted the conical bras, corsets and mannish women's suits for her Blonde Ambition Tour of 1990. Indeed, like so many designers before him Gaultier found his reputation and his sales enhanced by a widely photographed celebrity fan base. But with Gaultier, essentially for the first time, the phenomenon was pushed to its logical extreme: the designer himself became a superstar, his name a determining factor in the quest for prestige that marked the 1980s as a whole. Yves Saint Laurent retained his primacy along these lines as well. Like the broad-shouldered women's 'power suits' and pantsuits that he was busy producing for a nascent class of ambitious professional women, his much-publicized socializing with the likes of Andy Warhol, Loulou de la Falaise and Mick and Bianca Jagger enhanced his already formidable reputation for timeliness and glamour.

Although he began the decade working as the relatively unknown artistic director at the house of Patou, the young Christian Lacroix soon joined the ranks of Gaultier, Saint Laurent and other cult designers, showing luxurious *couture* designs under his own name in 1987, and starting a ready-to-wear line in 1988. Wrought from the richest of fabrics and intricately embellished with tassels, lace and beads, Lacroix's extravagant styles became synonymous with the consumer decadence of the age, even as they referred back to the sumptuousness of earlier French costumes, notably those of the eighteenth-century *ancien régime* and the nineteenth-century *belle époque*. This historically inflected sensibility manifested itself with particular vividness in a whimsical dress called the *robe à la folie*, which featured a tightly fitted satin bodice atop a short, ostentatiously flounced skirt. The skirt portion in particular, supported by a huge crinoline, was endowed with an exaggerated bubble shape or *pouf* that recalled not only the vast gowns of centuries past but also, more recently, the stiff, sweeping shape of the Dior era. In all events this *pouf* sent shock waves through the fashion community at home and abroad, and became one of the era's most emblematic forms. The labor intensivity that such confections demanded was extreme even by the *couture*'s standards; in making a dress for Sigourney Weaver to wear to the Oscars, for instance, one of Lacroix's *couturières* worked for a record-breaking 150 hours.

THE 1990S AND BEYOND: BIG BUSINESS AND FOREIGN TALENT

The pioneering impact of the house of Lacroix, however, was not restricted to design alone. Because his label was funded by Bernard Arnault, chairman of the vast luxury conglomerate LVMH (Louis Vuitton Moët Hennessy), Lacroix was also a forerunner of the business trend that would define the 1990s, in which a slew of 'independent' *couturiers* and fashion houses became absorbed by large multinationals. Print media, television, film and advertising having become, by the end of the 1980s, all-important factors in determining the success of a trend or a label, clothing designers found themselves increasingly unable to promote their product without recourse to hefty corporate marketing budgets. For their part, big corporations saw in the acquisition of prestigious *couture* names, and their ready-to-wear operations, a means of glamorizing their own brand name and realizing economies of scale in areas like marketing and distribution. Even in the face of exorbitant production costs and a shrinking clientele (2,000 women or less by today's count), the exalted names of the Parisian *couture* became, and remain, intangibly valuable assets for companies around the world. In France, Bernard Arnault has been the leading practitioner of this strategy, acquiring the houses of Givenchy and Dior in the early to mid-1990s and poaching hot young designers away from other labels to put their talents to work for LVMH. Conversely, many esteemed French labels were acquired during this period by foreign corporations, the most notable case of this phenomenon being Yves Saint Laurent Rive Gauche's acquisition by the Gucci Group in 1997, a move of which Saint Laurent himself heartily disapproved. In all events this corporate reshuffling of the fashion world betokened a conception of clothing design less French and parochial than cosmopolitan and international in nature. It was, for instance, the American designer Marc Jacobs who in 1997 transformed the once fusty, logo-based luggage and handbag line of Louis Vuitton into an edgy, contemporary new product line attractive not just to the French, but to the Americans, the British, the Italians, the Japanese, and so on. Similarly, it was the British-born prodigy Stella McCartney who revived the flagging allure of the House of Chloé in the late 1990s by resurrecting the rock-and-roll sensibility once pioneered by the likes of Mugler and Montana. More significantly still, in 1996 LVMH made the controversial decision to appoint two Englishmen, Alexander McQueen and John Galliano, as the respective artistic directors of Givenchy and Dior, thereby appearing to deprive these French style bastions of their Frenchness itself. Combined with the backlash against sartorial extravagance that had ushered in the 1990s, and with the economic crises that crippled the *couture* and the *prêt-à-porter* alike during the same period, this 'British invasion' was widely taken to herald the beginning of the end of France's dominance in the fashion world.

By the same token, to the extent that the Parisian *couture* remains to this day a trend-setter of international importance, this is largely attributable to the efforts of Givenchy's McQueen and Dior's Galliano themselves. Both men consistently outstrip their peers in exuberant creativity, iconoclastic daring and sheer virtuoso talent. What is more, along with their impeccable cutting abilities and their mastery of fabric, McQueen and Galliano create styles noteworthy for their unmistakable immersion in the history of specifically French fashion. From the structured shapes of the New Look to the vibrant 'ethnic' patterns and grungy chic of the 1970s, and from the textile experimentations undertaken in the 1960s to the unabashedly excessive and deliberately shocking modes of the 1980s, the garments these men produce play with the idioms of every decade – and, like Christian Lacroix's, with those of the eighteenth and nineteenth centuries as well. A case in point is a stunningly expansive ballgown included in McQueen's spring–summer 2000 line: a piece whose nipped waist and 3m (9ft) wide crinolined skirt recall the silhouettes of Dior, Givenchy and Lacroix, while its 'spun-sugar-like shell reinforced by plastic' (Koda, 2001: 125) evokes the wacky space-age engineering of Rabanne and Cardin. Making similarly creative use of past French fashion trends, Louis Vuitton's Marc Jacobs has recently revived the battered canvas jackets and long, loose-knit woolen scarves of the *babas*, while Tom Ford, also an American, has reintroduced the safari jacket, leopard-print caftan and *smoking* into today's Yves Saint Laurent Rive Gauche collections. Like so many styles before them, these looks have been pirated the world over (and disseminated, in Marc Jacobs's case, through his own line of cheaper 'youth' clothing), and have become fashion staples for the elite and the masses, the French and the non-French, alike.

CASE STUDY

THE ENGLISH INFLUENCE REVIVES *COUTURE*

In 1996, upon the retirement of Hubert de Givenchy, that long-time *éminence grise* of French fashion, the leadership of the designer's eponymous house fell to John Galliano, a 35-year-old Englishman with notoriously quirky and avant-garde sensibilities. Just one year before, a similarly iconoclastic English designer, Alexander McQueen, had been named the head of another bastion of French style, the house of Christian Dior. These appointments, which shocked the fashion world by placing foreigners at the highest echelons of the Parisian *couture*, historically an exclusive realm open to French designers alone, were the brainchild of businessman Bernard Arnault. Through these hiring decisions, Arnault, the president of Louis Vuitton Moët Hennessy (an umbrella organization that owns both Givenchy and Dior as well as the legendary luggage house, Louis Vuitton), led his company to post impressive figures, and prompted a considerable rebound in the luxury sector as a whole. While the fashion and textile sector worldwide had been in a slump since the 1987 stockmarket crash, on the Paris *bourse* in 1995 Christian Dior stock was up 22 per cent from a year earlier, and LVMH stock rose 18 per cent. Arnault's strategy thus proved an extremely savvy one, and other fashion houses benefited from the newfound sense of relevance and excitement that surrounded the output of the Parisian firms. In the case of Givenchy and Dior, even the negative publicity provoked in certain, more conservative quarters by the risky new styles of Galliano and McQueen drew massive attention to brand-names that the fashion world had long since written off as stale and irrelevant. Better still, the positive reviews that the young Englishmen's collections widely generated established their labels as undeniable sources of excitement and inspiration for customers and designers around the world. This case underlines the paradox that it was through foreign influence that the *couture* experienced a revival that remains under way to this day – as indeed does the influence of non-French designers in the lofty world of French style.

CONCLUSION

At the turn of the millennium, then, the Paris *couture* enjoys an international audience and a mass appeal that belie its perceived geographic and economic elitism alike. As in Dior's day and indeed throughout the past five decades, the *couture* continues, even as it is charged with catering to a tiny audience and reflecting a specifically 'French' sensibility, to shape popular tastes and dictate worldwide trends.

SUGGESTIONS FOR FURTHER THINKING AND STUDY

Yves Saint Laurent's business partner Pierre Bergé has been quoted as saying that 'once Yves has gone there will be no more couture ... above all, because there are no new designers with talent' (Steele, 1998: 288). In light of Saint Laurent's retirement in 2002, how is one to take this statement? Can the work of Tom Ford at Yves Saint Laurent Rive Gauche, work that has enjoyed an enormous popularity since the designer's arrival at that house, indeed be seen as an inadequate expression, or even a negatively distorting appropriation, of the master's legacy? To what extent might the disparagement of Tom Ford's abilities be linked to the fact that he is American, and to what extent might such attacks be refuted on the basis of the Parisian *couture*'s own general infusion with non-French talent? On what bases – commercial, sartorial, or both – might Bergé's comments be proven or disproven with respect to other 'new designers' like Galliano at Dior, McQueen at Givenchy, Marc Jacobs at Vuitton, Stella McCartney at Chloé, Martin Margiela at Hermès, and Nicolas Ghesquière at Balenciaga? In what ways can these designers, too, be said to betray or contrarily to embrace the fashion and the business savvy of Yves Saint Laurent himself?

BIBLIOGRAPHY

Alsop, Susan-Mary (1975) *To Marietta from Paris, 1945–1960* (Garden City, NY: Doubleday).

Howell, Georgina (1975) *In Vogue: Six Decades of Fashion* (London: Allen Lane).

Koda, Harold (2001) *Extreme Beauty: The Body Transformed* (New York: Metropolitan Museum of Art/New Haven: Yale University Press).

Madsen, Axel (1979) *Living for Design: The Yves Saint-Laurent Story* (New York: Delacourt).

Mendes, Valerie and Amy de la Haye (1999) *20th Century Fashion* (London: Thames and Hudson). (A comprehensive, richly illustrated account of western fashion's permutations from the beginning of the twentieth century to the end.)

Pringle, Colombe (1995) *Telles qu'Elle. Cinquante ans d'histoire des femmes à travers le journal ELLE* (Paris: Brasset). (A crisp, intelligent history of feminine culture in France from 1945 to 1995, with a particular emphasis on women's clothing.)

Robinson, Ethelbert (1953) 'Behind your Paris gown', *Holiday*, 17.3 (March), pp. 30–1.

Steele, Valerie (1998) *Paris Fashion: A Cultural History* (Oxford and New York: Berg). (An indispensable work that, unlike broader fashion histories, focuses on the specific importance of Parisian mode in the twentieth century.)

CHAPTER 15

Advertising

Sophie Bélot

THE EXPANSION OF ADVERTISING SINCE 1945: MODERNIZATION, GROWTH, CONSUMERISM

Modernization in France after the Second World War transformed the structure of the country and also the everyday life of French people. An important change was in consumption habits. Relying mainly before on agricultural products, France's economy suddenly saw a range of goods on the market such as labour-saving devices, television sets, electrical appliances and cars. Large manufacturing units began to produce cheap products for mass consumption.

From 1945, the strategic role of the state accelerated development of new technologies and the emergence of the new 'Fordist' production system. Effects were felt rapidly, as by the 1950s France was experiencing an economic boom known as *les trente glorieuses* (the 30 glorious years: 1945–75). The high level of production of modernized industries placed new goods on the markets, which the French could afford due to increasing income levels.

The increased flow of new consumer goods stemming from an advanced system of capitalist production had to be consumed quickly to guarantee production and economic growth. Gillian Dyer has suggested the need for a match between 'acquisitiveness' and the 'way of life' associated with consumer society' (Dyer, 1982: 5), and, as a result, French industrialists turned extensively towards advertising to ensure sales and create demand to stimulate the production of commodities.

The primary function of advertising in this period was to present consumer goods to the public. However, as the modern production system allowed more and more (similar) goods to emerge on the market, basic physical and social needs of the population were met. Manufacturers confronted advertising with the new challenge of avoiding markets being overwhelmed by large numbers of mass commodities, in order to ensure adequate returns on their investment. As a result, French advertising assumed both an economic and a cultural function – in the manipulation of social values and behaviours. By the mid-twentieth century, France had entered an era of consumption.

Consumption became the most important feature of the modern economy as manufacturers created demand, through advertising, in order to pursue private profit. The specificity of a consumer society is to be found in the way individuals see goods as the only satisfaction of all their needs, and the relationship between individuals and goods is the product of advertising, which in a modern capitalist society creates wants that not only did not exist previously, but which are also unfulfilled desires. Various critics, including Galbraith (1958) and Williamson (1981), agree that desire is central to modern advertising. Indeed, Williamson also accepts that, to sustain desire, advertising instils a sense of lack, of something continuously missing or absent. When buying material objects, people must feel that it is only by buying more and more that their lives could be better. More precisely, advertising perpetually creates new demand, and therefore produces new false ideals, which will lead people to feel dissatisfied with what they have already. The expansion of a consumer culture, and specifically how this happened in France, will be illustrated further by classic French advertising campaigns in the following sections.

THE ADVERTISING INDUSTRY

Agencies

French advertising reached its heyday in the 1960s, when advertising agencies shaping their structure according to the American model started appearing in France. However, since the 1960s French agencies have experimented with changes in their structure in order to accommodate themselves to phases of crisis (in the 1970s and 1990s) which questioned the role of 'traditional' agencies.

It is usual for advertisers to turn towards an agency – such as, in France, Publicis, RSCG and BDDP – to produce advertising and place it in appropriate media. It would be unfair to say that their function is limited simply to producing advertising and buying media space, as they can provide other services, such as helping their clients with marketing and sales operations; the basic activity of an advertising agency is to match audiences and markets through the use of media. The most important role of an agency is to produce ideas and to be creative within the client's requirements. However, it is not essential for advertisers to have an agency to advertise products. In France, Chanel produces its advertising in-house. There is a standard way to advertise, but it is also possible for the advertiser to do so itself or to use a compromise strategy. Therefore, in addition to their primary activity, agencies need not only to keep contact with existing clients, but also to find new business.

Clearly advertisers have always had a dominant position vis-à-vis agencies, but in recent years in France the advertisers' position has become even stronger, as the way agencies are paid has changed completely. From 1993 the Loi Sapin has limited interaction between agencies and the media. Before regulation, advertisers were not necessarily aware of the value of the commission paid from the media to the agency. Their knowledge was limited to the percentage on which commission was based and which was given by advertisers to the media through the agency. In the advertising industry, agencies are not the only body regulated by laws. In France, advertising has always been controlled by law much more than in the UK. This is not surprising as France is traditionally a country regulated more by the state in comparison with its European counterparts.

Government regulation

French advertising in the 1970s had to be more receptive to the views of the public and government. Following cultural and social changes, major laws in France were implemented. May '68 led to public concerns about misleading advertisements and also about humanist issues such as health. For its part, the government was concerned with the increasing foreign presence in French markets: French modernization had opened the French market to the world, but had also made France realize that the protection of French language and culture requires serious consideration.

The 1970s started with French consumers expressing wariness towards advertising. This hostile behaviour led to the Loi Royer on 27 December 1973 (amended and replaced by the Loi Scrivener on 10 January 1978). It had strict requirements concerning truthfulness (*la publicité mensongère* or misleading advertising). Advertising was henceforward required to be informative and clear, and not to contain deceptive messages. This was a reaction to May '68 when the public showed its dissatisfaction with the consumer society represented by advertising. It rejected mass consumption and wanted to put humanist issues to the fore.

As a result, French governments in the 1970s decided to take charge of consumers' health, and laws were passed regarding tobacco and alcohol. From 1976, the Loi Veil banned tobacco advertising from television and other media, including media for youngsters. Although tobacco advertising is permitted in the press, it is subjected to tight regulations. For instance, the amount of tobacco advertising is limited and since 15 June 1991 the following message has to appear: 'Fumer provoque des maladies graves' ('Smoking causes serious illness'), and later 'Fumer nuit gravement à la santé' ('Smoking damages health'). The same applies to alcoholic drinks, which, since 1991 must also warn: 'l'Abus d'alcool est dangereux pour la santé' ('Alcohol damages health'). The Loi Evin on 10 January 1991 forbade advertising for alcoholic drinks on television and in the cinema. Where these adverts are allowed to appear, they are required to adopt a very informative style.

Different regulations also came into effect regarding advertising for sectors such as energy saving, loans and travel agencies, but the next most influential law was the Loi Toubon of 1994. In an era when globalization was the main concern of western countries, the French government implemented restrictions on the use of languages other than French, focusing specifically on English. France saw globalization as a modern form of cultural imperialism by the Anglo-American world. To counter this, France focused on cultural diversity and started this process by protecting its language: any adverts containing English slogans or words were henceforward required to provide a legible, audible or intelligible translation.

All these regulations have affected the methods used to advertise products nowadays, which means that some French advertising has become extremely allusive – even more so than in the UK or USA. In addition to control from the government, the advertising industry in France runs its own self-regulatory system. The most famous aspect of this is the BVP (Bureau de Vérification de la Publicité), founded in 1935, whose objectives are to act in favour of a loyal, truthful and sound advertising ('agir en faveur d'une publicité loyale, véridique et saine'). This includes recommending what is acceptable and dealing with complaints from the public and firms. Adverts aimed at children or adverts representing women in a sexist manner are carefully viewed by the BVP before their release. The functioning of the BVP can be criticized: in one of the following sections, it will be revealed that the BVP has been extremely lenient towards negative representations of children – and above all women – in French advertising.

International competition

In the 1980s the French advertising industry experienced a process of concentration in search of competitiveness, which hit every domain of the advertising industry, from advertisers to agencies and media. Although on a worldwide scale, French agencies are behind their Japanese and American counterparts in terms of market share, they are doing well in France, whereas in many other countries American agencies dominate.

In their domestic markets, according to Duncan, France and Britain are the only European countries to have advertising agencies large enough to compete with American agencies set up in their respective territories (Duncan, 2000: 181–2). In France and in Europe, the French agencies Publicis and RSCG have an excellent position because of the protective barrier they and the State have imposed on foreign infiltration. The agency trade association, AACC (Association des Agences Conseils en Communication), was created to dissuade advertisers in France from using American companies on the grounds that French advertising culture is different from the advertising culture in Anglo-American countries. But can this still be a valid argument in the early twenty-first century, when advertising is more and more global?

Nowadays, the largest advertisers use common, unified marketing activity to reach the world market. Indeed, for brands such as Chanel, global advertising supports global marketing. Reasons to favour global advertising are that the number of creative ideas is limited, the cost of production can be kept low and, when one brand is a mass-market product, managers tend to centralize decisions and marketing activity. Despite these advantages, the few examples of global advertising that exist show that it is difficult for creative ideas to travel effectively around the world, for nuances disappear as cultural and linguistic boundaries are crossed. Global advertising stops here as international marketing companies prefer to adapt and modify creative ideas to fit individual markets. In a global market, the advertising industry works with the following motto in mind: 'think global, act local' – a philosophy which enables French companies to maintain market shares.

ADVERTISING AND THE MEDIA: PRESS TO INTERNET

To be effective, advertisements have to be prominent within the wide range of media currently available. Latterly, this range has broadened due to the appearance of new technologies such as the internet, and satellite and cable television. Competition between media to win advertising has intensified. The development of the different media in France in the post-war period (see Chapters 3, 4, 5 and 6) has thus intersected with changes in French advertising. Advertising used to be via posters and press, then cinema and radio were used and now, due to rapid advances, TV and internet. The changing importance of media has mirrored changes in the balance of forces between media and the socioeconomic development of France. When one looks at the five main media for advertising in France, which are press (51 per cent advertising expenditure), television (29.3 per cent), billboards (12 per cent for outdoor advertising and 8 per cent for posters), radio (7 per cent) and finally the least important, cinema (0.7 per cent), one realizes that, in comparison with countries such as the USA, new technologies have far less prominence in France.

The most popular advertising medium within French press is magazines. The number of news magazines, such as *Le Point*, *Le Figaro*, *L'Express*, *Le Nouvel Observateur*, shows that French people like reading magazines. Those that are read the most are television magazines like *Telerama*, *Télé 7 Jours* and *T.V. Hebdo*. It is in these magazines that expenditure by advertisers is the most significant. As far as newspapers are concerned, the best-selling paper in France is regional – *Ouest France* – and regional tabloids are hence attracting more advertising expenditure than national ones.

Advertisers also tend to turn to television, but this has only been possible in France since 1968, when advertising was finally allowed on television. Subsequently, advertisers' television expenditure has risen constantly, as television has become France's favoured leisure activity. Furthermore the audiovisual sector in France underwent important changes in the 1980s and 1990s which influenced the relationship between television and advertising. Television has become more and open to advertising. Indeed, in 1984, a new channel was launched, Canal Plus, which was the first private channel in France, and, in 1986, TF1, a public channel, was privatized and two other private channels were started: M6 and La Cinq.

In comparison with television, billboards have a long-standing relationship with advertising going back to the development of advertising art posters as early as the nineteenth century. The importance of poster advertising in France is partly explained by French advances in printing technology in the late nineteenth century and artists who played an important part in the creation of advertising posters such as Bonnard and Toulouse-Lautrec in the 1890s. Subsequently, art movements such as cubism, futurism and later surrealism have influenced poster designers. Art posters and advertising have, therefore, a long tradition which lasted until the 1950s, when France had to change the aesthetics of its posters to follow changes in the culture of modern society, i.e. the consumer society. The poster was totally renewed and simplified, as in advertisements for the soap Mon Savon by Sauvignac (1950), which used simple drawings of a cow in a bath. This feature has remained, since posters are now characterized both by their simplicity and also recently by their use of artistic photography.

From the 1950s, radio sets became widespread in French households (see Chapter 4) and the volume of advertising on radio has since risen to around 7 per cent. The private and most widespread radio channels have had to share advertising investment with stations called *les périphériques* – private radio stations broadcasting from neighbouring countries, such as RTL, Europe 1 (and Europe 2 and RFM), RMC and Sud Radio. Since the 1980s, such radio stations have been legalized in France and have allowed radio as a whole to maintain its position as one of the main advertising media, even more prominent than cinema. Cinema has suffered considerably, as the proportion of its advertising investment is now less than 2 per cent. In the eyes of advertisers, cinema has become a media attracting a specific, extremely young audience (15–35). Moreover, though it has been able to attract this young audience, cinema has seen its audience decrease due to technological advances (home videos, DVD) and also to high ticket prices.

In France particularly, the increasing role of new technology should be stressed. France was ahead of the USA and the UK concerning technology, as the Minitel predated the internet (see Chapter 6). The Minitel was originally conceived by France Telecom to replace the phone book but quickly offered different services, including advertising. However, as is also the case for the internet, the advertising investment is still low, 0.5 per cent, but is steadily increasing. Advertisers have up to now been reluctant to use the internet and Minitel, considering the number of users to be minimal and believing that these media had to be used in conjunction with other media for advertising to be effective (Mitrofanoff, 1999).

TRADITIONS AND STEREOTYPING IN FRENCH ADVERTISING

National and regional pride

French advertising, arguably more than other national advertising, seems to rely on evocations of nationality/national identity, particularly in luxury goods. Luxury goods stereotypically represent part of France's commercial and cultural identity in the world. Also, regional identities are often highly visible in advertising for other products, reflecting the complex relationship between the regional and national identities of individuals in France. Children – as in advertising worldwide – are used in French advertising but they figure in French advertising in ways which reflect a changing trend in French society since the 1970s. After decades of television adverts searching to seduce the 40-year-old housewife – as in the example of Moulinex – in the 1970s advertisers tried to appeal to French women through their children such as in adverts for Mamie Nova (desserts) and Pur Beurre l'Alsacienne (biscuits). The 1970s were also a period when French advertising – because of French attitudes towards women – entertained a specifically sexist approach towards depictions of women.

The French language has always played an important role in shaping national identity. This is even truer since the 1996 Loi Toubon (see Chapter 2) and its ambition to counter the threat of English in the media and to defend French and 'Frenchness'. The way in which English advertising slogans are now simply translated verbatim into French – for instance, the slogan for the Kenzo advert 'Time for peace' has been translated as 'Un temps pour la paix' – shows the will of the government to defend the French language.

France's sense of nationhood is not only related to language but is also expressed by luxury products such as Dior, Givenchy, Guerlain and Chanel, and more latterly Jean-Paul Gaultier, Yves Saint Laurent and Vuitton, and their advertising images convey a certain representation of France. Chanel advertisements have traditionally used the faces of famous personas in France. In addition to Catherine Deneuve, an actress renowned for sophistication, glamour and for her iconic status as model for 'Marianne' (France herself), the face of Vanessa Paradis, another famous but younger actress, has been used in posters and television adverts for Chanel products. Deneuve and Paradis have been carefully chosen to carry on Coco Chanel's role as a model of how French women should look. It is also not by chance that Sophie Marceau – a Bond Girl – has been chosen for a Guerlain advert (on television and in magazines) in which she walks, elegantly dressed, along the most sophisticated boulevard in Paris, the Champs-Elysées. The use of two strong symbols in French society – Marceau and the Champs-Elysées – in these advertisements for cosmetics reinforced a sense of nationhood.

The use of specific signs to create a sense of national identity can be seen in other specifically French products like food and drink, which are associated with values evocative of the French countryside, relating consumers to 'mythical roots in the soil of France' (Duncan, 2000: 187). Representations of the French countryside link people to a rural past. In the minds of many French people, the countryside relates to quality and healthy eating (see Chapter 13) and connotes a national *savoir-faire* and *savoir-vivre*. Hence, it is not surprising that this image is often used in adverts for French products – Elle et Vire (dairy products), Roquefort (cheese), Ricoret (instant coffee) and many others. This 'appeal to patriotism' (Duncan, 2000: 187) is sometimes reinforced by products named after their place of origin. This can denote French regions or the countryside: *le jambon Lorrain* (ham from Lorraine), *le beurre de Normandie* (butter from Normandy) or *Poulet fermier Loué* (free-range chicken Loué) and *la baguette, Baguépi* (the baguette Baguépi) – famous in the advert for its traditional manufacture.

Children

Nationhood is not conceptually, of course, the only prominent advertising strategy used to attract consumers. Since the 1970s, France has been concerned with the increasing appeal to, and use of, children in adverts – and specifically adverts for television. Indeed, in a time of women's liberation, advertisers no longer focused their attention solely on housewives, but became increasingly aware of the hours children spend watching television and of the economic force they represent. (Children are good consumers, and strongly influence parental spending patterns.) Advertisers have exploited this even further, as they use children in their films in order to sell products to their parents. Examples are numerous but include a 1994 TV advert in which Peugeot claims to be 'the car that children recommend to their parents'. The impact of this kind of film is strong, and the continuing use of children as actors in and targets of television advertising in France implies a weakness in the attempts of the government and the BVP to thwart this trend. In 2002 the authorities intervened by asking Monique Dagnaud, a media sociologist for the ministry of national education, for a report aiming to defend children against manipulative advertising.

Women and sex-appeal

Children are a controversial issue in contemporary French advertising, but representations of women are even more so. French advertising is known for its extensive use of women. In the 1950s women were mostly represented in the role of the good housewife or mother buying/making cakes and biscuits for her children, but from the 1970s onwards women have been shown in a more 'liberated' way, i.e. sexually liberated, according to the media. In a recent article, Jacobs shows her contempt for the use of naked or semi-clad women to advertise anything and everything in France: 'Marketing experts have known since time immemorial that sex sells, in France it is more than *de rigueur*, it has taken the place of just about every other marketing strategy' (Jacobs, 2002: 2). These kinds of images have proliferated in adverts for perfumes, for instance Dior, Lolita Lempicka and many others. This trend, also called *porno-chic*, intensified in the 1990s and the beginning of the current decade. For example, sexism in French advertising was accentuated by a poster advert for Babette cream in April 2001. Not only does the cream have a woman's name (and the advert plays on this ambiguity), but it shows a woman with no face, wearing an apron with the caption: 'Babette, je la lie, je la fouette et parfois je la passe à la casserole' ('Babette, I whip it/her, I beat it/her and sometimes I have sex with her'). The Babette advert sees women as sexual objects and implies domestic violence.

Such adverts in France are possible because sexism is not regulated by law. They are also facilitated by a lack of responsibility in the BVP and a lack of feminist research in media studies. However, this has changed slightly with the recent feminist movement's Les Chiennes de Garde (Female Watchdogs) interest in sexist adverts, and also with the creation in 2000 of a network called La Meute (The Pack), whose aim is to analyse and react against any objectifying representations of women in adverts ('Non à la publicité sexiste!'). Moreover Nicole Perry, state secretary for women's rights, has produced a report on 'the representation of women in advertising' ('L'image de la femme dans la publicité') (Foufelle, 2001). These actions move advertising towards showing individuals with neither gender (masculine or feminine) nor sex (man or woman) characteristics – as will be demonstrated in our case study. An advert for Emporio Armani in French magazines (1999) presents two individuals facing each other across opposite pages. It is difficult to decide if it is two women or two men, or one woman and one man. As the new millennium is marked by a concern over gender issues in advertising, this advert played cleverly on gender and sexual ambiguities. At this stage, though, it remains to be seen whether the proliferation of adverts featuring positive representations of men but above all women is only a passing fashion or a trend that will continue.

ICONIC ADVERTISING CAMPAIGNS: 1950–2000

Certain 'emblematic' advertising campaigns illustrate both trends in French culture and society, and developments in French advertising itself. As France industrialized and society and culture modernized through consumerism, new products and services typified different decades and new social trends. Central to changes in culture and society were – for instance – transport (the SNCF railways), the role of women in real life and in their use within advertising campaigns (Moulinex and 'Myriam'), the increasing youthfulness of French demographic structures and a rising interest in leisure (Hollywood chewing gum and Club Med). As a response to May '68, consumerism led to concerns with lifestyle and quality of life which mirrored pre-existing moves towards women's liberation and the rising importance of leisure, but which were also backward-looking in some instances – as in the case of French food.

Industrial modernization produced a new range of electrical products such as television and home electrical appliances. The main spending of French households in the 1950s–1960s was no longer on food and clothes, but on industrial products, and new electrical appliances such as those of the French company Moulinex now attracted women, who were responsible for family purchases. A famous advert for Moulinex represents how advertisers in the 1950s–1960s targeted a specific group of consumers: the 34-year-old middle-class housewife. Indeed, this television advert of the 1950s showed a housewife using Moulinex appliances in her kitchen, with the significant caption 'Moulinex libère la femme' ('Moulinex frees women'). The aim was to show how useful these new industrial goods were, as the everyday housewife would gain time to spend with her children or on leisure activities – and would be invited to consume even more.

French women could afford new industrial goods because of their husbands' rising salaries. The 1950s–1960s saw an increase in wages, which meant that, because of the greater purchasing power of households, French industries could also develop new luxury goods and services such as holidays (see Chapter 11). The Club Méditerranée is a typical example: it adapted itself to French people's insatiable desire to consume, but also to growing dissatisfaction with the new standardized consumerist society. This ideology is conveyed through the famous and long-lived caption, 'Club Med: la plus belle idée depuis l'invention du bonheur' ('The most beautiful idea since the invention of happiness'), on posters in the 1970s.

Industrial production increased thanks not only to the rising purchasing power of the French, but also because of the increasing population (baby boom, immigration and greater longevity). Industries mass-produced goods for a mass market, and immigration and the baby boom created a source of labour from which industrialists could draw. A well-known poster from the 1960s, for the railway route linking the north to the south of France ('Les trains du soleil Côte d'Azur, hivers chauds, étés secs' ('Trains to the Côte d'Azur sunshine, warm winter and dry summer')) demonstrates this point well as it presented a series of identical trains. These stood for industrial advances, which were linked, after the Second World War, to mass production.

The baby boom had another impact in 1960s France. It created a high proportion of young people, of whom a majority lived in towns. In comparison with their parents, these young people had high purchasing power, and, most importantly, rejected the traditional culture of their elders. This group became the target of industrialists and advertisers. In a celebrated television advert for Hollywood chewing gum in the 1980s – which despite the name is a French brand – a group of teenagers are participating in sports such as rafting or sailing and are chewing Hollywood gum together. Both the active sports and the Hollywood gum define these teenagers. They symbolize free behaviour, which contrasts with the traditional behaviour of their parents. This advertising strategy has become widespread and is still prevalent nowadays. To position their products among a multitude of others, advertisers use 'lifestyle' to create images that particular groups can aspire to. In France in the 1950s and 1960s this was a frequent strategy because of demographic changes.

The 1970s was a prosperous decade for French advertising as the market was flooded with new goods and advertisers found new ways to sell them. From this period onwards, advertising started relying heavily on representations of naked women. This trend, known as 'teasing', can be illustrated by a large number of adverts, but a typical and classic case from the 1980s is called 'Myriam', for the poster company Avenir. This campaign is characterized by three images of a woman, Myriam, at consecutive points in time. On the first poster, Myriam stood in a bikini, hands on hips, with the caption: 'Le 2 septembre j'enlève le haut' ('On 2 September I will take off the top'). On that date, Myriam appeared again keeping her promise – hands on hips, her top was removed, with a new caption: 'Le 4 septembre, j'enlève le bas' ('On 4 September, I will take off the bottom'). Once again her promise was kept as Myriam appeared – but showing her back, wearing neither top nor bottom – and with a last slogan: 'Avenir, l'afficheur qui tient ses promesses' ('Avenir, the poster company which keeps its promises'). This campaign aroused indignation in France because of its pioneeringly blatant use of a naked woman.

The 1970s was a time when new ideas flourished in advertising but it was also a time of growing nostalgia. As a result themes like the countryside and the French way of life became more noticeable. These are still widespread as a way to take a firm position against foreign culture. As discussed earlier, in the 1990s France took the protection of French language and culture extremely seriously. Examples of adverts which express such ideologies are numerous. A recent magazine advert (late 1990s) for 'le Beurre Grand Fermage, au sel de mer de Noirmoutier' (Noirmoutier butter made with sea salt) associates its products to Frenchness. The most important feature of this advert is a man gathering salt as his ancestors used to do 1,500 years ago – we are told – together with informative text. This reliance on an informative strategy is crucial, as the emphasis of the advert is on the product's qualities. The words are chosen carefully to evoke how this butter is made. Indeed, they refer to a mystical view of the special qualities embodied in the traditional French production method: *méthode ancestrale* (ancient method), *savoir-faire traditionnel* (traditional way of doing things), etc.

THE LUNETTES GIVENCHY (1999) ADVERTISING CAMPAIGN

An advert for Givenchy is analysed here to show how it relates to contemporary issues in French society. Changing representations of gender are worth contemplating in contemporary French advertising and it is interesting to look at a Givenchy advert with this in mind, as it is a brand which, like Chanel and other cosmetics and fashion names, symbolizes French sophistication. In tracking the changing approaches of such brands towards gender issues we can see how they reflect society's changing outlook on gender issues.

The advert features a close-up of two faces in profile, lying down one behind the other, but pointing in opposite directions. A shadow covers part of their faces and also forms the background of the picture. The Givenchy logo together with the brand name 'Lunettes Givenchy' (Glasses by Givenchy) appear written in white towards the bottom centre of the advert. Looking at the faces, only a few physical characteristics can be perceived, such as their mouths and noses. All the rest is hidden, even their eyes – which are covered by Givenchy sunglasses. Moreover the faces are in shadow, which reinforces the absence of any physical characteristics. The light on the face in the background makes the red of the mouth stand out, thereby revealing a feminine characteristic. However, because the viewpoint of the camera focuses on the face in the foreground and shows the other face in shadow, the fact that these faces are feminine is not confirmed.

The emphasis of the picture is on the striking cultural (masculinity and femininity) and physical (man and woman) similarities between these faces. An image of reciprocity is formed, by the face in shadow but also by the identical pair of sunglasses. The emphasis is put on two similar faces showing no strong signs of gender or sex characteristics which would otherwise differentiate them. The sunglasses are the only cultural signs, but on this picture they are not a key element to dissociate man from woman. Their similar shape together with their dark colour actually hides any differences and hence contributes to the non-categorization of these faces.

Usually in a picture, the look – eyes – is a means of contact with the outside world and also with others in society. Furthermore, the look acts as a code if one considers such theories as developed by Mulvey (1988). For Mulvey the pleasure of looking (or scopophilia) corresponds to a gender difference between an active look – the man – and a passive object – the woman. However, this Givenchy advert does not obviously convey a pleasure of looking, as it does not rely on a binarism/division between looking and being looked at. The eyes are averted upwards and not towards the audience and furthermore they are hidden with a pair of dark sunglasses. These are signs intended to emphasize the control of the two people in the advert over their identities.

The sunglasses can be read as a way of resisting the gender division and hierarchy in the 'pleasure of looking'. In contrast to an advert such as Myriam where the woman was offered to the gaze of a male audience, the Givenchy advert is characterized by a marked lack of detail concerning gender or sex characteristics. This therefore prevents the audience from looking at this advert in the same conventionally gendered way, i.e. to identify with a male subject or female object. The gender and sex ambiguity within this advert reverberates on the audience. The audience is not defined by sexual or gender characteristics, as in the Givenchy advert. The advert therefore addresses a heterogeneous audience which has the possibility to express its own individuality.

The issue of individualism is significant in the twentieth and twenty-first centuries. In particular, French advertising has addressed – latterly, in advertising such as the Givenchy sunglasses – changing attitudes towards gender and sexuality which were born in the 1960s and in May '68. The May movement was a protest against the ideology of economic modernization and economic growth after the Second World War, but it also amounted to a rejection of traditional social and cultural constraints. There was a will to preserve human values against the ideals of a consumer society, and there was a rejection of all forms of authority – family, state, church and traditional moral rules. As a result, different groups were formed to claim the recognition of, for example, a sexual diversity, of a choice to live one's life as one wanted. In the 1970s, the MLF (Mouvement pour la Libération des Femmes) and FHAR (Front Homosexuel d'Action Révolutionnaire) came into existence and had a significant impact on issues such as gender and sexuality in French society, with a new emphasis on the self-fashioning of a personal identity.

The period from the late 1990s onwards has been marked by governmental and public concerns about representations of women in adverts. French advertising clearly takes human issues seriously – as demonstrated by the Givenchy advert discussed here. Indeed, Givenchy shows and speaks to individuals regardless of any gender or sex categories, therefore disregarding traditional cultural constraints. Personal identity is alluded to here; it is also a theme which comes forward in the concept of globalization with which France has recently been concerned. In the advert for Givenchy there is a change in the representations of women and men, and also in the way it addresses its audience – changes which reflect trends in French society and its approach to the diversity of identities.

C O N C L U S I O N

The impact that post-war France – as a modern industrial nation undergoing rapid change – has had on advertising is considerable. Advertising as we now know it in France started with consumer society and has been following trends in French society over decades. Its big change occurred at the end of the 1960s with May '68 and also at the beginning of the 1970s, when it had to find new ways to attract consumers because of the rising discontent of French people about the growth of materialism, acquisitiveness and consumerism. Advertising adapted itself to the new situation in France by focusing on themes such as women, sexuality, children and attachment to values of the past, creating an ideological image of France and Frenchness. These values are still relevant in contemporary advertising campaigns, and, indeed, these themes and values are even more present nowadays in a period of global markets, when French advertising wants crucially to keep its Frenchness. The recent involvement of government in protecting the French language has made this an even more pressing issue.

SUGGESTIONS FOR FURTHER READING

An introductory text is A. Dayan, *La Publicité*, 8th edn (Paris: Presses Universitaires de France, 1998). For studies on advertising as a mirror of French society, see J. M. Penn, 'Advertising in France: Mirror of Society or Distorted Image?', in J. Ringford (ed.), *France: Image and Identity* (Newcastle upon Tyne: Newcastle upon Tyne Polytechnic, 1987); also P. Sorlin, who has written extensively on advertising in France, 'Is Advertising a Characteristic Element of Contemporary French Culture?' in R. Chapman and N. Hewitt (eds), *Popular Culture and Mass Communication in Twentieth Century France* (Lewiston, NY: Edwin Mellen, 1992). On analysing advertising and for examples of contemporary French advertising campaigns, A. Semprini, *Analyser la communication. Comment analyser les images, les médias, la publicité?* (Paris: L'Harmattan, 1996). For a critical view on advertising in French society, A. Matterlart, *La Publicité* (Paris: La Découverte, 1994) and, above all, F. Amalou, *Le Livre noir de la pub* (Paris: Editions Stock, 2001). Representations of women have been looked at by E. Goffman in his classic text *Gender Advertisements* (London: MacMillan, 1979). However, for studies specifically aimed at French advertising, see R. Günther, 'Equal but Different: Gender Images in Contemporary French Advertising' in Chapman and Hewitt, *Popular Culture and Mass Communication*; also M. V. Louis, 'Les Campagnes de l'AVFT contre les publicités sexistes en France: 1992–1995' in *Nouvelles questions féministes*, 18, 3–4 (1997). Useful websites are www.ucad.fr/pub/ (the Musée de la Publicité), www.culture.gouv.fr/culture/actualités (the ministry of culture). Another good source of information is La Maison de la Pub, 7, Boulevard Bourdon, 75004 Paris, tel: (33–1) 40.29.17.17, which has gathered 300,000 French advertising campaigns over the years. Weeklies are also available to keep up to date with changes concerning French advertising (agencies, laws): *CB News* and *Stratégies*.

BIBLIOGRAPHY

Brochand, Bernard and Jacques Lendrevie (1993) *Le Publicitor* (Paris: Dalloz).

Duncan, Alistair (2000) 'Advertising Culture in France: No Coca-Cola Please, We're French!', in William Kidd and Sian Reynolds (eds), *Contemporary French Cultural Studies* (London: Arnold), pp. 179–92.

Dyer, Gillian (1982) *Advertising as Communication* (London: Routledge).

Foufelle, D. (2001) 'L'image des femmes dans la publicité. Un rapport timoré', *Les Pénélopes*, 31 August. www.penelopes.org/pages/docu/sexisme/sexisme08.htm

Galbraith, John Kenneth (1958) *The Affluent Society* (Boston: Houghton Mifflin).

Jacobs, Suzanne (March 2002) in *Gender Agenda* (University of Cambridge, Women's Union), viewable on www.lameute.org.free.fr/complements/txt_1–5.html

Lury, Celia (1997) *Consumer Culture* (Cambridge: Polity Press).

Mitrofanoff, Kira (1999) 'Avis de coups de pub sur Internet', *Challenges* (September), pp. 88–90.

Mulvey, Laura (1988) 'Visual Pleasure and Narrative Cinema', in Constance Penley (ed.), *Feminism and Film Theory* (London: Routledge), pp. 198–209.

Reynolds, Sian (2000) 'How the French Present is Shaped by the Past: the Last Hundred Years in Historical Perspective', in William Kidd and Sian Reynolds (eds), *Contemporary French Cultural Studies* (London: Arnold), pp. 23–37.

Williamson, Judith (1981) *Decoding Advertisements: Ideology and Meaning in Advertising* (London: Boyars).

INDEX

A Strada, 95
Abbé Pierre, 9
Académie Française, 26, 137
Accord parental indispensable, 59
'Adam et Yves', 101
Adjani, Isabelle, 15, 122
advertising, 206–20
   agencies 207–8
   iconic campaigns, 214–16
   industry, 207–10
   media, 210–11
   modernization, 206–7
   press, 36
   television, 66
   traditions and stereotypes, 212–14
Affaire Francis Blake, L, 141
Agence nationale pour les chèques-vacances,
   159
Agence-France-Presse, 35
Agnès B, 199
Ah Nana!, 140
Aile ou la cuisse, L', 128
Ailleurs et demain, 112
Air, 2, 90
Akira, 141
Alaïa, Azzedine, 200
Algerian War, 8–9, 65, 93, 143, 153
alimentation, 178–9
Alizée, 90
Alliage, 92
Almanach des gourmands, 183
Almond, Marc, 92
Alouette radio, 50
Alsace, L', 40
Amant, L', 126
American in Paris, An, 158
'Amsterdam', 95
Anderson, Benedict, 34
Anémone, 122
Angélique series of films, 126
anglicisms, 27–8
Angot, Christine, 114
Annaud, Jean-Jacques, 123
'Annie aime les sucettes', 10
annuaire électronique, 79
Anquetil, Jacques, 173
Antenne 2, 60, 65, 71
Apostrophes, 114
Approximativement, 144, 145
Ardagh, John, 190
Ardant, Fanny, 122
Arletty, 130
Arnault, Bernard, 201, 202, 203
Art et décoration, 43
Arte, 63, 65–66, 68, 69
Arzach, 142
Ascension du haut-mal, L', 144

Association des agences conseils en
   communication, la, 209
Association, L', 141, 144
Astérix et Obélix: Mission Cléopâtre, 130
Astérix et Obélix contre César, 160
Astérix, 100, 132, 135, 137, 159, 160
athletics, 166
Attentat, L', 116, 124
Au revoir les Enfants, 8
auberges de jeunesse, 158
Aubert, Brigitte, 111
Audiard, Jacques, 8
Audience privée, 32
Audimat, 66, 72
audiovisual media and social change, 13
Aujourd'hui en France, 38–9
Auto-Journal, L', 43
Auto-Magazine, L', 43
Automobiles classiques, 43
Auto-Moto, 43
Autorité de régulation des
   télécommunications, 84, 88
'Aux armes citoyennes', 101
Avengers, The, 70
Aventures de rabbi Jacob, Les, 128
Aveu, L', 124
Aznavour, Charles, 90, 101

baba cool, 197, 198, 200
Babar, 43
Baker, Joséphine, 10
Balance, La, 124
Balasko, Josiane, 121, 122
Balenciaga, Cristobal, 195
Balmain, Pierre, 194
Bande dessinée et narration figurative
   exhibition, 136
bande dessinée (BD), 13, 95, 100, 135–49
   Anglo-American difficulties understanding
      BD, 135
   BD and the French cultural hierarchy of
      arts, 136–8
   BD as an industry, 140–1
   child, adolescent and adult readerships for
      BD, 139–40
   genres and key authors, 142–4
Barbara, 93, 102
Barbarella, 142
Barbusse, Henri, 6
Bardot, Brigitte, 123, 196
Barjavel, René, 107
Barnes, Julian, 168
Barthes, Roland, 176, 183, 185–6, 190
Baye, Nathalie, 122
Béart, Emmanuelle, 122
Beaumarchais l'insolent, 127
Bébête Show, Le, 74

Beineix, Jean-Jacques, 125
Belaid, Lakhdar, 113
Bellanger, Pierre, 59
Bellemare, Pierre, 54
Belmondo, Jean-Paul, 121, 122, 124
Bergé, Pierre, 195, 204
Berri, Claude, 122, 126, 160
Besson, Luc, 123, 125
Besson, Yvonne, 111
Beur FM, 50
Bhabha, 34
Bidochon, Les, 143
'blanc, black, beur', 172
'bleu, blanc, rouge', 172
Blier, Bertrand, 129
Blum-Byrnes agreement, 10, 95
Bluwal, Marcel, 69
Bocuse, Paul, 180
Bon appétit, bien sûr !, 187
bon chic bon genre (BCBG), 198–9
'Born to be Alive', 90
Borotra, Jean, 169
Bossu, Le, 126
boules, 170
Bouquet, Carole, 129
Bourdieu, Pierre
Bourges, Hervé, 62, 74
'Bourgois, Les', 93
Bourvil, 121, 122
Boussac, Marcel, 194
Bouvard, Philippe, 53
Bové en campagne contre burger, 190
Bové, José, 179, 188–90
boy-band phenomenon, 57, 92
Boyzone, 92
Brassens, Georges, 8, 93, 96, 99
Brel, Jacques, 90, 92, 93, 95, 96, 99, 101,
      115
Brétecher, Claire, 139
Breugnot, Pascale, 68, 73, 74
bricolage, 152, 155, 163
Bridget Jones' Diary, 123
Brigade mondaine, 106
Brillat-Savarin, Anthelme, 183
Bronzés, Les, 129
Brussolo, Serge, 107
Bureau de vérification de la publicité (BVP),
      209
Bureau export de la musique française, 90

'Ça fait d'excellents Français', 7
Ça se discute, 71
café-going as leisure, 154
Cahiers du féminisme, Les, 42
Cale, John, 94
Calvet, Jean-Louis, 24–6
'Camarade', 93
Camille Claudel, 126
Canal plus, 63, 65, 68, 69, 75, 119, 173
Canard enchaîné, Le, 12, 41

Caprice de Caroline chérie, Le, 126
Cardin, Pierre, 196, 197, 200
Carême, Antonin, 179
Carné, Marcel, 6, 121
Caroline chérie, 108
Carrefour, 110
Cars, Guy des, 108
Caunes, Antoine de, 2, 55
Cavanna, 139
Centre national de la bande dessinée et de
      l'image (CNBDI), 136, 137
Centre national de la cinématographie, 123
Centre national des arts culinaires, 181
Cercle rouge, Le, 124
Céréal killer, 106
Cerrone, 90
Certeau, Michel de, 4, 84
Cerveau, Le, 124
C'était la guerre des tranchées, 143
Chaban-Delmas, Jacques, 175
Chagrin et la pitié, Le, 8
Chambre syndicale de la couture parisienne,
      103, 195
Chancel, Jacques, 54
Chanel, 207, 209
'Chanson de Jacky, La', 91
'Chanson du maçon, La', 7
chanson (see Music)
Chapeau melon et bottes de cuir, 70
Charlie-Hebdo, 41
Charlie-Mensuel, 139
Charpentreau, Jacques, 95
Chase, Hadley, 106
Chasseur français, Le, 34
Chateauvallon, 70
'Cheese', 101
Cheney, Peter, 106
Chérie FM, 50, 54
Chevalier, Maurice, 7–8, 92
Chèvre, La, 128
Chiennes de garde, Les, 214
Chirac, Jacques, 12, 63, 88, 119
Chraibi, Driss, 113
Ciel mon mardi !, 71
Cigale concert hall, 98
Cindy-Cendrillon, 93
cine-clubs, 120
cinéma d'art et d'essai, 119
cinéma du look, 125
cinema, 119–34
      cinema in 1920s and 1930s, 6–7
      cinema-going as leisure, 154
      film stars in French popular cinema, 121–3
      political importance of French cinema,
            119–20
      trends in leisure and cinema audiences,
            120–1
      genres, 123–30
Cinq, La, 63, 65
Cinquième, La, 65

circus, 13
Civilisation, ma mère, La, 113
Clair, René, 6
Clan des Siciliens, Le, 124
classes de neige, 170
Clavier, Christine, 121
Cletus the slack-jawed yokel, 22
Club des bandes dessinées, 136
Club Med, 129, 159, 161–2, 214–15
coca-colonization, 10, 14, 27, 67, 151
Coco Chanel, 195
Cocteau, Jean, 121
Collins-Robert dictionary, 18
Colonel Chabert, Le, 127
colonies de vacances, 157, 159
Coluche, 1, 121, 128
Columbo, 70
Combat d'une mère, 112
Combustibles, Les, 116
comédie romantique,
'Comme d'habitude', 102
'Comme ils disent', 101
Commissaire Moulin, Le, 125
Communications, 137
Compères, Les, 128
Comte de Monte Cristo, Le, 126
Concombre masqué, Le, 139
Condé, Un, 124
Confédération paysanne, La, 179, 188
Confessions d'une radine, 113
congés payés, 152, 157, 158
Conseil supérieur de l'audiovisuel (CSA), 53, 56, 58–9, 67, 73, 74
Constantine, Eddie, 124
Cook, Malcom, 15
cooking, 13
'Copains d'abord, Les', 100
Corniaud, Le, 128
Cosby Show, The, 70
Coubertin, Pierre de, 166
Coucou c'est nous!, 71
Coup de torchon, 125
Courrèges, André, 196
Courrier de la nouveauté, Le, 42
Courrier de l'Ouest, Le, 30
couscous, 185
couture, 193, 198, 199, 202
Crime de Monsieur Lange, Le, 6
Crise, La, 129
Croix, La, 39
Crown Communications, 54
Cugière, La, 65
Cuisine actuelle, 43
Cuisine au beurre, La, 128
cuisine de marché, 182
Cuisine gourmande, 43
cuisine, 178, 179–81
culture de l'éloquence, 28
Curnonsky, 183
Curval, Pierre, 107

Cusset, Catherine, 113
cyberculture, 77–89
    competition between Minitel and internet, 83–5
    failed internationalization of Minitel, 79–80
    internet, 82–5
    Minitel messaging, 80–2
    US influences, 77, 78, 83, 86–7
cycling, 167, 168

Daeninckx, Didier, 111
Daft Punk, 2, 90
Dalida, 102
Dallas, 70
Dard, Frédéric, 106
Dauphiné-Libéré, Le, 40
Dawson's Creek, 70
Dechavanne, Christophe, 71
Défaite de la pensée, La, 95
Delanoë, Bertrand, 44–6
Delarue, Jean-Luc, 71
Delerm, Philippe, 186
Delon, Alain, 121, 122, 123, 124
demography, 9–10, 55, 160
Deneuve, Catherine, 121, 198, 212
Depardieu, Gérard, 69, 122, 128, 129
Dépêche de Tahiti, 40
Dépêche du Midi, 40
Dernier Métro, Le, 8
Dernières nouvelles d'Alsace, Les, 80
Dernières vacances, Les, 163
'Déserteur, Le', 49
Desproges, Pierre, 53
detective fiction, 106–7
Deux flics à Miami, 70
'Deux Oncles, Les', 93
Deuxième souffle, Le, 124
Diable au corps, Le, 6
Dick, Philip K., 107
Diên Biên Phu, 119
Difool, 58
Dîner de cons, Le, 128
Dior, Christian, 193, 194, 195, 196, 200, 212
Direction générale des télécommunications, La (DGT), 77
Diva, 125
Dix Commandements, Les, 93
Djian, Philippe, 111
Doc Spitz, 58
Dossier familial, 43
Double Face, 43
Doulos, Le, 124
Droit à la paresse, Le, 153
Droit de réponse, 71
Ducasse, Alain, 182
Dumas, Alexandre, 105, 126
Dumazedier, Joffre, 150, 151–2, 153, 161, 163
Duneton, Claude, 31
Dylan, Bob, 93

Dynasty, 70

Echo des savanes, L', 139, 140
Echos, Les, 39
Ecole de Bruxelles, L', 138
Ecole des vedettes, L', 154
Editions gaies et lesbiennes, 113
elite culture, 2
Elle, 42
En cas de bonheur, 70
En cas de malheur, 123
'En groupe, en ligue, en procession', 93
Enfant magazine, 43
Entremetteuse, L', 114
Equipe, L', 37
ER (Urgences), 70
Escoffier, Georges-Auguste, 180
Essel, André, 109–10
Et si cétait vrai? 114
Eté meurtrier, L', 124
ethnicity and language, 25
Euro Disney, 160
Europe 1, 50, 52, 54
Europe 2, 50, 59, 92
European integration, 14
Eurotrash, 2
Evénement du jeudi, L', 41
everyday life, 4–5
Express, L', 40, 210

F2, 63, 68, 69, 70, 71
F3, 63, 68
F5, 63, 68
Fabuleux Destin d'Amélie Poulain, Le, 101, 131, 132
Famille Duraton, La, 54
'Fan de sa vie, La', 99
Fantomas se déchaîne, 128
fastfood, le, 183
Fédération des familles de France, 81
Fédération Internationale du Football Association (FIFA), 166
Fédération Internationale du Sport Automobile (FIA), 166
Fédération nationale de la presse française, 47
Fée carabine, La, 114
Femme d'aujourd'hui, 43
Femme trombone, La, 94
Femme-Actuelle, 43
Fernandel, 121, 128
Ferniot, Vincent, 187
Ferrat, Jean, 9, 93
Ferré, Léo, 93, 96
Festina drugs scandal, 168
Fête de la musique, 96
Fête de l'internet, 84
Fête du livre, La, 104
fête, 7, 152
fêtes légales, 156
Feu, Le, 6

FG Radio, 55
fiction, 104–18
    Anglo-American influences on French fiction, 104, 105, 106
    contemporary developments in popular fiction, 111–15
    importance of reading and books in France, 104–5
    making reading affordable, 109–11
    popular fiction genres, 105–8
Fièvre d'Urbicande, La, 143
Fifth Republic, 9
Figaro, Le, 38, 211
Fignon, Laurent, 173
Filipacchi, Henri, 41, 109
Finkielkraut, Alain, 95
FIP Radio, 50
Fleuve noir, 107
Fluide glacial, 139, 140
Fnac, 91, 110, 111, 135, 141
Foch, Marshal, 6
food and advertising, 212–13
Forbes, Jill, 15
Forest, Jean-Claude, 142
Fourastié, Jean, 8–9
Fourmis, Les, 114
Fourth Republic, 8–10
FR3, 65, 69
France Telecom, 78, 79, 85
France, Régis, 137
France-Antilles, 40
France-Bleue, 50
France-Culture, 49, 50
France-Dimanche, 41
France-Football, 42
France-Info, 50, 52
France-Inter, 49, 50, 54
France-Loisirs, 110
France-Musiques, 49, 50
France-Télévision, 62, 63
franglais, 27–8
Fréquence gaie, 50
Fréquence protestante, 50
Fresnault-Deruelle, P., 136–7
Frith, Simon, 97
Front homosexuel d'action révolutionnaire, 218
Frou-Frou, 71
Fruit défendu, Le, 124
Frustrés, Les, 139
Fugitifs, Les, 128
Fun Radio, 50, 53, 56, 57, 58–9, 92
Fun TV, 92
Funès, Louis de, 121, 122
Futur, 43
Futuroscope, Le 159

G Squad, 92
Gabin, Jean, 121, 123, 124
Gadet, Françoise, 22
Gainsbourg, Serge, 10, 90, 99

Gai-Pied, 42
Gall, France, 10
Galliano, John, 202–3, 204
Garde à vue, 124
gastronomad, 108
gastronomie, 179, 180, 182–3
Gaulle, Charles de, 9, 10, 11, 47, 64–5, 140, 175
Gaultier, Jean-Pierre, 2, 197, 199, 200–1, 212
Gault-Millau, 182
gay popular fiction, 113
Gazon maudit, 129
Gendarme à New York, Le, 128
Gendarme de Saint-Tropez, Le, 128
Gendarme et les extra-terrestres, Le, 128
gender identity, 5–6
generation gap, 10
Géo, 43
Georges et Louis, 143
Germinal, 119
Giard, Luce, 184–5
Giff-Wiff, 136
Giovanni, José, 106
Girardot, Annie, 122
Giraudoux, Jean, 175
Giscard d'Estaing, Valéry, 10, 11, 63, 140, 160
Givenchy advertising, 217–19
Givenchy, Hubert de, 194, 203,
Glob 'off, 144
globalization, 112, 182
Goldman, Jean-Jacques, 57
Gordon-Lazareff, Hélène, 42
Gorille vous salue bien, Le, 123
Goscinny, 139, 159, 162
Gotlib, 139
Grand Prix de la ville d'Angoulême, 136
Grand Secret, Le, 85, 86
Grande bouffe, La, 129
grande cuisine, 179
Grande illusion, La, 6
Grande vadrouille, La, 128, 130
Grimaud de la Reynière, Alexandre, 183
Grosses têtes, Les, 53
Gubler affaire, 85–86
Guide bel air, Le, 43
Guide cuisine, 43
Guignols de l'Info, 75

Hachette group, 35
Halloween, 156
Hallyday, Johnny, 93, 150, 153
handball, 172
Hara-Kiri, 139
Hardy, Françoise, 196
Harlequin, 108, 112, 113
Hayward, Susan, 62–3, 70
Heartbreak High, 70
Hebdo Hara-Kiri, 140
Hélène et les garçons, 70

Heliot, Johan, 112
Hendrix, Jimi, 93
Hergé, 115, 138
Hernandez, Patrick, 90
Héros très discret, Un, 8
Hersant, Robert, 35
'Hier encore', 102
high culture, 2
Highmore, Ben, 4, 14
Hinault, Bernard, 173
hip-hop and rap, 3
Hippopotamus restaurants, 183
Hiver '54, 9
Hommes préfèrnt les grosses, Les, 129
Horne, Alistair, 9
Hugo, Victor, 93
Humanité, L', 39
Humanoïdes associés, Les, 140
Huppert, Isabelle, 122
Hussard sur le toit, Le, 127
Hygiène de l'assassin, L', 115

IAM, 94
Ici et maintenant, 53
Ici-Paris, 41
IFOP, 92, 135
Ile des gauchers, L', 105
Inceste, L', 114
Indochina, 126, 153
Indochine (film), 129
Indochine, (group) 94
Inspecteur Barnaby, L', 70
Inspecteur la bavure, 129
Institut national de l'audiovisuel (INA), 65, 71
Institut national du sport et de l'enseignement physique (INSEP)
internet, 36–7, 114
IPSOS, 51
Izzo, Jean-Claude, 112

Jacks, Terry, 92
'Jacky', 91
Jacques Brel is Alive and Well and Living in Paris, 91
J'ai Lu, 109, 113
Jardin, Alexandre, 105
J'attends un enfant, 185
'Je t'aime moi non plus', 90
Jeanne d'Arc, 126
'J'écris quand j'ai mal aux autres', 101
Jeu des mille francs, 54
Jeunet, Jean-Pierre, 101
Jeux de notre temps, Les, 43
'Joe le taxi', 90
'Jojo', 100
Jospin, Lionel, 83
Jour de Fête, 128, 155, 163
Journal de l'Ile de la Réunion, 40
Journal de Mickey, Le, 138
Journal de Paris, Le, 34

Journal des dames, Le, 42
Journal d'un album, 138, 144
Journal, 144
Juge Fayard, dit le 'Shériff', 124
Justicière, La, 108

Kelly, Mike, 5, 15
Kenzo, 199
Kerr, Jim, 94
Khaleb, Ched, 94
Khaled, 94
Khanh, Emmanuelle, 196, 199
Kidd, Bill and Reynolds, Sîan, 15
Kilborn, Richard, 71–2
Klein, Gérard, 107, 112
Kojak, 67, 70
Kopa, Raymond, 173
Kuhn, Raymond, 34, 35

Lacombe Lucien, 8
Lacoste, 198–9, 200
Lacroix, Christian, 201
Lafargue, Paul, 153
Lagerfeld, karl, 199, 200
'Laisse les filles', 154
Lang, Jack, 6, 12–13, 67, 70, 125, 136
language, 17–33
    formal and informal French, 20
    geographical variations, 20
    non-standard French, 18–21, 24–6, 28–31
    popculture products, 23, 32
    prescriptivism and standardization, 18,
        18–21
    role of State, 26–8
    slang, 21
langue de culture, 27
Lapidus, Ted, 197
Lapin, 141
Lavilliers, Bernard, 93
Le Pen, Jean-Marie, 101
Lebreton, Auguste, 106
Leclerc hypermarkets, 91, 110
Leenhardt, Roger, 162
Leforestier, Maxime, 93
leisure, 7, 150–64
    35–hour working week, 150–1
    definitions, 151–2
    post-1945 growth of leisure, 152–5
    privatization of tourism, 157–61
    secularization of holidays and vacations,
        155–7
Lelouch, Claude, 123
Lemerre, Roger, 173
Lenglen, Suzanne, 173
Lennon, John, 5
Léon la came, 143
Léon, 125
Lesbia, 42
Lévy, Marc, 114
Lhermitte, Thierry, 121

Liberation and press, 35
Libération, 12, 38
Liberté, égalité, fraternité, 5
Librio, 109
licence, 166
literature and heritage cinema, 125–7
littérature-trash, 113
Livre de Poche, 109, 110
Livret de Phamille, 144, 146–7
Lloyd, Chris, 7
Loft Story, 68
Loi Evin, 208
Loi Lang, 110
Loi Royer, 208
Loi Sapin, 207
Loi Scrivener, 208
Loi Veil, 153, 208
loisirs, 151
Looseley, David, 67
loucherbem, 29
Louis-Vuitton-Moët-Hennessy (LVMH), 202
Lovin' Fun, 58–9
luxury goods, 212

M6 Music, 92
M6, 63, 68, 92
Mac Orlan, Pierre, 175
Madame-Figaro, 42, 43
'Made in love' 101
Madonna, 201
Maigret tend un piège, 123
Maigret voit rouge, 123
Maigret, 123
maisons de la culture, 3, 67, 96
Majumdar, Margaret, 15
malbouffe, la, 188–90
Malle, Louis, 8
Malraux, André, 3, 12
Mamie Nora, 212
Manchette, Jean-Patrick, 111
Mano Negra, 94
Marais, Jean, 121
Marceau, Sophie, 122
Marie-Claire, 42, 43, 78
Marielle, Jean-Pierre, 125
Mariés de l'an II, Les, 125
Marius-Fanny-Trésor trilogy, 69
Marshall, Bill, 70
Marshall aid, 10
Masque et la plume, Le, 54
mass culture, 2, 3
Match, 49
Matin, Le, 34
Maurad, 59
Mauresmo, Amélie, 173
Maxi, 43
Maxi-Poche, 109
May '68, 2, 5, 9, 10, 11, 12, 41, 65, 79, 93,
    111, 120, 127, 128, 131, 153, 181,
    197, 208, 214, 218, 219

Mazdon, Lucy, 71
MC Solaar, 94
McCartney, Stella, 202
McDonalds, 183–4
McGuigan, Jim, 14
MCM, 92
McQueen, Alexander, 202–3, 204
media studies, 3
Médiamétrie, 51, 52
Mélodie en sous-sol, 123
Melville, Jean-Pierre, 124
Ménie Grégoire, 53
Mennell, Stephen, 179
Menu, Jean-Christophe, 144, 145
Mercure, 116
messagerie rose, 81
messageries, 80–2
Messieurs les enfants, 114
Métal hurlant, 140, 142
Meute, La, 214
Michelin guidebook, 157
Midi-Libre, Le, 40
Midi-Olympique, 42
Mille et une nuits éditions, 109
Millet, Catherine, 110, 113
Minicom email service, 80
Minitel, 78, 82
Miou-Miou, 122
Misérables, Les, 126
Mistinguett, 7
Mitterrand, François, 12, 47, 49, 85, 93, 119, 136, 150
modernization, 8–9, 206
Modes et travaux, 43
Moebius, 139, 142
'Moi... Lolita', 90
Moins d'un quart de seconde pour vivre, 145
Môme vert-de-gris, La, 124
Mon carnet de recettes, 187
Mon Oncle, 128
Mon Savon, 211
Monde, Le, 3, 9, 38
Mondino, Jean-Baptiste, 99
'Mondrian' dress, 195
Monoprix supermarket, 109
Monsieur Jean, 143
'Monsieur Tout-Blanc', 93
'Montagne, La', 9, 40
Montana, Claude, 199
'Moribond, Le', 91
Moulinex, 212, 214–15
Mouv', Le, 50
MTV, 92
Mugler, Thierry, 199, 200
music, 90–103
    1920s and 1930s, 6–7
    Anglo-American dismissal of French music, 90–1
    artists and mass media, 92
    British influence on French music, 93–4

music festivals, 96
music industry, 91–2
music radio, 52, 54–5
popular music and French cultural debates, 95–7
Muvrini, I, 94
'My Way', 102
Mylène Farmer, 102
'Myriam' advertising campaign,
Mythologies, 185, 186–7, 190

Nagui, 71
Napoléon, 125
National Federation of the French Press, 37, 39
national identity, 5–6
Navarro, 125
'Ne me quitte pas', 99
Négresses vertes, Les, 94
néo-polar, 111
New Kids on the Block, 92
New Look, 193–4, 196
newspapers/magazines as leisure, 155
Nikita, 125
Nikopol, 142
Nora-Minc report, 77, 83, 86
Nostalgie, 50
Nothomb, Amélie, 105, 115–17
Notre Dame de Paris, 93
Notre Temps, 43
Nous deux, 107, 108
Nous sommes tous des assassins, 124
Nouveau détective, Le, 43
Nouveau politis, Le, 43
Nouvel observateur, L', 40, 139, 210
nouvelle cuisine, 179, 180
Nouvelle république du centre-ouest, 40
Nouvelle république, 40
NRJ, 50, 55, 56, 57, 59, 92
NTM, 102
Nuit des héros, 72
NYPD Blue, 70

Office national du tourisme, 157
Oliver, Raymond, 186
Olympic Games, 166, 170, 171, 173
Ophuls, Marcel, 8
Oreille en coin dimanche matin, L', 53
ORTF, 49
Ouest-France, 39–40, 210
Ouï FM, 55
Ouvroir de bande dessinée potentielle (OUBAPO), 145
Oxford-Hachette dictionary, 18, 30
Oyyo, 162

Pagnol, Marcel, 69, 70
Papy fait de la résistance, 129
'Parachutiste', 93
Paradis, Vanessa, 90

Parc Astérix, Le, 159, 160
Parisien, Le, 38–9
Paris-Match, 41, 44–6
Paris-Normandie, 40
Paris-Saint-Germain (PSG), 167
Paris-Turf, 39
Parole de flic, 125
Passagers du vent, Les, 143
Passe le temps, 144
patronages, 174
Pedley, Alain, 34
Pelchat amendment, 56, 95
pelota, 167
Pennac, Daniel, 114
Péplum, 116
Pérec, Marie-José, 173
Pernoud, Laurence, 155
Persepolis, 141
pétanque, 170
Petit Echo de la mode, Le, 42
Petit monde de Don Camillo, Le, 128
Petite collection, La, 109
Petit-Journal, 34
Petit-Parisien, 34
Petit-Robert dictionary, 18
Pétroleuses, Les, 42
Philipe, Gérard, 121
Phosphore, 43
Physiologie du goût, La, 183
Piaf, Edith, 92
Pilote, 139, 160
Pionniers de l'espérance, Les, 142
Pivot, Bernard, 6
Place des Victoires, 199
Plan télématique, le, 47
Platini, Michel, 173
Point (-Seuil), 109
Point, Le, 40, 210
Poiré, Jean-Marie, 128
Polac, Michel, 71
polar, 106, 107, 123–5
Pompidou, Georges, 11, 65
Popstars, 92
Popular Front, 5, 7, 6, 169
porno-chic advertising, 214
poster advertising, 211
Poulidor, Raymond, 173
poulpe, le, 111
Pour la peau d'un flic, 125
Pradel, Jacques, 74
Première gorgée de bière, La, 187
Premiers baisers, 70
press, 34–47, 167
    declining readership, 36–7
    historical development, 34–7
    news magazines, 40–4
    Paris-based dailies, 37–9
    press groups, 35
    regional dailies, 39–40
Presse-Pocket, 109

prêt-à-porter, 196–7, 198, 202
price of newspapers, 36
Prima, 43
Prisma press, 35
Prisunic supermarket, 109
produits de terroir, 181
Progrès-La Tribune, Le, 40
Proust, Marcel, 137
Prouvost, Jean, 35
Provençal, Le, 40
public service mission of sport, 169
punk, 199
Pur beurre l'Alsacienne, 212

Queneau, Raymond, 23, 98, 145
Qu'est-ce que la littérature?, 8
'Qui m'aime me fuit', 100

Rabanne, Paco, 196–7
Radiguet, Raymond, 6
radio, 48–61
    advertising, 55, 211
    development of sector, 49–50
    everyday routines, 51, 59–60
    genres, 52–5
    music radio and cultural identity, 56–8
    popular culture, 48–9
    presenters, 58
    radios associatives, 49
    radios libres, 49
    talk radio, 52, 53–4,
Radio Alfa, 50
Radio Arverne, 50
Radio Latina, 55
Radio Notre-Dame, 50
Radio Scoop, 50
Radio Shalom, 50
Radio Zinzine, 50
Radio-France, 50
Radioscopie, 54
rap and hip-hop culture, 57, 94
Reader, Keith and Hughes, Alex, 15
regional music, 94–5
Règle du jeu, La, 6
regulation of advertising, 207–8, 209
regulation of broadcasting, 13
Reine Margot, La, 126
Reiser, 139
Renaud, 1, 93
Renoir, Jean, 6
Republic and sport, 165
Républicain, Le, 40
République du Centre, La, 40
Resnais, Alain, 136
Retour de Don Camillo, Le, 124
Révoltée, La, 108
Révolution nationale, la, 8, 174
RFM, 50, 54, 55
Richard, Pierre, 121
Ricoret, 213

Ridicule, 127
Rigby, Brian, 15
Rimet, Jules, 166
Ripoux contre ripoux, 125
Ripoux, Les, 25, 125
Rire et chansons, 50
Rita Mitsouko, Les, 94
Riviera, 70
RMC Info, 52
RMC, 52
Robuchon, Joël, 187
Rochefort, Jean, 121
rock métissé, 94
roman à quatre sous, 105
roman beur, 113
roman noir, 106
Roméo et Juliette, 93
Rosier, Michèle, 196
Ross, Kristin, 10
Rousso, Henri, 8
rowing, 166
RTF, 49, 65
RTL, 50, 54
RTL2, 50
Ruda salska, La, 94
'Rue de la Paix', 100
rugby, 166, 167, 174–5
Ruquier, Laurent, 53
Ruy Blas, 69
Rykiel, Sonia, 198

Sadoul, Jacques, 107
Saint-Laurent, Yves, 195, 196, 198
Saint-Laurent-Rive-Gauche, 195, 202
Salon de la bande dessinée, 136
Salon du livre, 104
Salut les copains, 152
Samouraï, Le, 124
San Antonio, 1, 106–7
Sanson, Véronique, 93
Santé magazine, 43
Sartre, Jean-Paul, 8
Satrapi, Marjane, 141, 148
Schneider, Romy, 122
science fiction, 107, 112, 142
Sciences et techniques des activés physiques
    et sportives (STAPS), 171
Sciences et Vie découvertes, 43
Sciences et Vie, 43
'Seasons in the Sun', 91
Semaine de vacances, Une, 163
Sempé, Jean-Jacques, 162
sentimental fiction, 107–8
Sérail Killers, 113
Série noire, 106, 123
Serrault, Coline, 122
Seule la lune le sait, 112
Si Versailles m'était conté, 125
Signoret, Simone, 122
Silence de la mer, Le, 8

Simenon, Georges, 70, 106, 115, 123
Simonin, Albert, 106
Simpsons, The, 22
skiing, 157, 170
Skyrock, 53, 56, 57, 58, 59, 92
slang, 21, 24
Snow, Carmel, 195
soaps on TV, 69
soccer, 152, 166, 167, 170, 171, 172
Société française de production (SFP), 65
Souchon, Alain, 93
Spirou, 43, 138
Spoon restaurant, 182
sport, 6–7, 165–77
    French successes in international
        competition, 171–2
    geography, demography and the Tour de
        France, 167–8
    historical origins of French sport, 166–7
    mass media and sports stars, 172–3
    mass participation and the role of the state,
        168–71
    understanding the importance of sport in
        France, 165
standards, 3
Star Academy, 92
Stardust, 90
Starshooter, 94
Sting, 95
Stivell, Alain, 94
St-Laurent, Cecil, 108
Storey, John, 14
style atome, 139
Subway, 125
supermarkets and booksales, 109–10
'Supernature'. 90
Supreme NTM, 94
'Sur toi', 99, 100
Sylvestre, Anne, 93
Syndicat national de l'édition phonographique
    (SNEP), 92

'Tais-toi et rap', 101
Take That, 92
Tardi, 137
Tati, Jacques, 121, 128, 15, 163
Tavernier, Bertrand, 123, 163
techno music, 2, 90
technology, 6–7, 13, 211, 120
Télé-7–Jours, 42, 74, 75, 210
Télédiffusion de France (TDF), 65
Télégramme, Le, 40
Télé-Loisirs, 42
Télématin, 187
TéléObs, 40
Téléphone, 94
Télérama, 75, 210
Télétel, 77, 78
television, 62–76
    advertising, 210–11

U.W.E.L. LEARNING RESOURCES

channels and institutions, 63–5
cinema, 119–20
cultural values and debates, 65–8
food, 186
genres and programmes, 68–72
leisure, 154–5
magazines, 42
reality programming, 71–2, 72–4
soccer, 172–3
Témoin No. 1, 71, 72–4
tennis, 170
Tenue de soirée, 128
'Terru d'oru', 95
Têtu, 42, 44–6
TF1, 63, 65, 68, 70, 71, 73, 74, 75
theme parks, 159–60
Théry, Gérard, 77
Thibaud, Jacques, 67
thirty-five-hour work week,150–1, 160, 161, 163
Thody, Philip, 28
Thorgal, 142
Three Men and a Baby, 121
Tintin, 135, 138, 143
Tontons flingeurs, Les, 123
Top Santé magazine, 43
Töppfer, Rodolphe, 137
Torchon brûle, Le, 42
Toubon law, 27–8, 208–9, 212
Touchez pas au grisbi, 25, 124
Tour de France, 157, 167–8
tourism, 157–61
Tournier, Michel, 105
Tous les matins du monde, 127
'Tout le monde', 101
Trace, La, 73
Trainspotting, 119
Trautmann, Catherine, 96
Travail, famille, patrie, 5, 7
Trenet, Charles, 92
trente glorieuses, 8, 12, 150, 180, 188, 206–7
Tribunal des flagrants délires, Le, 53
Tribune de l'histoire, 54
Tribune. La, 39
Trigano, Gilbert, 161
Trois Hommes et un couffin, 122, 126, 127, 131
Trop belle pour toi, 129
Truchis de Varennes, Isabelle de (Zazie), 98
Truffaut, François, 126
Tueuse, La, 108
TV Magazine, 42
TV6, 64, 65

Uderzo, Albert, 159
Union, L', 40

Vacances de Monsieur Hulot, Les, 164
Vacances du petit Nicolas, Les, 162

Vaillant, 142
Valise, La, 54
Valseuses, Les, 128
Vargas, Fred, 111
variétés françaises, 92
variétés,
Vartan, Sylvie, 153
Vélo, 42
Vendredi et les limbes du Pacifique, 105
Vendredi-Samedi-Dimanche (VSD), 41
Ventura, Lino, 121
Vercors, 8
verlan, 25, 30–1, 114
Vermeil, 43
Verne, Jules, 105, 107
Vers une civilisation du loisir?, 151–2, 153
Vian, Boris, 49
Vichy 'syndrome', 8
Vichy, 7, 35, 106, 124, 168–9, 174, 193–4
Victoires de la musique awards, 98
Vie est à nous, La, 6
Vie sexuelle de catherine M., La, 110
Villeurbanne, 167
Villiers, Gérard de, 106
Visiteurs, Les, 120, 121, 122, 128, 130–1
Vivendi-Universal, 14
Vogue, 42, 195
Voix du Nord, La, 40
Voleuse, La, 108
Voltage FM, 55
Voulzy, Laurent, 93
Vulcania, 160

Walker, Scott, 92
Weaver, Sigourney, 201
Werber, Bernard, 114
Westlife, 92
Wit FM, 50
Wolinski, 139
womens' liberation and press, 42–3

'Yesterday when I was Young', 102
yéyé, 2, 92, 93, 96
Youpi, 43
Yousso N'dour, 94
youth culture, 13

Zazie, 97, 98–101
ZB3, 92
Zazie dans le métro, 23–4
Zebda, 94
Zenith concert hall, 96, 98
Zidane, Zinedine, 173
Zidi, Claude, 122
'Zizanie, La', (song and album) 97, 98–101
Zizanie, La (film), 129

U.W.E.L. LEARNING RESOURCES